Culture and Technology

Culture and
Technology

Andrew Murphie and John Potts

palgrave
macmillan

First published 2003 by
PALGRAVE MACMILLAN
Houndmills, Basingstoke, Hampshire RG21 6XS and
175 Fifth Avenue, New York, N.Y. 10010
Companies and representatives throughout the world

PALGRAVE MACMILLAN is the global academic imprint of the Palgrave
Macmillan division of St. Martin's Press, LLC and of Palgrave Macmillan
Ltd. Macmillan® is a registered trademark in the United States, United
Kingdom and other countries. Palgrave is a registered trademark in the
European Union and other countries.

ISBN 978-0-333-92927-8 hardcover

ISBN 978-0-333-92929-2   ISBN 978-1-137-08938-0 (eBook)
DOI 10.1007/978-1-137-08938-0

This book is printed on paper suitable for recycling and made from fully
managed and sustained forest sources.

A catalogue record for this book is available from the British Library.

Library of Congress Cataloging-in-Publication Data
Murphie, Andrew
    Culture and technology / Andrew Murphie and John Potts
        p.   cm.
    Includes bibliographical references and index.
    ISBN 978-0-333-92927-8 – ISBN 978-0-333-92929-2 (pbk.)
    1. Technology – Social aspects.   2. Culture.   I. Potts, John, 1959–
II. Title.
HM846 .M87   2002
306.4'6 – dc21

                                                                    2002074824

10   9   8   7   6   5   4   3   2   1
12   11   10   09   08   07   06   05   04   03

Contents

List of Figures

Acknowledgements

The authors wish to thank Catherine Gray for her editorial assistance. We especially thank the artists for their kind permission to reproduce their works: Robyn Backen, Jane Edden, Phillip George, Nigel Helyer, Rosemary Laing, Patricia Piccinini, Robyn Stacey, Stelarc, Anne Zahalka. The image of Stelarc is from his *EXOSKELETON, Event for Extended Body and Walking Machine* at Cyborg Frictions, Dampfzentrale, Berne 1999. Photo: D. Landwehr. Luigi Russolo's *Music* is reproduced courtesy of the Estorick Collection, London. Anne Zahalka's *Gestures* is reproduced courtesy of the artist and Roslyn Oxley9 Gallery, Sydney. The image from *The Noon Quilt* is reproduced courtesy of The trAce Online Writing Community, The Nottingham Trent University. *The Noon Quilt* is edited by Teri Hoskin and Sue Thomas.

We are grateful to the School of Media and Communications at the University of NSW and the Department of Media and Communication at Macquarie University for supporting the authors with research leave and other assistance.

Finally, we thank Lone Bertelsen and Renata Murawska for their support and encouragement during the writing of this book.

Introduction: 'Culture' and 'Technology'

Culture and technology; technology and culture. These two terms circumscribe a field incorporating many interests and disciplines. It is a dynamic field, reflected both in the rapid changes in technologies themselves, and in the growing range of relevant theoretical approaches. In academic terms, disciplines such as media studies, cultural studies and sociology have conducted theoretical inquiry into the complex relationship between culture and technology. The emergence of new media art – also called multimedia, cyberculture and digital media – is a central theoretical and practical concern of art schools, and of multimedia and media arts departments.

More broadly, the pervasive influence of technology makes the culture/technology issue pertinent to any number of other pursuits and disciplines – including medicine, sport and leisure studies, and of course information technology studies. Indeed, it is difficult to conceive of any contemporary pursuit untouched by developments in technology. Philosophy and psychology explore models of mind and consciousness significantly shaped by medical technologies used to examine the brain; they are shaped also by the cultural force of certain metaphors based on technology – such as the mind as computer. Dispersed throughout this book are discussions of many such areas, in which new technologies have played a prominent role – from intellectual property to the changing notion of community.

We have taught in this field for some years now, and have learnt a few things along the way. One is the folly of making predictions based on specific technologies, or on new cultural formations stemming from technological innovation. During the writing of this book, dot com companies have soared then crashed, Napster has

terrorized the music industry then been tamed. The cultural ramifications of technological change are multiple and volatile, making
fools of modern-day prophets. We have also learnt that any theoretical engagement with this thing called technoculture needs to be
as dynamic as its object. Theory needs to be supple, not monolithic.
It must be able to adjust to changing social circumstances; it
must be able to recognize when a theoretical model has reached its
use-by date. Perhaps the most appropriate course is to draw on
those theoretical approaches – no matter how diverse – that offer
the most illuminating perspectives on their particular patch of
technology-and-culture.

This is the approach we take in this book. We do not provide a
dominant 'line' to explain the cultural impact of technology. Rather,
we discuss a wide range of theoretical perspectives, assessing their
strengths and weaknesses in the context of recent technological
developments. Our aim is not tell readers how to interpret technological change; it is to give readers enough to go on in analysing
this extremely complex area. The topic of each chapter is sufficiently broad to accommodate divergent – often opposed – theoretical viewpoints. There is no chapter dedicated specifically to a
discussion of gender; rather, questions of gender, power, technology and culture are addressed at numerous points throughout the
book, in various contexts. One of our emphases in this book is the
cultural expression of technology and its social impact, which is
why we devote a chapter to science fiction. It is also why we consider the relation between art and technology in two chapters: we
see new media art in particular as a revealing and creative engagement with rapidly developing technologies.

There is no shortage of material when it comes to new technologies, as any contemporary media bulletin will demonstrate.
The news is full of technological breakthroughs, whether they are
new military technologies, or cloning and other products of genetic
science. In this book we shall be looking at specific technological
forms, and specific new media; but we are not so interested in how
things work technologically, as how they work culturally. How
do technologies from the printing press to the Internet function
culturally? How do they affect the manner in which we think
about ourselves and the world? From which cultural shifts do
such new technological forms arise? Do they bring new cultural
possibilities into being? We shall consider these questions and
others, making reference along the way to influential theoretical
approaches that have informed discussion of this field. Before

considering these arguments, however, we need to define our key terms.

What is technology?

The current range of meanings of the word 'technology' arose in the modern era. These only emerged in the second half of the nineteenth century; earlier nineteenth-century writers such as Karl Marx did not even use the word. Use of the word 'technology' developed, along with other terms like 'Industrial Revolution', to describe the radical restructuring of Western societies as a result of industrial processes.

If the current meanings of the word are a relatively recent development, its components are ancient. The Greek *tekhne* meant art or craft; *logos* had a range of meanings from 'word' to 'system' or 'study'. The gulf between the ancient Greek sense of *tekhne* as art or craft, and the present meanings of 'technology' testifies to the process of change undergone by significant words over time. Such changes often reflect fundamental social developments, or internal conflicts within a society.

Words can be sites of contests between competing social groups, as they attempt to assign and control specific meanings. For example, the word 'technocrat' emerged in the 1920s to describe a proponent of technocracy – the administration of society by technological experts – as a viable alternative to conventional democracy. To call someone a technocrat could be to criticize or praise that person, depending on the political point of view; the meaning of the term oscillated between its negative and positive senses. Later in the twentieth century the word lost much of its political edge, as the notion of technocracy lost ground; yet it remains today to describe someone who values highly the potential of technology. All important words, especially widely used words such as 'technology' and 'culture', carry the traces of social changes, which have operated around and through those words.

To return to our brief history of the term, 'technology' was used sparingly in the seventeenth and eighteenth centuries, referring to a study of the arts; its meaning at this stage remained closely related to its Greek roots. But by the 1860s its meanings began to shift to its modern usage; the word had come to mean the system of mechanical and industrial arts. This shift occurred in the wake of the rise of science, which had demonstrated over the previous two centuries its ability to measure, predict and control natural forces. Technology was understood as the application of a body of knowledge, or science, in specific areas. In particular, the application of science to production, in the form of engineering and the design of industrial systems, was summarized by 'technology', endowing the word with a wider range of meanings. It could refer either to the study of these new forms of production, or to the general complex of machinery, tools and apparatus itself. Over the succeeding decades, this second variant of meaning became dominant: 'technology' has come to describe the overall system of machines and processes, while 'technique' refers to a specific method or skill.

The contemporary meaning of 'technology' is both more abstract and more specific than the late nineteenth-century senses of the word. Throughout the industrial and post-industrial periods, technology has become so ubiquitous that it has been said that we now live in technology, surrounded by technological systems and dependent on them. 'Technology' has been generalized to the point of abstraction: it suggests an overarching system that we inhabit. But individual machines or devices are also described as technologies: a television set may be called a technology, or a computer. In this book we will use the word 'technology' in both these senses, and more; we will also explore the various ideas and beliefs that have influenced current attitudes to this thing, or things, called technology.

A common definition of technology would refer to its artificial character: that is, a technology is not a natural object but one made by humans. Throughout this book, however, we shall use a more expansive notion of technology. Many recent theorists have argued that a working definition of technology needs to be as broad as possible. As an example, Lorenzo Simpson defines technology as 'that constellation of knowledge, processes, skills and products whose aim is to control and transform' (1995: 16). This definition is typical of the broad-based approach to technology found in critical theory and cultural studies; it encompasses both concrete forms (products or artefacts) and abstractions (knowledge, processes and goals). Technology has become so central to so many societies that it needs to be considered as much more than a collection of tools and machines. For Arnold Pacey, technology entails 'ordered systems that involve people and organizations, living things and machines' (1983: 6). Technology in the contemporary world involves cultural values, ideologies, ethical concerns; it is also shaped by political and economic determinants.

What is technique?

Before we move on to the term 'culture', we need to clarify the distinction between 'technology' and 'technique'. Several of the theorists discussed in this book refer to the importance of technique, sometimes in relation to technologies, at other times not.

Technique can be defined simply as the use of skill to accomplish something. Beyond this, however, it is a little more complicated. William Barrett, for one, emphasizes the centrality of technique to culture/technology relations. He thinks that all technology is intimately involved with the techniques by which we use it, and writes that '. . . if our civilization were to lose its techniques, all our machines and apparatus would become one vast pile of junk' (1978: 18). This is a valuable point and we would like to take it a little further.

First, techniques are both a question of physical techniques and one of associated techniques of thought (one thinks differently when involved with different technologies). 'Losing' our techniques would imply the loss of direct operational skills *and* of a means of appropriate thinking to go with particular technological developments. Second, sometimes it seems as though we do invent technologies that can operate themselves (automatic pilot, a timer that waters the garden at a particular time of the day). These may lead us to rethink the question. A serious example in this context is a nuclear reactor. It would pose a major problem to whatever was left of either humanity or any other life on the planet if it ceased to be under the technical control of humans.

What of technique and the body? In his work 'Techniques of the Body', Marcel Mauss (1992) points out that in fact *anything* to do with the working of our bodies involves technique. As such, he notes that techniques are as crucial to culture and to the transmission of culture as technologies. What, for him, is a technique? He calls a technique that which is first, *effective* (it works) and, second, *traditional* (it can be passed on through culture). The inference here is that many of the things that we think are just 'natural' are in fact quite technically and culturally specific. This includes things such as the way we swim, run, walk, take care of our bodies, even sleep, all of which imply different techniques in different cultural contexts. This means that, to quote Mauss:

> The body is man's (or woman's) first and most natural instrument. Or more accurately, not to speak of instruments, man's (or woman's) first and most natural technical object, and at the same time his (or her) first technical means, is his (or her) body (p. 461).

Subsequently, he begins to extend this into the realm of thought and culture:

> ... we are everywhere faced with physio-psycho-sociological assemblages of series of actions. These actions are more or less habitual and more or less ancient in the life of the individual and the history of the society (p. 473).

In other words, questions of technology, machines and technique are crucial to any understanding of culture, to its physical techniques but also to its psychology, to its modes of thinking. To take just one quick example, it is arguable that, whatever the 'truths' of current technological change, whatever it 'means', you will understand digital technology the more once you have learnt to move your body to sampled and sequenced music. Or perhaps even when you have learnt to control a computer mouse. A deeper understanding of technique enriches our experience – and analysis – of technology.

What is culture?

'Culture' is a notoriously difficult word to define. Most universities in the world now have several departments devoted to it, teaching, among other things, the discipline of 'cultural studies'. Yet Raymond Williams, who in many ways is the founder of this discipline, called *culture* 'one of the two or three most complicated words in the English language' (1983: 87).

At the very least, we can distinguish two main senses to its contemporary meaning, one specific and one general. It is possible to speak of self-contained cultures, such as 'French culture' or 'youth culture'. On the other hand, the more general sense can become so wide as to embrace all human activity around the world: 'culture' as opposed to nature. Indicating a further distinction of meaning, many newspapers carry sections called 'Culture', bracketing off this area from news, politics, finance or sport: this reflects the tendency to think of culture as pertaining to the arts, or entertainment. With so many variants of meaning circulating at the same time in the same place, we begin to see some of the complexity buried within this term.

The diverse shades of contemporary meaning can at least be related to the root of the word. The Latin *cultura* meant tending or cultivation; when 'culture' entered the English language via French in the fifteenth century, it referred to tillage. This agricultural reference was later transferred metaphorically to other pursuits: by the sixteenth century, 'culture' extended to the cultivation of mind or body. By the early nineteenth century the intellectual aspect of such cultivation was favoured; 'culture' referred to the intellectual or artistic side of civilization. The Romantics in particular embraced culture as the positive dimension of civilized societies, while the industrial base of those societies was criticized for its alienating, dehumanizing effects.

This Romantic opposition of 'culture' – as uplifting and ennobling – to the degrading social results of the Industrial Revolution, established a dichotomy between culture and technology (even if, as we saw earlier, the word 'technology' was not yet widely in use). It also entrenched the notion of 'high culture' as spiritually enriching, superior to mass or 'low' culture. Both these conceptions of culture were challenged in the twentieth century, so that a word like 'technoculture' entails not a division between technology and culture, but rather a fusion of the two. Similarly, the distinction between high and low culture eroded in the age of cinema, while pop art and later art movements deliberately blurred the line between fine art and mass produced popular culture.

Yet earlier attitudes have persisted, supported by enduring class distinctions. The idea that culture means high art can be internalized by members of any class, with the result that a working-class person may associate 'culture' with opera and ballet, without considering working-class activities as worthy of the name. In the same way, marking off cultural pursuits from other facets of society – as represented by the newspaper 'Culture' sections – perpetuates the notion of culture as somehow separate from the technological or political components of civilization.

Our approach in this book, by contrast, is to regard culture as a dynamic and multiple thing. We certainly do not have a singular notion of culture, whether as cultivation of the mind, or artistic pursuits, or high art. We do not see culture as neatly separated off from the political, or more 'serious', aspects of civilization. And we do not consider technology and culture as polar opposites within contemporary societies.

Culture is dynamic because, as the preceding paragraphs have indicated, ideas and values change, often quite quickly, over time. Older attitudes to culture may be superseded, or they may overlap with new ideas, or the older values may re-emerge at a later time.

The various resurgences across two centuries of Romanticism, with its rejection of technology and its empathy with nature, constitute an example of the latter possibility.

Culture is multiple because it contains the activities of different classes, of different races, of different age groups. It is conditioned by political and economic forces: government policies, corporate research and development, market competition. It is full of oppositions and contradictions. Subcultures, for example, whether mod, punk, rave, hacker or any other, are indicators of the conflicting forces within the culture at large. As members of the subculture no doubt like to see it, they are resisting the dominant forms of culture, indicating how those dominant values may be opposed. Yet a different point of view may regard the proliferation of subcultures as a sign that culture accommodates various forms of dissent. The political means, including legislation, by which mainstream culture deals with alternative or oppositional groupings, is not separate from culture; rather, it is part of the cultural dynamic.

As distinct from the elitist nineteenth-century notion of culture as a stable, idealistic realm, we see culture as messy, confused and riven with contradictions. Above all, it is unpredictable, as is its relation to technology. Many technologies end up being used in ways never foreseen by their inventors. The Internet is a perfect example. Invented by the United States military as a means of decentralizing military authority in case of attack, it became an anarchic sphere populated by alternative lifestylers, political subversives, hackers, pornographers, cyberartists, anyone with any kind of cause, or simply anyone relishing the untrammelled freedom of communication offered by this vast network without a centre. While corporations attempted to wring new profits out of this huge entity, governments sought to impose regulations on what they saw as an ungoverned system. The latter attempt, at least, was made difficult by the properties of the Internet as a global network. As one instance of the globalization process, the Internet does not respect national boundaries or jurisdictions.

There are many remarks to be made about the cultural significance of the Internet, but in this introduction we shall restrict ourselves to two. First, the explosion of unrestricted cultural expression across a network that originated as a military project, is an indication of the dynamic and unpredictable aspects of culture. The central dictum of the cyberpunk subculture puts this succinctly: 'The street finds its own use for things.' Second, the complex knot of issues arising from the Internet's success exposes the folly of treating 'culture' as a separate stratum within society. The Internet is at once a technological, a cultural, a political and an economic phenomenon. A technological development of computers and communications, it produced an extraordinary volume of cultural expression, while confronting legal and political frameworks around the world.

Culture/technology

If we have so far avoided a precise definition of 'culture', it is because, as the preceding discussion has suggested, precision is not often a characteristic of cultural activity, including commentary on culture itself. We could offer a utilitarian definition of culture – as the signs, beliefs and practices of a group or society – but such a definition does not say very much. It covers everything from religion to architecture, but is annoyingly vague in its generality. We prefer, as a simple explanation of why there always seems to be 'more' culture, the definition proposed by the composer/musician Brian Eno. He defines culture as 'everything we do not have to do', and notes, for example, that

> . . . we have to eat, but we do not have to have 'cuisines', Big Macs or Tournedos Rossini. We have to cover ourselves against the weather, but we do not have to be so concerned as we are about whether we put on Levi's or Yves Saint-Laurent. We have to move about the face of the globe, but we do not have to dance. These other things, we choose to do. We could survive if we chose not to . . . (1996: 317).

Eno's basic and informal definition has the advantage of condensing many dimensions of 'culture' and its meanings into one accessible explanation. It incorporates human activities such as art, music and building, while also relating to the everydayness of culture. It is what people do, beyond the basic necessities of survival and bodily function. Much of this cultural activity is conditioned by the economic system in which it takes place; an affluent capitalist society, for example, will target the 'culture industry' as a means of making huge profits. Advertising, merchandising, marketing and other aspects of the consumer society take their place as shaping forces of contemporary culture.

Finally, this discussion has made evident the interaction of culture and technology at all levels. The earliest human societies used technology, in the form of tools and weapons, to transform their natural environment. Civilizations are based on, among other things, the technologies of building and writing. Cultural activities from cooking to music making are dependent on technology. Contemporary mass culture is made possible by the technologies of communication and production.

All the old meanings of the word 'culture', as identified by Raymond Williams, still live in the contemporary relations between culture and technology. The cultivation of plants and animals we now call biotechnology; 'couture' is the work of the fashion industry, based on the textile industry that was central to the industrial revolution; the improvement of the human mind uses artificial memories such as books and computers, not to mention 'smart drugs'; even religious practices, as in cults, persist in the various technomysticisms and 'technopagan' groups scattered across the Internet.

Technology plays a crucial role as well in the large-scale and popular forms of culture. Tourism became the world's biggest industry in the twentieth century, largely as a result of new technologies of transport: car, ocean liner and jet aircraft. Sport is probably the most popular cultural activity; certainly the Olympic Games and the football World Cup are the world's largest cultural events, in terms of both global audience and expenditure. Huge stadiums are built for these and other events; beyond that, technology is significant in all sports. This is most evident at the elite level, in which rival sports shoe and apparel corporations compete in a race of technical innovation. Specially designed suits, shoes and helmets draw on scientific research to improve athletes' performances. Another technological industry produces illegal performance-enhancing drugs, while sport officials develop drug-testing equipment in a desperate technological race with the drugs industry.

Now that we have offered at least provisional definitions for our key terms, we are ready to move on. As we have indicated in these first pages, the area covered by the terms 'technology' and 'culture' is expansive and elaborate. It is also highly pertinent to an understanding of contemporary societies. In the following chapters, we shall assess the range of issues operating within the culture/technology dynamic. To assist us in exploring these issues, we devote the first chapter to a discussion of the most relevant theoretical frameworks, perspectives and orientations for the study of culture and technology.

CHAPTER 1

Theoretical Frameworks

In this chapter we survey influential theories of culture and technology. This survey ranges across many perspectives on the social and cultural significance of technology. We consider debates within media theory and cultural studies; we discuss various theories of technology and society. We also introduce a number of approaches that have been termed 'poststructuralist'.

Our survey will address many complex issues arising from the interplay of technology and culture. How do we live with technology? What impact does it have on our lives? How should we conceive of technology? Are technologies neutral in themselves, that is, does the way in which they are used determine their cultural impact? Or do technologies have intrinsic properties that shape the cultures into which they are introduced?

We commence this chapter with the debate arising from the last two questions. This debate can, in very broad terms, be said to involve a contest between a technological determinist position and a cultural materialist one. After considering the various arguments involved in this dispute, we move on to some of the broader perspectives on the interaction between culture and technology.

Technological determinism

Technological determinism refers to the belief that technology is the agent of social change. It is both a popular attitude – reflected in such expressions as 'you can't stop progress' – and a theoretical position. The term was coined by social scientist Thorstein Veblen in the 1920s, at a time when social policy in industrialized nations was increasingly influenced by technical capacity – but the notion is older than this. Technological determinism is linked to the idea of progress; in this sense it was forged as a social attitude in the

Victorian period, in which progress was measured in industrial terms: speed of movement, volume of production. Of course, technological determinism is still with us. It is equally significant in the post-industrial era: the terms 'information society' or 'computer age' betray the technological determinist notion that society is shaped by its dominant technologies.

Technological determinism tends to consider technology as an independent factor, with its own properties, its own course of development, and its own consequences. Technological change is treated as if autonomous: removed from social pressures, it follows a logic or imperative of its own. This viewpoint holds that a successful technical innovation, if implemented on a sufficiently wide scale, will generate a new type of society: hence 'the steam age', 'the age of electricity', 'the information age'. The choices open to societies undergoing a technological 'revolution' are limited to restricting the upheavals caused by the 'culture shock' induced by the new technology. One example of this view is the 'future shock' predicted in the popular writings of Alvin Toffler, who warned that post-industrial societies need to protect themselves from the more dislocating effects of automation and computer-based technologies.

Technological determinism usually refers to the present, projected onto the future, as expressed in claims that 'we have no choice but to adopt this technology'. But as a theoretical approach it is also used as a means of interpreting cultural history. Several significant theorists, from a range of disciplines, have made studies of the cultural effects deriving from technological developments, often with regard to media. Eric Havelock (1963), for example, argues that the technology of writing, using the phonetic alphabet, made possible profoundly new modes of thought, first expressed in Plato. Walter J. Ong, a scholar of orality and literacy, similarly insists on the deeply significant consequences of writing as a media technology: 'More than any other single invention, writing has transformed human consciousness' (1982: 78). Elizabeth Eisenstein's (1979) study of the printing press analyses its key role as an 'agent of change' in European culture, with ramifications in religion, science, economics, exploration and politics. Jack Goody developed the notion of 'intellectual technologies' such as writing, print and electronic media, each of which creates a different 'cognitive potentiality for human beings' (1977: 128). Most recently, Pierre Levy has appraised digital networking as the latest intellectual technology to modify the 'intellectual ecology' (1994: 10) into which it has been installed.

Not all of these authors would agree to the description 'techno-logical determinist', but in tracing the far-reaching cultural effects made possible by certain technologies (writing, print, the Internet), their focus is on the way in which a new technology creates a new potential and possibility for human thought, expression or activity. One theorist who was not at all reticent in pursuing a technologi-cal determinist line was Marshall McLuhan, the most well-known, and most controversial, exponent of a cultural theory emphasizing the properties of specific technologies.

Technologies of media

McLuhan's basic premise is that all technologies are extensions of human capacities. Tools and implements are extensions of manual skills; the computer is an extension of the brain. McLuhan adopted this and other concepts from the earlier work of Harold Innis, whose *Empire and Communications* was published in 1950. McLuhan's fame – or notoriety – arose from his observations in the 1960s on the cultural effects of mass media and other technologies (his *Understanding Media* of 1964 is a collection of his popular essays). His writings received renewed attention in the 1990s and beyond, when several commentators and theorists of the Internet hailed McLuhan as a prophet of digital networking. Paul Levinson's 1999 book *Digital McLuhan* is a prime example of this interpretation. For Levinson, McLuhan's most famous idea – the global village – makes most sense in the age of the World Wide Web.

For McLuhan, media are technologies that extend human sense perceptions. In proposing that 'the medium is the message', McLuhan argues that the cultural significance of media lies not in their content, but in the way they alter our perception of the world. The impact of any technology is in 'the change of scale or pace or pattern that it introduces into human affairs' (1974: 16). The par-ticular impact of media technologies is in the way they alter the 'patterns of perception steadily and without any resistance' (p. 27).

McLuhan is emphatically a technological determinist, defining history by technological change. The technology of writing induced a fundamental shift in the way human beings relate to each other, emphasizing vision over sound, individual readership over collec-tive audiences. The cultural effects flowing from the shift from orality to literacy (which occurred over a long transitional period) have been itemized in the works of McLuhan, Ong, Havelock,

Goody and others: they include the development of analytical thought, the cultivation of artificial memory, of abstraction and linearity.

McLuhan's main focus, however, was the electronic mass media, which generated their own cultural consequences in the twentieth century. For him, radio, cinema, hi-fi and television constituted a shift away from the cultural conditioning of print, with its intellectual legacies of linearity and rationality. The globalized flow of information, which commenced with the use of satellite broadcasting in the 1960s, created the 'global village'. The 'electric speed' of communication, its primarily audio-visual basis, and the saturation of society with images and sounds from around the world, produced a total perceptual field, in contrast to the ordered patterns of print-dominated cultures. For McLuhan, the cultural effects of the print medium were rationality and social fragmentation; audio-visual mass media, by contrast, provided a continuous and instantaneous stream of information from an enormous variety of sources. The result was a cultural implosion, in which people were more aware of the world as a 'village' community: they could begin to think 'mythically' once again, throwing off the straitjackets of a culture determined by the properties of print.

McLuhan interpreted the cultural discord within Western societies in the 1960s as the result of culture lag: the older generation, determined by the hierarchical values of print ('a place for everything and everything in its place'), was threatened by the spontaneity and collectivity unleashed, within youth culture, by the new electronic media technologies. Walter J. Ong, a like-minded but more cautious scholar than McLuhan, also finds in the culture shaped by electronic mass media a 'secondary orality', reflecting the communal sense and instantaneity of preliterate culture.

McLuhan's writing is deliberately provocative and often simplistic; it also ignores the socio-economic factors underpinning these cultural developments, as his many critics have pointed out. Other theorists, however, have pursued a similar line of inquiry in more scholarly fashion. One of the most thorough analyses of the cultural effects of electronic media has been conducted by Joshua Meyrowitz, whose book *No Sense of Place* (1985) examines the impact of television in particular. For Meyrowitz, like McLuhan, the key to a medium's cultural effect is not found in its content, but in the way it conveys information. Unlike literacy, which demands the lengthy acquisition of reading and writing skills, electronic media are far more accessible to people of all ages. As a result, television continually reveals hitherto hidden or private behaviour: children are exposed to adult behaviour; the private lives of individuals become public property. Meyrowitz therefore asserts that age and gender divisions have blurred in the age of TV; he also claims that the continuous exposure of politicians' private and public failings has destroyed the possibility of the Great Leader.

The staples of TV – the close-up, the probing camera, the revealing of private spaces – have been generalized, according to Meyrowitz, into a contemporary cultural condition: the obsession with exposure.

> The Victorian era – the height of print culture – was a time of 'secrets'. Our own age, in contrast, is fascinated by exposure. Indeed, the *act* of exposure itself now seems to excite us more than the content of the secrets exposed (1985: 311).

The intrinsic properties of TV also favour emotion and spectacle over reason and argument. TV news incorporates footage designed to trigger emotional responses: sorrow, fear, amusement. Reality TV raises the 'act of exposure' to the level of mass entertainment. The widespread international mourning at the death of Princess Diana, whose career was played out in front of cameras, is testament to the emotive power of the TV medium in particular.

Baudrillard and the technologies of simulacra

The influential cultural theorist Jean Baudrillard follows on from McLuhan in several respects. Baudrillard's theories are provocative and controversial, as were McLuhan's; both push a theory of technology, media and culture to extreme positions. For Baudrillard, contemporary culture is increasingly determined by an array of technologically produced 'simulacra', which has come to hijack reality itself.

Baudrillard's theory of simulacra (signs which are copies of other signs), based as it is on the generative power of media technologies, owes a great deal to McLuhan. One difference between the two is that McLuhan's optimism regarding the effects of electronic media gives way to pessimism in Baudrillard. Yet both draw on the role of mass media in representing reality. Baudrillard explicitly modifies McLuhan's 'the medium is the message' dictum, so that it becomes 'the medium is the model'. It is the model for behaviour, perceptions, knowledge of the world, sense of self, reality itself. In societies more mediated than ever before, bombarded with images of themselves, reality is reproduced so many times that it produces a 'hyperreal' condition: more real than the real. This is what Baudrillard means by 'the precession of simulacra': the representation of the real comes before the real, so that it becomes the real. Simulations no longer refer to real objects, people, facts and societies. They increasingly refer only to each other, moving faster and faster. Think of advertising. Think of the video clip. In this maelstrom of simulation the real disappears. No meanings, just media-produced simulations. No coherent society – just a whirl of signs through a now inconsequential ground of bodies. The Internet.

It is important to realize that reality was not hidden by this simulation – quite the opposite. It was hijacked by simulation and made obscene – too much of it was seen too fast. In its increasingly rapid movement the real was converted into something much more portable – the sign, the simulation. Wildlife and travel documentaries are a small part of this; reality TV is the 'pornography of everyday life' beamed back at us. This does not mean that people, objects and so on, have ceased to exist. It is just that it is no longer the exchange of objects, a common or known history, an assumed social cohesion or conflict that holds the social together. For Baudrillard, what moves through it is simulation. There is no more object and, subsequently, no more subject. Just saturation in simulation, in which everything is now everywhere and yet nothing can be pinned down.

What transports these simulations? How do they move through us? The answer is that they move through the screen and the network in the 'ecstasy of communication' (1988). We are more and more 'wired' to our interfaces. We react to simulations – to the television news rather than the world, to a computer program rather than social interaction, to email rather than vocal communication. In all of these we react to simulations rather than to the immediate environment. In the meantime we still consume – but now, where once we consumed objects, we consume signs.

Baudrillard thinks the obsession with communication for its own sake eradicates the message. There is nothing to be communicated but communication itself. This is like those many conversations on a mobile phone that are about the fact that one is talking on a mobile phone. As Baudrillard puts it:

Ecstasy is all functions abolished into one dimension, the dimension of communication. All events, all spaces, all memories are abolished in the sole dimension of information: this is obscene (1988: 85).

For many critics, Baudrillard's position – even more extreme than McLuhan's – is untenable. It is certainly hyperbolic, and gives the appearance of fatalism, whereby nothing can be done to prevent the precession of simulacra. A more charitable reading of Baudrillard might point to a 'fatal strategy' in his work, which at least alerts readers to the influence of these media-generated simulations (we discuss his controversial *The Gulf War Did Not Take Place* in Chapter 7). For our purposes here, Baudrillard is significant as a latter-day technological determinist, founding his theories on the technologies of information and media. For him, like McLuhan, these technologies have exerted a profound effect on culture, an effect largely beyond social control.

Cultural materialism

It is readily apparent that technological determinism, for all its insights into the specific properties of technologies, offers a one-sided perspective on the relation between technology and culture. In removing specific technologies from their social and political contexts, this approach treats technologies in isolation, as if they come into existence of their own accord and proceed to mould societies in their image. There is an alternative perspective, however, which is concerned to situate those technologies, at all times, in their social and cultural context.

We shall give the name 'cultural materialism' to that theoretical approach which foregrounds the complex interplay of factors associated with cultural change. Other terms could serve just as well: two such terms are 'the sociology of technology' or 'critical theory', which cover a range of critical thought within various disciplines. We shall concentrate for the moment on the genesis of 'cultural materialism' as a means of analysing the relationship between technology and culture.

Raymond Williams used the term 'cultural materialism' with reference to his own work, which has been highly influential in the discipline of cultural studies. The 'materialism' component of the term signifies that cultural change is to be interpreted as part of a historical process, in which economic, political and institutional pressures play an integral part. Williams distanced his approach, however, from conventional historical materialist (Marxist) analysis, which overplayed the economic determinants of social and cultural forms. While he was critical of economic determinism, he was also vigorous in his refutation of technological determinism; his critique of McLuhan is especially significant for our purposes here.

Williams's criticism of the technological determinism articulated by McLuhan is concerned with all the things that McLuhan leaves out of his analysis. For Williams, such a narrow focus on the technology and its intrinsic properties constituted 'an attempted cancellation of all other questions about it and its uses' (1975: 126). Williams opposed McLuhan's reductionist version of cultural history, which posited each new medium as a cause from which inevitably flows a stream of new cultural effects:

> . . . if the medium is the cause, all other causes, all that men ordinarily see as history, are at once reduced to effects (p. 127).

Whereas in McLuhan all media operations are desocialized, Williams emphasizes social need and political intention as significant factors involved in technological development. His book on television, for example, is subtitled 'Technology and Cultural Form'; in it he explores the cultural and social forces that created both the need for broadcasting, and the institutional frameworks that oversaw its implementation. Rather than simply accepting (and celebrating) the marvellous advent of radio and TV and the consequent shaping of culture in their wake (the McLuhanite approach), Williams looks for the particular circumstances into which these technologies were introduced. Developing social conditions after the First World War – larger cities, more mobile populations, greater emphasis on the family home – necessitated more extensive systems of communication. To meet this need, the technology of radio, originally used as a means of point-to-point communication in a manner similar to telegraphy (or the Internet today), was redeployed as a form of mass broadcasting.

The other pressing concern uncovered by a cultural materialist analysis is the political context of technological development. Broadcasting was an economic and political entity as much as a technological and cultural one. The transformation of radio into a mass broadcasting medium suited two sets of interests. Manufacturers of radio technology made profits from the large receive-only sets that were installed in homes; state authorities nervous about the political potential of radio were concerned to limit its range of uses. A complex of government policy-making and capitalist economic interest was responsible for the implementation of radio (and then television) broadcasting. This complex differed in specific contexts: European governments exercised stricter controls than were applied in the United States, for example. But in all cases, political decision-making determined the technology's implementation, and its cultural shape (formats, content).

Williams's critical account of broadcasting history is one example of his cultural materialist approach in action. It can easily be observed that he fills in all the factors that McLuhan leaves out: social need, economic interest, political control, specific decision-making, the broader sociocultural context. McLuhan's assertion that radio 'created' Hitler in Germany and the teenager in the United States is condemned by cultural materialism as a gross form of shorthand at best, a collusion with conservatism at worst. Williams's critique of McLuhan indeed contended that 'the medium is the message' took its place within an active ideology of progress, a depoliticizing of technological innovation. The need to expose the political and economic decision-making behind new technologies is probably the greatest legacy of Williams's work. As we have seen, considerations such as these are virtually absent in technological determinist accounts. Although McLuhan prophesied the global village, he had nothing to say about ownership and control of that village; Baudrillard likewise writes in generalities, ignoring the specifics of political economy.

Brian Winston's historical study of media technology follows the cultural materialist path laid down by Williams. In his book *Media Technology and Society*, Winston analyses the development and implementation of media from the telegraph to the Internet. His concern is with the pre-existing social formations in which technological developments occur. Unlike McLuhan, Winston's analysis is historically based, focusing on the 'social sphere . . . conditioning and determining technological developments' (1998: 2). This orientation is able to provide answers to questions arising from the history of technology: why do some inventions succeed while others do not? Why are some inventions created simultaneously by inventors who have no contact with each other? Winston answers the second question as would Williams, by referring to the 'social necessity' to which inventors of any one period will respond.

The matter of the success or failure of inventions entails several factors. Winston gives the name 'supervening social necessities' to those diverse social forces that affect the process of innovation. A technology prototype may not be taken up because no use for it can be foreseen; on the other hand, one technology may create the need for another (trains and telegraphy, aircraft and radar). Perfectly useful technologies may fail in commercial competition (Beta vs VHS videotape), while others are actively suppressed by market rivals through litigation or the securing of patents.

In the case of media technology, government regulation can play a major role. Winston proposes a 'law' of the suppression of the radical potential of media technologies, a process most clearly seen with the emergence of new media forms. The advent of digital television in the late 1990s created consternation in the media sector, as rival organizations bade for control of the radical new potential of this technology. Governments in Britain, Australia and elsewhere 'licensed the technology to established industrial entities', thus stabilizing the sector by 'constraining the radical potential of the latest development . . .' (1998: 14). The regulation of datacasting, which has largely protected established media proprietors from the threat of Internet broadcasting, is another example of this process.

The considerable body of work devoted to the social context of technologies operates as an antidote – or corrective – to technological determinism. *The Social Shaping of Technology*, a collection of essays edited by MacKenzie and Wajcman, summarizes in its title the orientation of this work. It opposes the doctrine of progress – 'we have no choice' – that has been invoked in the name of technological development since the nineteenth century. MacKenzie and Wajcman state their denunciation of technological determinism: 'a new device merely opens a door; it does not compel one to enter' (1988: 6).

The characteristics of a society play a major part in deciding which technologies are adopted, and how they are implemented and controlled. The research and development facilities of transnational corporations control much technological development in the contemporary world. Military research has contributed a myriad of technological devices to civilian society, not least digital computers. In other areas, as we have seen, the state has direct decision-making powers regarding technology and its development. This can mean that within any culture, specific technologies may be either developed or repressed. Many of the technological inventions associated with Europe – including the printing press and the clock – had been pioneered centuries earlier in China, but these inventions were given no support by the ruling Chinese elite, which favoured stability over innovation.

The 'social shaping of technology' approach, then, is careful to consider the overall dynamics of society. For MacKenzie and Wajcman, the relationship between technology and society cannot be reduced to a simplistic cause-and-effect formula: it is, rather, an 'intertwining'. By highlighting the 'social shaping' of technologies, they support a 'politics of technology' in order 'to shape technological change with human betterment and environmental protection in mind' (1999: xiv–xv).

Stephen Hill, in his book *The Tragedy of Technology*, describes this subtle interplay of forces as the 'cultural text' that includes new technologies as one of its elements. Any cultural ramifications of a new technology must be appraised within the many strands of this text.

> Technological change . . . is not, by itself, productive of social change.
>
> Instead, the direction of change is a product of the particular alignment between the technological possibilities and the society and culture that exists (1989: 33).

Hill discusses the proposition that 'barbed wire destroyed the aristocracy in Britain', in that it rendered the traditional fox-hunt much more difficult. On the surface this seems an instance of technology (barbed wire used to parcel off property) generating cultural effects (the decline of the aristocracy). But Hill argues that this connection can only make sense if analysed as part of a long, involved social process, keyed by the changing nature of class relations during the Industrial Revolution. Economic and political factors are entwined with cultural activities and their use of various technologies.

Barry Jones, in his book *Sleepers, Wake!* discusses the example of the motor car, and the shaping of twentieth-century urban development in its wake. A city like Los Angeles may seem to be a huge cultural effect of a technological cause: the advent of the car as an alternative mode of transport. Jones, however, exposes the economic and political decision-making that lay behind this model 'car-based city of the future' (1988: 214). The public transport infrastructure of Los Angeles was purchased by the car and rubber-tyre manufacturers, then eliminated; citizens came to accept that the use of their own vehicles was a superior alternative to a deficient public transport system. But this was not, as Jones points out, the inevitable cultural result of a new technology. One can imagine different cultural choices and outcomes.

The 'cultural text' includes many other elements beside the technology and decision-making such as those mentioned above. Existing patterns of ownership, class relations, gender relations, the role of advertising and public relations, the flux of social attitudes and beliefs: each of these contributes to the way in which technologies are developed, introduced, used, even resisted. The nineteenth-century Luddites – English cloth workers who smashed textile frames in protest at the industrialization of their craft – have their equivalents in the twenty-first century. Contemporary Luddites share with their predecessors the concern that technological innovations may work to the detriment of society, rather than its improvement. Large-scale developments often meet resistance from protestors suspicious of the developers' economic and political motivations, and alarmed by the developments' social and environmental consequences. Apart from 'neo-Luddism', a well-documented adverse reaction to technological innovation is 'technophobia'. Mark Brosnan summarizes this condition as a fear or anxiety towards new technologies, particularly computers; it is estimated to affect up to a third of the industrialized world (1998: 36).

Is technology neutral?

Those theorists concerned to refute technological determinism affirm the importance of choice in implementing, or opposing, new technologies. Integral to their case is the claim that technologies may be used in a number of ways, resulting in a number of possible cultural effects. Technologies do not determine; rather, they operate, and are operated upon, in a complex social field. It is the way technologies are used, rather than any intrinsic properties of those technologies, that is crucial. In defusing technological determinism, then, we are often left with the notion of technology as neutral, awaiting deployment for specific ends.

Barry Jones, for instance, regards technology in this way. He proposes that any technological change 'has an equal capacity for the enhancement or degradation of life, depending on how it is used' (1988: 231). This argument is certainly common in theoretical discourse; it also has a common-sense appeal as a social attitude: 'it's not the thing itself, but the way it's used that counts'. The argument strikes against the generalizations of technological determinism; it also rebuts the idea that a new technology generates inevitable consequences.

How do theorists sympathetic to technological determinism respond to this criticism? McLuhan is forthright in his rejection of it; in fact he treats this view with contempt. Discussing media technologies, and the idea that 'it is the way they are used that counts', he denounces this argument as 'the numb stance of the technological idiot' (1974: 26). For him, the most profound cultural change occurs due to the structuring role of new technologies – on cultural behaviour, on consciousness, on our perceptions. For McLuhan, technologies, especially technologies of media, radically alter the way we are; it is a petty distraction to isolate the way those technologies may or may not be used.

Other theorists, whose attachment to technological determinism may not be as complete as McLuhan's, are more circumspect. A weaker version of determinism might argue for a correlation between technological change and cultural transformation, or for a more complex engagement between the two. It may contend that a new media technology alters the 'communicative relationships' between individuals, allowing for a diversity of possible emphases within such new relationships (Bernadelli and Blasi, 1995: 10–11). Or that a new technology creates a 'precondition' for cultural change, which may then proceed in a number of different directions, depending on other circumstances. The technology is thus seen as one factor in a matrix of factors. The political ramifications of an unrestricted technological determinism ensure that many theorists are extremely cautious in their conclusions. Pierre Levy, for all his utopian flights regarding the potential of virtual technologies and digital networking, sounds such a note of critical caution. We must distinguish, he warns,

> . . . causal or determining actions from those that prepare the way for or make something possible. Technologies don't determine, they lay the groundwork (1998: 128).

Other influential writers on technology and culture have attempted to expose the political consequences of technological determinism, often with a sense of resignation. The 'liberal pessimist' tradition of criticism is intensely critical of the 'technological imperative', while acknowledging the grip of this imperative on contemporary culture. This tradition of critical writing takes its cue from the earlier sociological theory of Max Weber, which lamented the imprisoning nature of rationalization in early twentieth-century society. The Frankfurt School of critical theory developed an influential critique of the 'culture industries' of contemporary societies. Theodor Adorno and Max Horkheimer, leading Frankfurt School theorists of the 1940s and 1950s, proposed a view of mass culture as an industrialized apparatus, in which science, technology, media and consumerism are elements of a heavily administered social system. A number of like-minded studies of technology appeared in the 1960s, all critical of the technological obsession which had suffused Western societies. Herbert Marcuse's *One Dimensional Man* (1964), Jacques Ellul's *The Technological Society* (published in English in 1964) and Lewis Mumford's *The Myth of the Machine* (1967) all pursued a critical agenda. None of them, however, was content with the notion of technology as neutral; they argued, rather, that technology had become a powerful regulating system in itself.

Ellul's *The Technological Society* typified this strain of critical pessimism, asserting that 'technique has become autonomous' (1964: 14). (Ellul uses 'technique' in the abstract sense of 'technology'.) For Ellul, technology has become the system in which we live: rationalized, all-encompassing and dehumanizing. Technique has produced 'Technical Man'. Technology is a self-running system to which humans have adapted themselves, without even being aware of it. 'In the modern world, the most dangerous form of determinism is the technological phenomenon' (p. xxxiii). Like the cybernetic systems deployed in automation, technique runs according to its own rules, and humans – the inventors of these techniques – have submitted to these very rules. Ellul's writing is both politically motivated and fatalistic: he analyses the extent of technological determinism but is overwhelmed by its sway over contemporary life.

Another recent commentator along similar lines is Neil Postman, who has described in pessimistic detail the cultural decline furthered by an irresistible technical apparatus. Postman contrasts electronic media unfavourably with the print culture of an earlier era in his book *Amusing Ourselves to Death* (1985). For Postman, the enormous volume of information unleashed by mass media has had negative consequences: the trivializing of political and ethical thought, the degradation of civil values. (In this respect, Postman is diametrically opposed to McLuhan.)

Other recent writers, however, are less pessimistic. The advent of digital media technologies, and the spread of the Internet, have encouraged certain theorists to celebrate the potential of these technologies. The non-hierarchical, uncontrollable nature of the Internet, and the ease of access to much digital information, have been seen as enabling rather than restricting in their potential. Sadie Plant (1997), for example, argues that the intrinsic properties of digital media are favourable to those citizens traditionally marginalized in society. Regarding access to technology, this marginalization has historically included women. The structured political hierarchies of gender, race and class are much less oppressive in the emergent technosphere (we shall examine claims such as these in more detail in later chapters).

Andrew Feenberg, in his book *Critical Theory of Technology* (1991), continues the critical analysis of technological society, while resisting the fatalism of Ellul. On the one hand, Feenberg agrees that contemporary technology is so influential that it cannot be regarded as 'neutral': 'Modern technology is no more neutral than medieval cathedrals or the Great Wall of China; it embodies the values of a particular industrial civilization...' (1991: v). Yet rather than succumb to a generalized sense of 'the immanent drift of technology', Feenberg identifies the specific political character of technological systems:

> The values and interests of elites are installed in the very design of rational procedures and machines even before they are assigned a goal ... technology is not destiny but a scene of struggle (p. 14).

This approach couples the political awareness of the 'social shaping of technology' criticism with the 'cultural critique of technology' established by earlier writers.

Such an approach was prefigured, to some extent, in the work of Lewis Mumford. His monumental lifelong study of technology and society (his *Technics and Civilization* was published in 1934) became progressively more critical of the direction taken by Western societies. His *Pentagon of Power*, published in 1970 as the second volume of *The Myth of the Machine*, makes some interesting distinctions regarding technologies and their sociocultural contexts. Mumford is scathing of the 'technological imperative': for him it is as binding, yet as arbitrary, as 'the most primitive taboo'. Supported by consumerism and a blind devotion to progress, this imperative demands that we 'surrender to these novelties unconditionally, just because they are offered, without respect to their human consequences' (1970: 185–6). Yet while acknowledging, like Ellul, the pervasive power of 'megamachine' society, Mumford is more hopeful that political choice may be exercised in the quest for alternative versions of technological development. He discerns an alternative to the 'megatechnics' of the 'military–industrial–entertainment complex', that joining of corporate, government and bureaucratic interest. Mumford gives the name 'polytechnics' to that deployment of technology that is more conducive to a small-scale, pluralistic and decentralized power base.

This notion has been taken up by Langdon Winner, one of the most subtle theorists of technology, politics and culture. Winner is certainly dismissive of the naive form of technological determinism, yet in his book *The Whale and the Reactor* he also rejects the single-minded social determination theory, whose central premise he summarizes as: 'What matters is not technology itself, but the social or economic system in which it is embedded' (1986: 20). For Winner, this approach is deficient in that it eliminates altogether the characteristics of technical objects. It needs to be complemented by attention to those characteristics, which may in themselves have political ramifications. Winner points out that certain technologies necessitate political and cultural responses by their very structure: Haussmann's broad Parisian boulevards, designed to prevent revolutionary activity in narrow streets, require a different form of political activity, as do the huge plazas and ugly concrete buildings on American university campuses of the early 1970s, constructed to defuse student activism. These technological systems, and many others, were of course designed with these express intentions, yet they support Winner's initial premise that technologies are ways of building order in the world. Once the initial choices have been made, these technologies will continue to invoke certain responses; they become part of the 'order of things'.

Winner goes further, however, in wondering if certain technologies may be considered 'inherently political'. That is, are there some technologies that demand political and cultural responses in themselves, irrespective of social control or intention? Do 'intractable properties in the things themselves' lead to 'unavoidable social responses' (1986: 27)? Or does a governing body, social elite or institution need to insert such devices into a pre-existing social pattern, thus determining their use and effect?

Taking his cue from Mumford, Winner suggests the examples of nuclear energy as opposed to solar energy. The former, by its very nature, demands a highly centralized and regulated system to implement it. The related technology of nuclear weaponry demands a rigid, authoritarian chain of command. Solar energy, by contrast, is 'decentralizing in both a technical and political sense'; it encourages communal and individual use on a small-scale, self-sufficient basis. Winner admits that this dichotomy is exceptional, based on extreme examples. But he proposes as a general principle that certain industrial technologies have required certain patterns of power and social organization to administer them. Railroads, construction and manufacture have been attended by specific 'aggregates of people and apparatus' – hierarchies and infra-structure. Winner suggests that if there were alternatives to these socio-political patterns, they were less effective in managing the technologies' potential, and hence not pursued.

Winner is certainly aware of the contentious nature of these claims. By no means is he an apologist for irresponsible progress or authoritarian control of technologies. He is simply concerned that in discussing the cultural context of technologies, we do not lose sight of the specific characteristics of those technologies them-selves. In a way, his writing forms a synthesis between the techno-logical determinism of McLuhan and the cultural materialism of Williams. It provides a sophisticated means of considering tech-nologies' cultural and political impact.

From this perspective, it is difficult to maintain the notion that technologies are neutral, that it is simply the way they are used that matters. The common-sense aspect of such a viewpoint has often been used by theorists and activists critical of conservative decision-making in society. But it should not be forgotten that this 'common-sense' idea is employed by other political programmes as well.

The idea that technologies are in themselves neutral is also used for conservative political ends. It is the argument presented by the gun lobby in resisting tighter gun ownership controls: 'Guns don't kill people, people kill people.' This political argument proposes that the gun technology itself is neutral; it is the way it is used – responsibly or irresponsibly – that counts. The counter-argument to this position is that the gun, by its very presence, alters a situa-tion. A violent conflict may be dangerous but non-fatal without a gun involved; the addition of a gun drastically increases the possi-bility of fatality. The gun creates the precondition for extreme harm, achieved much more easily than with knives or other objects. As well, a potentially violent person armed with a gun is something quite different from a person armed with a knife, or an unarmed violent person. With a gun, one can kill or harm from a distance, without the need to engage the other with one's own body. The act becomes disengaged from physical contact; violence becomes impersonal. The fundamental changes introduced by the gun technology would seem to refute the claim that the technology is in itself neutral.

Knowing the world differently: poststructuralist thought

If technologies carry within them a certain kind of politics, they also seem to imply particular 'configurations' of our relations to the world at large. In other words, we know the world differently through different technologies, and different technologies themselves are in turn a response to knowing the world differently. Although this is obvious, the less obvious implication is that technology may dwell closer to the very heart of whatever we call the 'human' than we might like to admit. As technologies change, it becomes important to assess the challenges made, through technology, to basic definitions of the human. Some theorists have been recently led to write, for example, of the 'posthuman' as a contemporary exceeding of the human by entities thoroughly merged with machines.

Notions such as the posthuman have arisen out of a broader set of ideas that acknowledges the entire world as one of fundamental change, instability and variation. The label 'poststructuralism' has been given to a diverse set of theoretical approaches (emerging from the challenge to structuralist thought in the late 1960s) that refutes the existence of a universal underlying structure determining social or cultural behaviour. Poststructuralists are more likely to focus on the contradictory, dynamic elements of culture, emphasizing the unpredictability of language, culture or social systems. For these thinkers, there are no eternal values, and change no longer occurs between stable entities. Everything is change, and changes occur only between other changes.

The thinkers of interconnection and flux, and of the radical cultural breaks afforded by recent cultural developments, are not always those involved with 'high tech'. Rather they are linked in an attitude that favours leaving older attitudes and practices behind in order to enjoy what is good about a general dynamism. How do we enjoy dynamism normally? Central to this is the element of technique discussed in the introduction.

That technique is central to a consideration of technology and culture is obvious. However, difficult questions soon arise. For example, although we know that machines imply techniques, there is the question of whether they can be used without them. On the other hand, there is the question of whether techniques exist unattached to specific technologies. If so, this implies a much broader scope for the technical. Then there is the question of thought, which could be considered just a series of techniques – such as mnemonics, the art of memory. If thought is only a series of techniques, this might imply that machines could think as well. Could we say that animals possess technique, or mountain ranges, or thunderstorms, or even technologies themselves? A full consideration of technique raises all these issues and more. For some critics then, the unravelling of eternal truths in favour of cultural practices suggests a manner of understanding culture – and indeed the world at large – as a series of forces to be dealt with technically, rather than a series of meanings to be attacked or defended. In this way, meanings become means.

We can follow some of the examples given by Michel Foucault, one of the most influential poststructuralist thinkers. One example (1988) is that the opposition set up between madness and civilization at a certain point in history has no essential basis in truth – a true madness or sanity. Neither madness nor sanity have any intrinsic meaning but are instead produced in the world by a series of technical operations by which we know the world, and each other, through the concepts and practices of madness and sanity. Foucault follows this by arguing that psychoanalysis and other forms of psychiatric regimes do not so much discover neuroses and psychotic behaviours as contribute to their production. These forms of production concerning mental disturbance are subsequently extended into general culture, in the form of notions of mental health, or intellectual performance in IQ tests, magazine self-help quizzes and so forth. Or, the techniques give birth to related technologies: of restraint, from hospitalization and medicinal developments up to contemporary pharmaceuticals or electro-convulsive therapy. In all this, practices and judgements to do with sanity, civilization and madness are the result of cultural and technical *forces*. This is not to say that madness and sanity do not exist. It is rather to comment on how and why they exist as they do. For Foucault, their existence is contingent and technical before it is anything else. Likewise, other supposed essential aspects of the human such as sexualities are produced at certain points of history as a series of techniques that form discourses and bodies in a certain fashion (Foucault 1978).

Foucault's theory is based upon the circulation of techniques as culture. As these techniques shift we know the world – and, we could say, are known by it – differently. For Foucault all knowledge is therefore technical knowledge. Knowledge does not innocently contemplate the world from a distance. Knowledge is instead a series of techniques that participate in, and to some extent organize, a series of forces in the world. This is especially true of abstract knowledge, which is unique only in that it allows a certain portability to the force with which knowledge expresses itself. For example, the abstract concept of the panopticon as developed by Jeremy Bentham – a form of incarceration in which prisoners are disciplined through technologies of surveillance – is portable in that it can be instantiated in a range of institutions and technical practices, from prisons to schools to the monitoring of individual use of the Internet. Foucault pointed to the urgent necessity of a constant re-evaluation of various techniques as a way of the individual being able to respond to the culture in which he or she is immersed, in a kind of 'art of the self'. This takes the way in which the world is given to one – and one is given to the world – and recombines the techniques involved according to one's own needs. In this environment culture can be creative, not in that it consists only in what happens in the arts, but in that it may consist of 'a proliferation of inventions in limited spaces' (De Certeau 1998: viii). The more complexities that move through a small space, the more possibilities there are for invention – in the realm of the everyday especially.

Certainly these ideas have their critics. For the prominent German theorist Jürgen Habermas, for example, these may not be the right questions. He opposes what he called the 'technocratic consciousness' (1996: 53–65) – which he finds in thinkers such as Foucault – to something outside of it. He suggests if we take the technical as the basis for ethics or politics there is the danger of seeming to solve problems without the need for public discussion. This masks the real problem for him, which is precisely one of communication and democratic participation in the life of the society. He proposes the nurturing of what he calls 'communicative action' as a counter to this.

Going with the flow – 'machinic' thought

Yet there is perhaps not such a division between technology and communication as Habermas suggests. Neither is culture perhaps so threatened by the technical as both Foucault and Habermas propose in their different ways. Another perception of the technical would be one perhaps of its adaptability. Much of contemporary cultural life is indeed about adapting our thinking, our perceptions, our techniques and our technologies to accelerating, and more and more interactive, flows. These flows include the movement of planes, trains and automobiles, but they are more generally about what they facilitate. This would include the flow of goods and information around the world in globalization and transnational capital, and the flow of cultures and languages around the world in massive migration and tourism. These flows would also include the urban flows in which each day many individuals travel further from home than many in previous centuries may have travelled in their entire lives.

These ideas can also apply to the *relations between* technologies, animals, humans, and the world, in what we could call the broader 'machinic' way of thinking about the world. This is a manner of thinking most clearly described by Gilles Deleuze and Felix Guattari (1987). What we would normally conceive as specific and isolated technologies are participants in a broader natural and cultural flow in a 'machinic' dimension. This machinic dimension will be a major theme in this book, both as a way of understanding the integration of technology into everyday life, and of accessing some of the more surprising examples of the relations between culture and technology. The latter can, for example, be found in the work of some contemporary artists. Jane Edden's art works often fuse the natural and the technological in startling ways: her *Lemon Field* installation (Figure 1.1) uses 100 lemons as 'batteries' to power mechanical insects. Nigel Helyer's *Silent Forest* installation (Figure 1.2) constructs a 'forest of media technologies', producing a thoroughly technologized naturescape.

In general, technologies are as much relations between cultural and physical forces as they are objects, if not more. This means that technologies can be studied not only in terms of their specific form, but also in terms of their function and their various contexts. What does this mean in practice? Here technologies that look quite similar can in fact function quite differently. Think of a car and a tank – they have quite different functions. Think of the television and the computer monitor, the audiotape and the video cassette, the music compact disc and the CD-ROM (often these two functions are on the same disk these days). Some of these look exactly the same but they often express quite different cultural and natural

Figure 1.1 Jane Edden, *Lemon Field*, 2001

forces. They function quite differently because of the way that they connect to the rest of the world. To sum this up, sometimes it is more important to think of the actual function of a technology – materially and culturally – than its form.

Perhaps one of the reasons that contemporary life seems so determined by technology is not as fundamentally technological as it might seem. It is rather that our thought and culture have finally aligned themselves with flow, become even obsessed by it – in other words, our thought and culture now align themselves with that which technology does best. How do you make people flow? You invent traffic or escalators. How do you fly? You work the flows of air turbulence over a wing. How do you win wars? You work with logistical flows. Most of the technologies developed in the

Figure 1.2   Nigel Helyer, *Silent Forest*, 1996

twentieth century were developed in response to the increasingly complex problems of flows – from air turbulence to the fluctuations of the stock market.

How then does technology fit into all these flows? It is perhaps in thinking about such questions that we rethink the world once again. Here we come to one of the main themes of this book, which is that technological change is both continuous and discontinuous. Technology indeed introduces dramatic changes, but even these changes are not totally removed from what has come before. The computer as a specific idea is at least 300 years old. The effects of plumbing lay the ground for the domestic transformation of kitchens and bathrooms, leading to the developments of kitchen appliances and huge shifts in interior design and urban design. Not the least of these has been the very possibility of satisfactory living in large urban concentrations – something that many technologies both depend upon and make possible – such as the telephone system. Some technologies, like the Walkman, only subsequently become necessary in such an urban space.

As a further contribution to this urban consolidation, with all its benefits and problems, consider the rise of food processing (in cans, for example). Or consider other forms of hygiene development such as the medicalization of the house, the rise of the hospital, urban security technologies. This leads not only to the possibility of the city, but the conquest of the world by the city. The rise of the city as a kind of technology in itself into which humans are inserted leads to some surprisingly machinic claims about humans. In 1937, an ad for a laxative proclaimed that in the modern metropolis where 'high speed living' and 'unfavourable eating and working conditions' make unhealthy demands on the human body . . . The bowel, like a modern railway, must have a regular schedule of operation' (Lupton and Miller 1992: 512).

Technologies do not then, of course, arise magically from out of nowhere, but where do they come from? Here we shall suggest – following Deleuze and Guattari and other thinkers – that technologies, like rivers and streams or developments in the arts, also flow. Like rivers and streams, they are produced by particular contexts and change as these contexts change. Like rivers and streams, they flow into each other, accumulate in larger rivers or split into deltas. Some are like creeks that emerge from hidden underground sources and sink back into them quite quickly. In this light one can look at particular technologies as singularities – in some ways like weather formations – relations of forces that arise from a particular context and flow into one another within that context. Think, for example, of the manner in which the car, the field gun, the terrain of the battlefield and the specific problems of a particular war come together in the development of the tank in the First World War. This is subsequently transformed into other faster tanks, the mobile missile launcher and so on. Or, think of the meeting of photography and the Gatling gun in the cinema (moving still images quickly through a mechanism in the way that a machine gun moves bullets). Think of the subsequent meeting of the cinema and long-distance communications technologies – in the telephone or the radio – which come together in the television, which then enters into a new set of variations – video, digital TV, cable television and the computer interface.

In all these flows singularities form, and although we sometimes focus on these singularities, it is also important to note the flows themselves as primary. There are constant mutations and new developments in these flows but only because they are flowing. When one thinks this through some of the connections become particularly interesting. To take a particularly striking example, Guattari asks, were not the world's

> ... monastic machines, which passed down memories from antiquity to the present day ... the computer programs, the 'macroprocessors' of the middle ages? (1992: 18).

In all this, what is natural and what is artifice? Do the 'natural' and the 'artificial' converge, or, to put this another way, which leads which in technological development?

Deleuze and Guattari (1987: 409) point out that the artisan (or craftsperson who makes swords, locomotives) – and here we can include the new technologist or even the cultural theorist – is involved with following these flows as much as developing them. In this 'following', as with carving some wood, to take a very simple example, there is quite an exchange between what we might normally consider 'natural' and what we might normally consider 'artificial'. At this point it may not make any sense to talk about a division between the two. Deleuze and Guattari point out that even the artisan who appears to work with wood in one location must follow it in other ways. For example, through buying it from someone who logs it, transports it, stores it and so on.

There is a whole network of 'following' surrounding the work with the wood, and we can see that activities such as commerce are a development of this process of following. Artisans, for example, pay people to do some of their 'following' for them. One can link this to the use of wood in the contemporary world that leads to the decimation of forests, the various conflicts of cultures involved, the need to provide employment to whole towns dependent upon logging, and some of the linked effects such as those upon climate and species biodiversity. This shows how complex the flow of movement matter can be. It also shows that an ethical approach to technology/culture issues might be a question of how one follows the flow of forces rather than a question of finding deeper meanings or trying to oppose nature to culture. We shall consider the ramifications of Deleuze and Guattari's 'machinic' thought at various other points in this book.

Virilio and the technologies of speed

Another theorist who will appear in various contexts in this book is Paul Virilio. Virilio is a distinctive thinker who is difficult to categorize: he is, among other things, an urbanist, a Christian, a political theorist and a historian of the military. Virilio shares the pessimism of earlier critical theorists, while his writing could be called poststructuralist in its fragmentary and nonlinear form. He is an interesting thinker for the purposes of this book, as his work is a continuous engagement with the effects of technology on culture; indeed, he sometimes describes himself as an 'art critic of technology' (Madsen 1995: 78).

Lewis Mumford claimed that the clock was 'the key-machine of the modern industrial age', and that the clock remains, in all its phases of development, 'the outstanding fact and the typical symbolism of the machine' (1934: 14). Much of Virilio's writing is concerned with the technologies of speed, which exert a major impact on our sense of time, of space, even of our consciousness. For Virilio, there was nothing confused or complex about the twentieth century. It was 'as brutal as a fist in the face' and was pervaded by 'the horror brought about by technologies that have become autonomous' in a final rush to escape what he calls terminal velocity. Behind all this is a desire to increase speed, which lies behind all politics, all wealth (1986). In short, he asserts that we are losing our sense of space as we more and more push the speed at which things move.

Virilio thinks that the effect of this rush to terminal velocity is that space – the space of the city, of the environment, of the body – is being sacrificed to time. Moreover, having destroyed space, even time begins to implode as everything, particularly communications, accelerates to the speed of light. Space is imploding as we more and more empty it out in order to move communications, weapons and images at the speed of light (1991a, b). Space begins to be swallowed up when weapons systems (and the systems that follow them) reach absolute speed – the speed of a missile that cannot be comprehended. Or the speed of information networks. Space – and our sense of space – is hollowed out by these speeds, and vision at the speed of light becomes little more than a blur. We have absolute vision as we dash around the world as fast as we can carry our signals, or ourselves, but as with a blinding light, we cannot actually 'see' anything. The result is that there is a 'pollution of distances' (Madsen 1995: 80) in the new information networks. This is the 'accident' of the Internet (Virilio 1997). This is the meaning of his resonant phrase 'the aesthetics of disappearance': we have invented machines whose systems are so fast and so complex that they operate beyond human capacity. We program our own disappearance.

Virilio explores the last moments of the struggle between metabolic speed and the technological speed into which we seem to be disappearing. We treat the body as if it was something to 'accelerate' constantly. It is increasingly given rhythms that are imposed technologically (the rhythms of work, of the edit on the screen, of the video clip, of dance music). One instance of this is the alteration of bodily rhythms occasioned by industrial technology, even the use of electric light. An example familiar to modern travellers is jet lag, in which the body is moved through time zones in a disruptive manner. Virilio coins terms to describe the saturation of contemporary culture with technological speed: we live, he says, in a 'dromosphere', or speed-space. The same applies to the mind. Consciousness itself becomes subject to 'cognitive ergonomics' (Madsen 1995: 80), where the realm of metaphysics and of memory are given over to machines. Our consciousness is 'taken by speed', as our media technologies flash information at us in ever faster and shorter bites: a 'picnolepsy', or set of frequent breaks (1983: 30). We have been conditioned to see the world as a series of interruptions, much like the montage of the cinema.

One of Virilio's political projects is to try and recapture some of this time – to 'politicize speed' (1983: 30). This is what he refers to as 'chrono-politics'. The industrial strike, for example, is a 'break' in the machine time of industry. Another of his political projects is to draw attention to what he calls the 'accident'. For Virilio, we do not see that every technology has both its positive and negative sides (this is not initially meant morally). The latter are what he calls generally the 'accident'. These are built into every technology. We have nuclear testing in the Pacific Ocean and elsewhere that fractures coral atolls, and so on. We have crashes, derailments, drug-induced psychoses or crossed telephone lines. One can think of many of these 'accidents'. In fact, Virilio constantly calls for a museum of accidents to remind us about them.

The accident is not just an incidental aside to the main game here, although this is the way that we like to think of it. It is as intrinsically a part of the technology as everything else. Indeed many technologies, one could say, are based upon it – particularly information technologies, which are constantly lauded for the way in which you never quite know what is going to happen – whom you will connect up with on the net, where the Web will take you next. The accidents are built into the system. Risk management, for example, has developed as a profession to oversee such systems. Virilio notes that the accident of the new technologies in particular is that we are now 'killing "present" time' (1997: 10) in a further disruption of a more natural relation to time. The accident is like the unconscious of the technology – that which drives it but which we try to repress. Virilio's work is a vivid reminder that no technology – no matter how 'smart' or sophisticated – is perfect or free of accidents.

CHAPTER 2

Art and Technology

We lay a special emphasis on art in this book for a number of reasons. Contemporary artists are quick to explore the potential of new technologies, which are often used in surprising ways. The cultural ramifications of technology are often examined in artistic works. Several commentators, including McLuhan, have regarded artists as the 'antennae' of society, foreshadowing in their art the social impact of technological change. And the history of art is, after all, also a history of technology. All art employs technology of some kind, whether the materials of visual art, or the instruments used to create music, or the structures and materials of architecture, the art most readily associated with the shaping of technological form.

In this chapter we must limit our discussion. In the next chapter, we shall consider some developments in the many forms of contemporary art that use digital technology. Here we shall concentrate chiefly on the relationship between art and technology in modernism and postmodernism. The historical period involved – from the second half of the nineteenth century to the beginning of the twenty-first – embraces rapid and large-scale technological developments: the growth of industrialism and urbanism, the explosion of mass media, the shift to information economies and globalization. The technologies used to create art have themselves changed rapidly. We shall be inquiring into the role of art, in its many forms, in this period of profound transition. Does art reflect changes in technology and social organization? Does it respond to them? Does it engage with them, does it influence them? Is there any continuity between modernism and postmodernism, or do they represent radically different aesthetic orientations? Finally, what have artists had to say about technology and the societies in which it operates?

The modern

Our first task is to clarify the relation between modernism and modernity – indeed to place some time frame on modernity itself. We shall treat modernity as a historical period, whose genesis and character can be analysed in terms of social, economic and techno-logical changes. We treat modernism as a cultural condition within that historical period. Modernism can then be discussed as first a general sensibility, reflected in the broadest cultural terms – a new way of seeing the world, perhaps, as experienced by people at that time. The more specific sense of modernism concerns its aesthetic expression – the way that art in all its forms represented the changed conditions found in modernity. By extension, we shall regard postmodernity as a historical period succeeding modernity, and postmodernism as a cultural condition and set of artistic practices within that period. This formulation comes with certain reservations, however; as we shall see, some theorists dispute or complicate distinctions between the modern and the postmodern, or indeed between the industrial and the post-industrial.

The relation between modernism and modernity was far from a straightforward one: it was riven with ambiguities and contradic-tions, as we would expect given the dynamic nature of the time. One qualification is already apparent in this context: modernism was certainly not a universal cultural condition in its time period. Modernism was generally restricted to those Western nations that had experienced large-scale industrialization. Even then, politi-cal factors may intervene to thwart the simplistic equation of industrialism, modernity and modernism. The Soviet Union, for example, adopted many features of industrialization developed in the United States, but after a brief flowering of modernism as expressed in Constructivism and other avant-garde movements, the political authority of the Soviet Union banished modernism as an inappropriate aesthetic for the new social order. Modernism was thus the intersection of many factors, not solely the technology factor.

When, then, was modernity? Jürgen Habermas, in his essay 'Modernity – an Incomplete Project' argues that although the term 'modern' had been used since the fifth century, modernity only emerged when developments in eighteenth-century Europe allowed for a new conception of history. Habermas insists that modernity could only emerge when the present was able to detach itself from dependence on the past:

Specifically, the idea of being 'modern' by looking back to the ancients changed with the belief, inspired by modern science, in the infinite progress of knowledge and in the infinite advance towards social and moral betterment (1983: 4).

It was the Enlightenment of eighteenth-century Europe that ushered in this changed consciousness of time, and set the ground-work for artistic modernism. The breakthroughs of science and the elevation of reason in philosophy engendered a new, optimistic orientation to the future. This was the forging of the doctrine of progress. The Enlightenment philosophers believed that through the application of reason they could create a new society unrivalled in its fairness and equality. Progress promised a more just society, liberated from the tyrannies of the past: monarchy, religion, super-stition, fixed social hierarchy. Reason had opened up new fields of knowledge, embodied in the Enlightenment media form, the encyclopaedia. It was felt, to an almost utopian degree, that a truly reasonable society would be achieved as the triumph of historical progress.

It was not until the second half of the nineteenth century, however, that the new *technological* definition of progress emerged. The Victorian period measured progress in industrial terms: speed of movement, volume of production. The train was a symbol of progress, in which contemporaries could feel pride. The historian of technology Leo Marx has discussed the thorough way in which the Enlightenment idea of progress was absorbed into the new inflection of technological progress, whose aim was 'the continu-ing improvement of technology' itself (1995: 20). It was assumed, according to the new doctrine of progress, that better technology would produce a better world.

Artists represent technology

It is now time to consider the various ways in which artists responded to these technological and social transformations. Most commentators agree that the first significant expression of moder-nity in aesthetic terms can be found in the work of French poet and essayist Charles Baudelaire, whose significant writings were published in the 1850s and 1860s. Baudelaire's poetry drew from the streets of Paris, while his essays sought to define a modern sensibility in opposition to the classical French tradition. But

Baudelaire's embrace of modernity only went so far. He ranted against photography as 'art's mortal enemy'; he rejected progress as 'a grotesque idea', evidence of the increasing 'confusion of material order with spiritual order' (Berman 1983: 138).

It would take another four decades before artists could wholeheartedly celebrate the potential of technology. Robert Hughes in *The Shock of the New*, his study of modernism, describes the 'romance' of technology that had developed in Europe and America by the turn of the century. By then, Hughes asserts, culture had been reinvented through technological innovation occurring at an 'almost preternatural speed'. Hughes describes the early modernist sensibility, between 1880 and 1914, as 'the sense of an accelerated rate of change in all areas of human discourse' (1991: 15). A list of significant technological inventions provides some indication of this rate of change: the phonograph (1877), synthetic fibre (1883), the box camera and pneumatic tyre (1888), the Diesel engine (1892), the Ford car (1893), X-rays, radio telegraphy, the movie camera (1895) and many other achievements including powered flight (1903). Sigmund Freud's *The Interpretation of Dreams* (1900) and Albert Einstein's *Special Theory of Relativity* (1905) opened up vast new spaces for thought, with profound consequences across culture. The rapidly growing cities and their proud technological emblems such as the Eiffel Tower (finished in 1889), combined with an optimistic faith in the benefits of science and technology, created a sense of the world being created anew.

This element of 'newness' was perhaps the defining element of the modernist experience. Old ideas were rejected if they could not meet the challenge of the new, whether expressed in science, technology or philosophy. Some modernists promoted the notion of the avant-garde, originally a military term, now used to suggest the daring of those who ventured into new cultural territory, leading the more cautious mainstream. Habermas finds in this groping towards an 'undefined future' the basic characteristic of modernism: its 'changed consciousness of time' (1983: 4). It was the artists of the first two decades of the twentieth century who most spectacularly charted the possibilities of a world oriented to the new.

It would be a mistake, however, to regard the modernists as a homogeneous group, especially concerning their attitudes to technology. Many of the great modernist artists, including the Abstract painters, explored an inner psychic space removed from technological development. The Dada artists who came to prominence in

1916 with their Cabaret Voltaire, celebrated the irrational in opposition to 'progress', a direction elaborated by the Surrealists under the influence of Freud. Other modernists drew on styles and motifs from the past or non-Western cultures. Andreas Huyssen has gone so far as to claim that the twentieth-century avant-garde may be defined by its attitude – positive or negative – to technology (1986: 9). Yet despite their differences, modernists in all the art forms shared one chief objective: to find new modes of representation that might reflect the changed world around them.

The Futurists

From the point of view of technology and art, the most pertinent – and the most interesting – group of modernists were the Futurists, who announced themselves in their founding manifesto of 1909. They exemplified the modernist avant-garde: provocative, often outrageous, contemptuous of tradition and respectability, self-promoting through their manifestos and staged public events. What made them distinctive was their infatuation with technology and its potential:

> We declare that the world's splendour has been enriched by a new beauty; the beauty of speed. A racing motor-car, its frame adorned with great pipes, like snakes with explosive breath, a roaring motor-car, which looks as though running on shrapnel, is more beautiful than the *Victory of Samothrace* (Marinetti 1961: 124).

This *Initial Manifesto of Futurism* was written by F.T. Marinetti, poet, entrepreneur and leader of the Futurists. Marinetti was excited by the industrialization taking place in northern Italian cities such as Milan; he devoted his prolific writing to dragging Italy from its agrarian past into a technological future. Having bought, and promptly crashed, an automobile, he was intoxicated by the thrill and danger made possible by technological speed – a dizzying beauty which he elevated above classical virtues as embodied in the ancient Greek statue *Victory of Samothrace*. For Marinetti, art now could only mean looking forward, never backward:

> Why should we look behind us, when we have to break in the mysterious portals of the Impossible? Time and Space died yesterday. Already we live in the absolute, since we have already created speed, eternal and ever-present (1961: 124).

Marinetti's turbulent prose has echoes of Einstein (Time and Space died yesterday) and the contemporary philosophy of Henri Bergson, which emphasized flux and dynamism over stasis. Futurist aesthetics valued the dynamic over the static, technology over nature. The city with its noise, movement and industrial rhythms was to be the new material of art:

> We shall sing of the great crowds in the excitement of labour, pleasure and rebellion; of the multi-coloured and polyphonic surf of revolutions in modern capital cities; of the nocturnal vibrations of arsenals and workshops beneath their violent electric moons . . . (1961: 124).

Electric light was to be preferred as subject matter to the moon – once beloved of the Romantics, but sickly and inferior for the Futurists. Marinetti declared war on the past and all its institutions: 'We wish to destroy the museums, the libraries,' he declared, likening them to cemeteries. Youth and vigour were to be celebrated, decay to be dreaded.

Marinetti's embrace of technological progress was complete. Science was seen not as the enemy of art but its 'vivifying current'. The artists who joined Marinetti in the Futurist movement looked to science and technology for their inspiration. High-speed photography, cinema and the X-ray revealed new dimensions of movement and perception; the paintings produced by Balla, Boccioni, Severini and Carra in the period 1909–14 were informed by these insights. Balla projected speed and movement into his paintings, most famously in *Dynamism of a Dog on Leash* of 1912, which depicted the dog's movement through space and time. Boccioni depicted the 'force lines' of objects and the rhythms of motion in many paintings, inspired by the energies and speeds of machinery.

The Futurists did not restrict themselves to painting: their resolve to develop an aesthetic of dynamism found outlets across a range of media. 'Photo-dynamism', a photographic technique to display movement, was used early; Marinetti developed 'words in freedom', incorporating experimental typography, as a literary technique; Boccioni's sculpture *Unique Forms of Continuity in Space* is an enduring Futurist work capturing dynamism in solid form. Russolo turned to music, publishing his manifesto *The Art of Noises* in 1913, in which he proposed the acceptance of noise into composition (Figure 2.1). He invented a number of Intonarumori (noise-organs that generated a variety of mechanical sounds) to be used in compositions such as *The Awakening of a Great City*. While the

Figure 2.1 Luigi Russolo, *Music*, 1911

instruments themselves did not survive, the Art of Noises concept exerted a profound influence on succeeding composition, including electronic music. There was also Futurist theatre, Futurist performance, Futurist film, Futurist food (pasta was condemned as too heavy and slow), Futurist clothing, even Futurist sleeping (briefly, standing up). For a brief period, the Futurists extended the radical avant-garde into a total way of life.

Several leading Futurists, including Boccioni and the architect Sant'Elia, were killed fighting in the First World War. This was one result of the Futurists' faith in the healing powers of technology, which extended to technological warfare – described by Marinetti as 'the world's sole hygiene'. Such a blind faith in technology, even its destructive potential, is untenable today; indeed it was untenable for many during the Great War. The Dadaists' celebration of absurdity in 1916, for example, was motivated by the horror of that war's battles. There are aspects of Marinetti's creed that are certainly repellent; his militarism and patriotism, combined with his glorification of technology and youth, fed into Fascist propaganda in the 1920s. Marinetti had earlier unsuccessfully launched a Futurist political party, with an anarchist programme of hopelessly unrealistic policies; Mussolini's Fascists offered a surer route to power.

This affiliation between the post-war version of Italian Futurism and Fascism blackened Futurist aesthetics for decades. The Marxist critic Walter Benjamin included a political critique of Futurism in his famous essay of 1936, 'The Work of Art in the Age of Mechanical Reproduction'. Marinetti's glorification of technological warfare, argued Benjamin, supported the Fascist aestheticization of a destructive, self-alienated politics. In more recent years, Paul Virilio has persistently connected Futurist imagery of speed and aerial assault with military propaganda, running from Fascism to the high-tech media shows since the Gulf War. This line of criticism is undoubtedly valid: Marinetti made no secret of his passion for imperialistic war. Yet it presents only part of the Futurist legacy. Futurist ideas spread quickly across Europe, taking on varying orientations in different environments. Italian Futurism was the direct inspiration for Russian Constructivism, which became for a short period the aesthetic wing of the Bolshevik Revolution. In 1921 the Italian Marxist theorist Antonio Gramsci saw the Futurists as cultural revolutionaries, praising their destruction of rigid traditions and values (Tisdall and Bozzolla 1993: 201).

How can we summarize the Futurists' cultural influence, apart from their mixed political legacy? Their espousal of technology may seem utopian, even demented at its more extreme points. Yet by absorbing the properties of the machine into their art, they built a prototype that is still being used by artists. Technology and technological processes could now be both the subject and material of art, as cyberartists continue to demonstrate in the digital age. The Futurists' shock tactics and self-promotional use of the media set the template for all other avant-gardists and provocateurs to follow. Their alternative values, as expressed in multifaceted public events, were echoed decades later in the counter-culture 'happenings' of the 1960s, and later in rave culture. The celebration of youth and danger was revived in the 'Hope I die before I get old' ethos of rock and youth culture, while the love of technological speed is evident in cultural forms as diverse as game parlours, Formula One racing and techno-music. We are removed today from the Futurists' unbridled belief in technology and its liberating power, yet aspects of their romance with the machine remain with us.

The Constructivists

The other group of modernists with a direct relation to technology were the Constructivists, who flourished in the decade following the 1917 Russian Revolution. Like the Italian Futurists before them, the Constructivists longed to drag their rural nation into the machine age; like the Futurists they had a utopian faith in the powers of industrial technology to shape a marvellous new world; like the Futurists they were mainly young artists who revered the new at the expense of tradition. But unlike the Futurists, they dedicated their art to the service of the state, in their case the new Soviet state.

The abiding metaphor of Constructivism in all its forms was the machine. The artist was an engineer; art had to be a useful object in the radical reconstruction of society. The film-maker Eisenstein, for example, developed a theory of montage (editing) as a series of shocks, which he likened to the explosions of an internal combustion engine. In theatre, Meyerhold devised an anti-naturalistic technique of acting he called 'bio-mechanics'. The artists Tatlin, Lissitzky and Rodchenko, working in a range of media, saw themselves as artists/technicians, contributing directly to the emergent state. Agit-prop trains took Constructivist art to the provinces; the works – whether posters, sculptures or films – were meant to be accessible to all. Radical formal effects were often married to propaganda purposes, most brilliantly in Dziga Vertov's film *Man with a Movie Camera* (1929), in which a dizzying array of technical devices was placed at the service of documenting the revolutionary state. The 'hero' in this film was as much the camera – the 'mechanical eye' – as it was the Soviet people.

Constructivism enjoyed the support of the Soviet authorities in the heady years succeeding 1917. But official approval of avant-garde techniques did not last long: by the ascent of Stalin to power in 1924, avant-garde practice was criticized as decadent formalism, and the more formally radical of the Constructivists were suppressed. Some, like Eisenstein, were officially marginalized; others, like the poet Mayakovsky – former 'Moscow Futurist' then enthusiastic revolutionary artist – committed suicide in despair; others, like Meyerhold, defiantly critical of the authorities to the end, never returned from state labour camps.

Machine modernism

In the early optimistic years of the Soviet Union, however, the enthusiasm for all things modern and technological is striking, as Peter Wollen has remarked in his essay 'Cinema/Americanism/ The Robot'. Progress through technology was given the term 'Americanism', a force to be championed. As Wollen observes, 'Americanization stood for true modernity, the liquidation of stifling traditions and shackling life-styles and work-habits' (1989: 7). Central to this 'Americanism' was the system of industrial production known as Taylorism, enshrined in Frederick Taylor's *Principles of Scientific Management* (1911). Taylor devised a method based on simplified movements for workers, as determined by rigorous time-and-motion studies. Taylorism was the rationalization of labour on the model of the machine. Each movement was meticulously timed and planned to generate maximum efficiency; the system 'heralded a new epoch in which the worker would become as predictable, regulated, and effective as the machine itself' (Wollen 1989: 8).

Taylor's method was implemented in Henry Ford's automobile factory. Ford organized the production process around an assembly line and a Taylorized workforce: each worker had one basic and highly repetitive task to perform. By extension, 'Fordism' represented a new form of social organization, in which industrial production was 'a kind of super-machine in its own right, with both human and mechanical parts' (Wollen 1989: 8). This highly mechanized system, with its attendant boredom and alienation for the labour force, was the target of Charlie Chaplin's satirical film *Modern Times* (1936). Chaplin plays the Taylorized worker – a mere cog in a giant machine – driven mad by the constant repetition of his mechanical task. Unable to switch himself off even in leisure time, he is compelled to tighten noses and buttons as if they were bolts. The film's famous image – of Chaplin being physically absorbed into the machine – is one of the most powerful artistic critiques of Taylorism and its human cost.

The German critic Walter Benjamin provided some of the most interesting insights into the intersection of modernity and technology. Benjamin's cultural criticism has proven enormously influential, its richness springing from the contradictions in Benjamin himself (he was a Marxist with something of a mystical bent). 'The Work of Art in the Age of Mechanical Reproduction' is Benjamin's sustained attempt to base a Marxist aesthetic on the cultural effects of media technology. He finds something intrinsically liberating in one of the basic constituents of mass culture – the mechanical reproduction of images – which withers the 'aura' of art works:

> ... the technique of reproduction detaches the reproduced object from the domain of tradition. By making many reproductions it substitutes a plurality of copies for a unique existence (1970: 223).

By 'aura' Benjamin meant that sense of distance, of unattainability and uniqueness, surrounding great works of art. The aura of mystification had sustained social hierarchies – religious and political – for centuries. Now photographic reproductions of unique works shattered that aura: a widely distributed photo of a great work can be physically handled and owned by anyone. Benjamin applauded the democratic consequences of this process, in which the work of art is 'emancipated' from its 'parasitical dependence on ritual'. Benjamin extended his analysis of mass media technology to cinema, whose 'constant, sudden change' of images may induce a 'heightened presence of mind' in spectators (1970: 240). In the rapid discontinuity of film editing, Benjamin saw the incorporation of avant-garde practice into mass culture. The Dadaists had used shock tactics which 'hit the spectator like a bullet', destroying art's complacency. Benjamin discerned a generalized shock effect in the very form of the industrial mass art of cinema.

Wollen describes this essay by Benjamin as 'the high point of the modernist theory of cinema'. Inspired by the Soviet film-makers, Benjamin ascribed to cinema – and to the camera in general – a progressive role in mass culture. As Scott McQuire has observed in his book *Visions of Modernity*, Benjamin located the camera's 'revolutionary effect' in its ability to break the spell of 'cult value', even that of the commodity culture which had developed in the nineteenth century. Benjamin 'posited the historic role of the camera as its ability to "awaken" the masses from their commodity-induced slumber' (McQuire 1998: 187n.). Yet Benjamin was supple enough to note that capitalist cinema could employ the same technical apparatus for the opposite effect – the manufacture of celebrity, with its spellbinding appeal:

The film responds to the shriveling of the aura with an artificial build-up of the 'personality' outside the studio. The cult of the movie star, fostered by the money of the film industry, preserves not the unique aura of the person but the 'spell of the personality', the phony spell of the commodity (Benjamin 1970: 233).

Benjamin was grappling in theoretical terms with the paradoxes of technology in the modernist age. He and other theorists of the Left such as Gramsci hoped to make something positive of the mechanization of life, even of Taylorism. A similar impulse can be found in various artists apart from the Futurists and Constructivists. The French painter Fernand Leger, for example, depicted humans and machines in the same visual terms, embodying 'an idea of society-as-machine, bringing harmony and an end to loneliness' (Hughes 1991: 36). But the most influential embrace of technology and its transforming powers was found in modernist architecture. Twentieth-century architects had new materials to work with – the steel frame, sheet glass, the elevator – components which made possible that awe-inspiring icon of modernity, the skyscraper. Yet the driving force of modernist architecture, a force that moulded buildings and cities around the world, was the set of aesthetic principles promulgated by a key group of defiantly modern architects.

These aesthetic principles fused a utopian impulse with technological rationalization. They rejected traditional aesthetics, venerating the properties of the machine with a zeal equal to that of the Futurists. Strict economy of design was wedded to a will to improve social conditions by technological means. This idealistic programme was articulated by the Bauhaus school in Germany, founded in 1919 under the leadership of architect Walter Gropius. Bauhaus design was austere, minimal, in line with a machine aesthetic. Non-functional decoration was outlawed, as was every trace of the past. Whether designing furniture or mass housing, Gropius demanded 'a decidedly positive attitude to the living environment of vehicles and machines – avoiding all romantic embellishment and whimsy' (Hughes 1991: 195). Similarly, 'form follows function' and 'less is more' were the aesthetic tenets implemented on an international scale by the architects Le Corbusier and Mies van der Rohe. Le Corbusier, who described the house as 'a machine for living in', extended the machine model to mass housing and town planning:

You will inevitably arrive at the 'House-Tool', the mass-produced house, available for everyone, incomparably healthier than the old kind (and morally so too) ... (Hughes 1991: 195).

The architecture historian Charles Jencks characterizes this hugely influential Modern Movement, known also as the International Style after 1932, in religious terms – but a religion of the future rather than the past. He notes that Gropius called the Bauhaus 'a cathedral of the future'; Le Corbusier saw his work as a 'crusade' for 'a new spirit' (Jencks 1989: 25). This spirit was defined by Mies as 'art and technology: a new unity'. In a secular age these high modernists were prophets of a new faith. Mies proclaimed that industrialization, guided by the spirit of modernism, could solve all problems, even social ones. The urban slums of previous centuries would, it was assumed, be eradicated by the modernist purity of design enacted on a grand scale – that is, high-rise buildings and vast housing projects. Modernist architecture provides a spectacular demonstration of the contradictions within modernist culture: a belief in progress and rationalization on the one hand, a utopian desire on the other. For those modernists who embraced it, the machine was far more than a tool. It was infused with a spiritual dimension, as the means for forging a new, superior, world.

Modern to postmodern: Pop Art

The shift from a modernist cultural condition to a postmodern one is extremely difficult to chart with precision. The term 'postmodern' was first mentioned in the 1930s, but it was not until the 1970s that it was used with any great frequency. Jencks described a break from modernist architecture in the 1970s, with characteristics that seemed reflective of more general cultural trends. Daniel Bell's book *The Cultural Contradictions of Capitalism* (1976) discussed the 'post-modernist temper' as a function of advanced capitalism's emphasis on consumption over production. By the 1980s, the commentary of Lyotard, Jameson, Baudrillard and many other theorists had set the parameters of postmodern culture; the term became increasingly used in the mass media, gaining acceptance outside academic circles.

'Postmodernism' remains a highly contentious concept, much

discussed and disputed. There are in fact many versions of it, drawing on a range of theoretical perspectives; this confusion over postmodernism may well be part of the condition itself. We shall simplify the issue in this chapter by restricting our overview to the relation between technology and culture. We discuss the 1960s as a transitional period between the modern and the postmodern. Significant changes in technologies of production, including that of the media, were expressed in that decade on a cultural level, most notably in Pop Art. Electronics industries, information systems and the prominence of the mass media were all exerting cultural influence. Cultural theory of the time engaged with the restructuring of societies: Peter Wollen sees McLuhan as the 1960s prophet of the emerging electronic age. Another theorist to document these changes was the French writer Guy Debord. In his 1967 book *Society of the Spectacle*, he argued that the commodification of culture had reached such a degree that life itself had become mediated by mass-produced spectacles. As a result, lived experience was alienated, as consumers preferred the copy to the thing:

> In societies where modern conditions of production prevail, all of life presents itself as an immense accumulation of *spectacles*. Everything that was directly lived has moved away into a representation (Thesis 1).

This idea, subsequently developed at length by Baudrillard, was Debord's critical insight into the proliferation of consumer and media culture in the 1960s.

Consumer culture and media saturation were two themes that found expression in the Pop Art movement of the 1960s. For our purposes, Pop Art is significant for at least two reasons: it represented a break from the artistic principles of modernism, and it related directly to the image-making technologies of mass culture. By the 1950s, modernist art had overcome much of its earlier opposition; Abstract Expressionism in particular had become accepted as an authentic mode of expression, its leading practitioners such as Jackson Pollock revered as great contemporary artists. The critic Clement Greenberg upheld modernist art for its depth and intensity, for the way it conveyed the essence of each art form.

In the late 1950s and early 1960s, the appearance of Pop Art works – laden with irony and imitation of commercial forms – was an affront to these lofty ideals. Richard Hamilton, for example, produced collage works drawing directly on advertising imagery. Their titles, such as *Just What Is It That Makes Today's Homes So*

Different, So Appealing? (1956), were ironic commentaries on the language of consumerism. In his book *Art in the Age of Mass Media*, John A. Walker discusses the 'quotational' techniques of Pop artists like Hamilton, techniques that were to become a staple of post-modern art. For Walker, Pop Art's significance was its concentration on the artificial world of signs and images, at the expense of nature or the inner depths of the psyche. Pop Art reflected a 'media-saturated environment', a 'humanly constructed world of buildings, interiors, roads, traffic, signs, posters, newspapers, radio and television broadcasts' (1983: 22). The silk-screen works of Robert Rauschenberg, for example, were composed of fragmented images taken from the media and reassembled by the artist. Other Pop artists were more brazen, accommodating popular imagery without the lyricism of Rauschenberg's works. Roy Lichstenstein produced paintings that reproduced the look and the content of comic books; Andy Warhol exhibited reproductions of soup cans and Brillo boxes.

The response from the modernist establishment was predictably critical: for Greenberg these works betrayed a lowering of art's standards by mass industrial culture. But it was precisely that industrial culture with which Pop Art was engaged. Pop Art blurred the distinction between high and low culture: the artists, many of whom came from commercial backgrounds, used popular culture as their material in a way which defied modernist expectations. Whereas modernist art was 'deep', Pop was deliberately shallow; modernism was intense, Pop was cool; modernism could be spiritual, Pop was ironic; modernism might express angst, Pop was more likely to tell jokes. Pop Art had no quest for transgression or transcendence; it seemed content to appropriate hot dogs, Coke bottles and other artefacts of mass culture. Yet much of this appropriation was made with an ironic double edge. At times Pop seemed to be affirming the exuberance of popular culture, at others it presented at least the possibility of a critique. Lichtenstein's simulations of violent comic book imagery, for example, point to the extreme violence cheerily depicted in popular entertainment. Warhol, often dismissed as an apologist for consumerism, could suggest the numbing effect of media representation in his *Disaster* series, featuring repeated media images of car crashes and other accidents.

Warhol's use of extreme repetition in his silk screen-works negotiated some of the concerns expressed by Walter Benjamin three decades earlier. Working in his studio known as 'The Factory',

Warhol imitated the mechanical reproduction of images in mass culture, demonstrating the lack of 'aura' in standardized mass production and consumption. Yet his famous serial images of Marilyn Monroe and Elvis Presley depict the other process noted by Benjamin: the mechanical production of celebrity. The mass media creates 'stars', bestowing an artificial aura through persistent exposure and marketing – that is, repetition. Celebrities are at base commodities like any other; Warhol's repetition of their image lays bare the mechanical construction of these contemporary icons.

Walker emphasizes the subversive effect of Warhol's explicit machine aesthetic. Warhol professed that he wanted to be a machine; his technique elevated the repetition, banality and boredom of automated production, refuting notions of originality and craftsmanship. If we compare Warhol's art with that of the Futurists, we find some continuity regarding the role of technology. Both self-consciously absorb mechanical properties into their art, both express admiration for machines, both use technological processes as material for their art. Yet there is none of the evangelical zeal of the Futurists in Warhol, no avant-garde conviction that art can change the world. Warhol was coolly detached, ambiguous at most. He declared outright that art had no revolutionary capacity; in the later stages of his career he was content with celebrity status. In his use of found materials, his denial of originality, and his ironic concept of art, Warhol pointed not back to the Futurists, but forward to postmodernism.

What were some of the other developments in the 1960s and 1970s that contributed to the advent of postmodernity? Changes to the technical conditions of production and consumption culminated in a generalized condition known as 'Post-Fordism'. Production became less regimented, developing greater flexibility in response to more diversified markets. Technologies of automation assumed significance; 'cybernetics' – concerned with automatic or self-regulated systems – was pursued on a number of fronts, while the figure of the 'cyborg' (cybernetic organism) began to exercise the popular imagination. Satellite technology marked a major step towards globalization, extending the role of media and popular culture (the international satellite broadcast of 1967 featured the Beatles performing 'All You Need Is Love'). Feminism advanced a critique of the traditional role of women, using the media itself to question images of femininity – a successful 'deconstruction' of conventionally accepted meaning that would inspire subsequent developments in identity politics. The environmental movement, marginalized at first, gradually assumed a more commanding social role, partly due to its skilful manipulation of the mass media. The growing public awareness of environmental damage due to pollution, industrial accident and ecological insensitivity, contributed to an erosion of the faith in technological progress. Conservation, recycling and care for the environment were proposed as alternatives to unchecked 'progress'. Mass culture was becoming increasingly plural, whether due to the influx of immigrant cultures, the reach of global media, or the hunger for alternative ideas.

In artistic terms, modernism no longer seemed capable of engaging with this cultural flux. The 'shock of the new' had been absorbed into museums and academies as an official, prestigious aesthetic language. Modernist purity, whether in painting, music or architecture, had solidified into convention, or worse, elitism, alienating both the mass audience and new generations of artists. Popular culture, meanwhile, was becoming more sophisticated, as experimental techniques were used in popular contexts, most evidently in music. Following the example of Pop Art, artists and theorists looked to the mass media and popular culture for inspiration. The architect Robert Venturi declared in *Learning from Las Vegas* (1972) that architecture could learn valuable lessons from the 'intensified communication along the highway'. Rejecting the 'heroic' modernist ideals of purity of space and structure, Venturi and his colleagues celebrated the plurality of styles, tastes and signs found in popular culture and commercial design. For these and many other artists and critics, modernism was no longer the undisputed way forward; indeed, the notion of going 'forward' was itself under challenge.

Postmodern aesthetics

While most theorists are cautious about dating general cultural shifts, Charles Jencks is prepared to pinpoint the death of modernism, at least in architectural terms, down to the minute. Many of the large-scale housing projects built according to modernist principles had not turned out as planned. Rather than uplifting their inhabitants and improving the social climate, they had proved alienating and unpopular. By the early 1970s, several had been abandoned as failures; some were detonated. Jencks regards the demolition of one massive project as symbolic of the death of modernist architecture and its ideals. Modernism 'expired finally and completely in 1972,' or, more specifically:

> ... [it] died in St Louis, Missouri on July 15, 1972 at 3.32 pm (or thereabouts) when the infamous Pruitt-Igoe scheme, or rather several of its slab blocks, were given the final coup de grace by dynamite (1987: 9).

For Jencks, modernism failed as mass housing in part because it failed to communicate with its inhabitants, who did not like the style, understand it or even know how to use it.

Postmodern architecture emerged partly as an attempt to redeem this failure of communication. The rigorous austerity of modernist aesthetics was dismissed as elitist. Postmodern design and architecture instead sought, according to Jencks, to communicate to its observers and users 'through a variety of styles and devices'. Often these styles came from the pre-modernist past, as architects turned to history for inspiration, thus marking an emphatic shift away from the modernist obsession with newness. The embellishment and decoration outlawed by the International Style returned in postmodernism, in the form of quotation. A postmodern building was a mix of styles from different historical periods; eclecticism replaced purity as the governing artistic principle. Modernist style was now simply one style among many from which to choose.

Jencks defines postmodernism as 'the continuation of Modernism and its transcendence'. Modernist ideas were still employed, but in combination with others, in a process termed by Jencks as 'double coding', by which he means:

> ... the combination of Modern techniques with something else (usually traditional building) in order for architecture to communicate with the public and a concerned minority, usually other architects (1989: 19).

'Double coding' thus has a double meaning: the combination of the new and old; and the ability to communicate with both elite and popular opinion. A postmodern building may appeal to the general public due to its decorative design; at the same time, observers familiar with the history of architecture may derive additional pleasure from identifying the various historical quotations incorporated into the building.

Jencks's discussion of postmodern architecture may be usefully extended to postmodern culture in general. Whereas modernism looked forward, postmodernism is often oriented to the past. The notion of the avant-garde was jettisoned by postmodern artists; its forward drive was replaced by an interest in recycling previous cultural forms. This orientation to the past is different from the reverence for the past of the Renaissance, or the sentimental attitude found in Romanticism. Postmodernism looks to history as a data bank of styles, images and techniques. Postmodern works are often hybrids, composed of fragments drawn from the range and history of culture. Whether a building, a novel or a piece of music, the postmodern work is an amalgam of styles, an intertextual 'tissue of quotations' in Roland Barthes's phrase (1977: 146). Influences are foregrounded rather than disguised; in this multiplicity there is no one dominant style.

Postmodern artists desired to produce art that was more accessible to a general public than had been the case in much of modernism. Postmodern works often speak to different audiences, with different knowledges and expectations, at the same time. This is evident in much of popular culture – in *The Simpsons*, for example, with its sophisticated quotations and parodies of media culture, or in the intertextual cinema of the Coen Brothers. This aspect of postmodernism – its ironic yet affectionate appropriation of past works – is perhaps the feature that distinguishes it most clearly from modernism.

Critical approaches to postmodernism

The range of interpretations of postmodernism covers a very broad spectrum. Jean-François Lyotard's well-known definition of the postmodern as an 'incredulity toward metanarratives' (1984: xxiv) has been influential in fostering a positive appraisal. For Lyotard, certain grand narratives of the West have been put into crisis. One of these is that of humanity as the hero of liberation through historical struggle, that is, through the revolutionary activity by which the production of knowledge and of the social is seized from those who would oppress the mass of humanity. The other is that of the gradual triumph of the speculative spirit, through higher education for example, but generally through the processes developed in philosophy and socially neutral science rather than politics. Recent events have brought two realizations. The first is that the revolution – as a final step towards human liberation – is not coming. We shall always have to struggle for justice and move backward in this respect as well as forward. The second is that we are not a society heading for enlightenment in the sense suggested by the Enlightenment project that began in the West 300 years ago. Lyotard argues that these 'heroic' narratives have failed, leaving societies and social acts based on 'little narratives' (*petits récits*) (1984: 60). Partly due to the enhanced technical determination of knowledge, these little compartmentalized narratives function in specific contexts. We shall return to the *petits récits* at the end of the book.

The fragmentation and pluralism of postmodernism are, for the critical approach following Lyotard, preferable to the totalizing tendency of modernist thought. Postmodernism is favoured because it 'refines our sensitivity to differences' (Lyotard 1984: xxv). Thus postmodernism is welcomed by many artists and theorists for its inclusive nature, as opposed to the elitism and arrogance of much modernist culture. Female artists and artists from non-English-speaking backgrounds have certainly become more prominent in the West in the postmodern era, a development reflected in the growing interest in feminist and post-colonial studies in poststructuralist theory. The playful irreverence of postmodern art similarly appears attractive to many observers, contrasting with the monolithic authority typified by the International Style modernists.

Yet this enthusiasm is far from universal. Habermas contests the 'neoconservatism' of postmodernist thought; for him modernity is 'an incomplete project' which should not be abandoned in a reflex rejection of reason. Other critics, including Terry Eagleton and Christopher Norris, have attacked the apolitical, even fatalistic character of much postmodern thought. The relativism of values and the protective screen of irony can result, it is asserted, in art and theory with no critical or oppositional edge, compliant in commodification and mainstream values. The most influential exponent of this line of criticism has been Frederic Jameson, who calls postmodernism 'the cultural logic of late capitalism'. Postmodern eclecticism is, for Jameson, an expression of capital's need to generate 'new' forms and patterns of consumption; the relativism of values is already implicit in the relativism of consumer capitalism, in which every item can be reduced to a monetary value. The appropriation of the past in postmodern culture is for Jameson merely 'pastiche', which he defines as 'blank parody' (1983: 114). Pastiche is a recycling of the past without the critical edge of satire or the subversive role of parody; it is a gesture to the past in a media-saturated culture that lives 'in a perpetual present'.

Jameson's criticism has been contested by other theorists, including Zygmunt Bauman and Linda Hutcheon. Bauman considers postmodern art 'a subversive force', in that it acts 'as a sort of intellectual and emotional antifreeze', laying bare the process of meaning-making and interpretation (1997: 107). Hutcheon finds in postmodern art levels of subtlety and subversion unacknowledged by Jameson. Hutcheon sees paradox as the defining feature of postmodern cultural politics. Contemporary artists engage with the complex systems of the media and the market with strategies of 'subversive complicity', by which she means the ability to operate within dominant codes of representation while at the same time questioning them. Unlike Jameson, Hutcheon identifies parody, satire and other critical mechanisms at work in postmodern irony; she also notes the sophistication of its artistic strategies. For Hutcheon, postmodern art uses an 'insider' position to 'de-toxify' cultural conventions (1989: 119).

Postmodern media art

The 'subversive complicity' identified by Hutcheon may be observed in the work of many postmodern artists who use media technologies in their work. It is significant that Barbara Kruger, Cindy Sherman, Sherrie Levine, and many other early postmodern artists, have worked with the technologies and strategies of mass media. Following the Pop artists, postmodern practitioners often situate their art in the terrain of mass-produced signs, in the technologies of representation. Thus Kruger's postmodern photographic art operates within the language and iconic system of consumer culture, while offering a critique of that mode of representation.

Postmodern artists often exploit the seductive power of images, appropriating them to speak within and against conventions of representation. The 'Untitled Film Stills' of Cindy Sherman are an excellent example of this approach: Sherman literally embodies the stereotypes of femininity found in TV, film and advertising. By photographing herself in simulations of diverse media images of women, she appears to 'become' a different woman each time – but of course she 'is' none of them. Each image is a mask, constructed by the technological means of photography and art direction. By appropriating these different images, Sherman makes the viewer aware of their constructed nature.

Multimedia performance art exemplifies the postmodern aesthetic at work, in its hybrid nature, its foregrounding of media technologies, and its fragmented or multiple narratives. Nicholas Zurbrugg considers the 'multilinear narratives' found in the works of Robert Wilson, Heiner Muller and others, 'peculiar to postmodern culture's multimedia sensibility' (2000: 118). Multimedia performance draws on a tradition of mixed media production, spanning the avant-garde events of early modernism (Futurism and Dada), the mixed media works of the Fluxus movement in the 1960s (Nam June Paik's sculptures made from TV sets), and the media-based interventions of the Situationist movement in the 1960s. From the 1980s on, digital technologies were incorporated into performance, as in Laurie Anderson's concerts and projects. Anderson's inventive use of sampling and other sound treatment effects, including lowering the pitch of her voice, are part of her exploration of technology's effect on gender and subjectivity, in the context of concerts that are both entertaining and intellectually engaging.

The postmodern multimedia performance works of Muller and Wilson incorporated an imposing machine aesthetic. Muller's productions, including his *Hamletmachine*, deliberately dehumanized characters, elevating lighting and sound effects as components of the production. Technology itself becomes a character, while actors work within a restricted emotional range. In this way, characters were seen to participate in architectural and spatial arrangements: technology assumes an elevated role. Wilson draws on much of the non-narrative avant-garde, especially Surrealism, in his productions, while utilizing contemporary technologies. Video and projected images are involved in a staged universe where actors move slowly or conduct repetitive tasks. His collaboration with Philip Glass in *Einstein on the Beach* (first performed in 1976) is perhaps his most influential work, transforming notions of music theatre, performance and design in an epic work of fragmentation and extended repetition.

The legacy of this machine aesthetic may be seen in many contemporary multimedia performance groups, including Knowbotic Research and Dumb Type. The latter group's events are powerful syntheses of performance, dance and technological effects. Lighting, amplified sound and other technological forms create an environment that continually impinges on bodies and psyches, both literally and figuratively. Other contemporary multimedia art uses technology in more accessible, or playful, ways. The group Audiorom develop interactive technologies that allow for the collaboration of a number of users in triggering sound samples, thereby becoming multiple authors of a musical composition. Sound, image and tactility are invoked in a constantly evolving relationship according to the input of multiple users.

The multimedia performance group Blast Theory stage their events in the public eye – that is, on the media. One of their most notorious events was *Kidnap* of 1998. This allowed for members of the public to enter a lottery in which first prize was to be abducted without warning and held captive for 48 hours. The hostage process was webcast live, while the entire event, including sur-veillance of prospective kidnap victims, was publicized widely in the British media. The media's reaction, a mixture of moral outrage and fascination, was the most revealing aspect of the event. Blast Theory's publicizing of this kidnapping, achieved by a skilful handling of media and public relations, parodied and subverted the media's role in terrorism. It was an effective instance of the 'sub-versive complicity' characteristic of postmodern art at its most provocative.

Continuity or discontinuity?

In making distinctions between modern and postmodern, indus-trial and post-industrial, we are engaging in a periodization of history. This implies a concept of cultural history as a series of distinctive epochs, separated from other periods by their radical difference. Such a discontinuous notion of history has been heavily influenced by Thomas Kuhn's analysis of science history as a series of 'paradigm shifts' (in *The Structure of Scientific Revolutions*, first published in 1962), and by Foucault's study of intellectual history as a series of 'epistemic breaks' (*The Order of Things*, published in France in 1966).

This view is challenged, however, by those who see cultural history not as a procession of breaks or revolutions, but as a long, continuous process incorporating change. Brian Winston argues that Western civilization has displayed, over the last three centuries, 'fundamental continuity', despite 'enormous changes in detail' (1998: 2). John Feather regards the contemporary 'information-dependent society' as a result of 'both profound change and fundamental continuity' (1998: 7). In the long view taken by these and other theorists, technological innovation occurs in the context of 'pre-existing social formations' (Winston 1998: 2). Technical and social 'revolutions' may just as easily be seen as repetitions: the Internet, for example, runs on the telephone network developed in the nineteenth century.

Several cultural critics have questioned the modern/postmodern division, suggesting – as does Nigel Wheale – that the aftermath of modernism constitutes not a break but a continuity (1995: 31). There is an overlapping of techniques and concerns into the 'postmodern' period that often goes unremarked. For one thing, modernism still exists as a style, not least in architecture, even if it is now merely one option among many. As well, different art forms have different timescales, which makes a generalized account of the shift from modern to postmodern difficult, if not impossible: rock music may well have its modern and postmodern periods, for example, but they do not correspond to those of architecture, film or literature. Certain key figures – such as John Cage or Jean-Luc Godard – occupy positions that bear traces of both modern and postmodern aesthetic values.

It is important to acknowledge that the division of cultural history into discrete periods – such as modern and postmodern – has theoretical disadvantages as well as advantages. The relationship between technology and culture may just as usefully be seen in terms of continuity, taking in the sweep of cultural and technological shifts from the eighteenth century to the twenty-first. The doctrine of progress, for instance, is still potent today, even if it lacks the unquestioned status it enjoyed in the Victorian and early modern periods. Contemporary advertising invokes consumers to keep up with technology's advances; progress is still measured in speed, only now it is computer processing speed. Marinetti's utopian faith in industrial technology may now be untenable, yet much of the excitement has been transferred to its post-industrial successor, the domain of information technology. Utopian hopes in the transforming powers of technology now reside in cyberculture, where mysticism often fuses with belief in technological progress. Erik Davis, in *TechGnosis* (1999), and Margaret Wertheim, in *The Pearly Gates of Cyberspace* (1999), both chart this new field, in which techno-mystics such as the Extropians dream of transcendence and immortality through the immaterial means of cyberspace. It is certainly possible, therefore, to identify constants underneath the changes in technology and culture.

Technology in music

We conclude this chapter with a brief survey of the use of technology in electronic music, in which we might well find both continuity and discontinuity in aesthetic terms. The Futurist Art of Noises has served as a conceptual underpinning for much electronic music, from the early avant-garde through to popular forms such as techno and its many variants (in the 1980s a British electronic pop group named itself Art of Noise). Composers such as Varese and Busoni pursued the compositional use of noise in early modernism, while electronic instruments including the Theremin (invented in 1919) and the Ondes Martinet (1928) augmented the conventional orchestra.

The composer John Cage was a pivotal figure because he combined innovative composition with technical invention (indeed the modernist composer Schoenberg denied that Cage was a composer at all, but an inventor, 'of genius'). Cage's 'prepared piano' interfered with the machinery of the conventional instrument, by the insertion of small objects into its mechanism. He incorporated a huge range of technologies into his works: his *Imaginary Landscapes*, commencing in 1939, featured recording and playback technologies, radio, film, circuitry; he also experimented with tape and computer-generated sound. Cage's prolific body of work is intriguing because its influence has been felt in many directions. His willingness to find a musical dimension in any new technology, no matter what its original purpose, as well as his involvement in mixed media productions, set a pattern for generations of composers to follow. Many contemporary sound-artists and electronic composers – including Scanner, who incorporates audio surveillance technologies into his works – operate in a field largely opened up by Cage.

The history of electronic music reveals a general pattern of experiment followed by absorption of experimental techniques into the musical vocabulary. In the early 1950s, the composer Pierre Schaeffer pioneered *musique concrète*, in which experiments with the newly available technology of magnetic tape transformed everyday sounds into new sonic events. William Burroughs and Brion Gysin applied a random cut-up technique to tape, while in the 1960s Steve Reich produced works based on tape loops. By the late 1960s, all of these techniques, as well as electronically generated sounds as used by the composer Karlheinz Stockhausen, had found their way into rock music, where the recording studio had emerged as a new 'instrument' for adventurous musicians and producers. The crossover between the avant-garde and popular music was embodied in musicians like John Cale, Frank Zappa and Brian Eno, who helped cross-fertilize rock music with the ideas of Cage, Varese and Stockhausen.

One other interesting development of the 1960s and 1970s was the rise of highly repetitive music. Generally associated with the compositions of Steve Reich and Philip Glass, this style was at first called 'minimalist' or 'process' music. There were several influences behind this musical direction, including non-Western ones (in Glass's case this came through a collaboration in 1965 with the Indian musician Ravi Shankar). Melody and harmony, the traditional building-blocks of Western music, were supplanted in importance by repetitive yet shifting rhythmic patterns. Reich's early tape loop compositions were inspired in part by Cage, in their use of everyday urban sounds and their incorporation of chance as the loops moved in and out of phase. Extending phase repetition to compositions for conventional instruments, Reich developed a compositional style based on repetitive processes. In his 1968 essay 'Music as a Gradual Process', he elaborated on this technique, which even downplayed the importance of the composer:

> Though I may have the pleasure of discovering musical processes and composing the musical material to run through them, once the process is set up and loaded, it runs by itself (Schwarz 1997: 8).

This statement is striking in its explicit incorporation of a machine aesthetic into musical composition. It exists as a musical parallel to the similar obsession with repetition emanating from Warhol's 'Factory' studio. Yet it goes even further in its interest in self-regulating, or cybernetic, systems. Several of Reich's works give the impression, both in live performance and in recordings, of mimicking the process of sophisticated cybernetic systems. To be fair to the composer, however, his later music, which draws for inspiration on non-Western musics such as the Balinese gamelan, is far subtler and more varied in its interlocking patterns than a machine metaphor may indicate. The extended compositions of Reich and Glass demand a type of listening, uncommon in Western music, in which perception reacts to small variations within extended sequences.

How can we assess this music of repetition? In its demotion of harmony and its emphasis on rhythmic patterns, often at great length (Glass's opera *Einstein on the Beach* runs for five hours without interval), it made demands which audiences were at first unwilling to accept. A common response was to find the music boring, even banal in its machine-like repetition. In this respect, minimalist music seemed to be a new permutation of the musical avant-garde; it was certainly marginalized, in the manner of avant-garde art, in its early years. However, minimalism brought back melody, albeit in extremely simplified form, to composition. Reich, Glass, Terry Riley and other composers of their generation rejected the atonality or serial techniques of modernism; their defiantly tonal compositions were attacked by the critical establishment in the same way that the simplicities of Pop Art were attacked by Clement Greenberg. The melodic nature of Glass's music, in particular, has enabled him to connect with large audiences, whereas the general public had been alienated by the difficulty of the modernist musical language. The return to tonality, the crossover with popular music (Glass wrote a symphony based on the rock album *Low* by David Bowie), and the synthesis of diverse influences from Western and non-Western sources, are characteristics of this music which we might justifiably term postmodern.

The technique of digital sampling has been used extensively in ways consistent with a postmodern aesthetic, as we shall discuss in the next chapter. This has largely been the province of electronic pop music, although Steve Reich sampled spoken word to great effect in his 1988 composition *Different Trains*, and other composers have used digital techniques in their works. The profound, widespread influence of Reich's experiments with technology was signalled in 1998 with the release of *Reich Remixed*, in which the composer's works were appropriated and reshaped by dance music DJs and producers. The embrace of noise and everyday sounds, the treatment of sound by technological means, and the creative use of repetition – all at one time avant-garde or modernist techniques – have all become staples of the contemporary musical landscape.

CHAPTER 3

Digital Aesthetics: Cultural Effects of New Media Technologies

Digital computers represent information as a series of on/off states, or zeros and ones. Unlike analog media, which maintain 'analogies' of patterns (such as sound waves) as they are transformed into other states (such as electrical signals), digital media encode all forms of information into long series of binary digits (zeros and/or ones). The advantages of digitization include: the speed with which huge volumes of digital information may be processed and manipulated; the ready convergence of diverse information types into digital data; and the speed and flexibility with which this data may be compressed and distributed through information networks.

The term 'aesthetics' refers to sense perception – to the circuits that our sense perceptions create between world, body and mind. In philosophy 'aesthetics' refers to sense perception in general. For example, the eighteenth-century philosopher Immanuel Kant discussed aesthetics as framed by the perception of natural beauty or the sublime. Yet aesthetics is most often raised as a question of the 'arts' – the question perhaps of what the arts do that is particular to them as a human activity. The discussion of a general aesthetics by Kant and others has been brought into the discussion of how art works, or of how particular styles work, including questions of design and other issues.

The question of digital aesthetics has arisen with the increasing importance of the computer to art, design and the way in which our sensory perceptions of the world in general might be changed by a more 'digital culture'. In this chapter we consider some of the ways in which digital technologies have affected the way we create, and the way we communicate. Later in the chapter we survey recent attempts to formulate in theoretical terms a specifically digital aesthetic. First, though, we turn to some of the cultural effects ensuing from the use of new media technologies. These are: the challenge to conventional notions of authorship brought by digital media and distribution; and the challenge to concepts of representation and reality brought by digital image-making. These themes may all be observed in the broad cultural domain; they are also present in the work of many contemporary artists. We shall discuss these cultural effects, then, with reference to artists and musicians who make use of digital technologies in their works.

Authorship, intellectual property and technology

The question of authorship has exercised many theorists and commentators; suffice to say here that there is no universal idea of the author. Rather, authorship is historically determined and culturally specific – as Foucault argued when describing the 'author function' in his influential essay 'What is an Author?' Many traditional and indigenous cultures, collectivist in orientation, have had no concept of individual authorship. Oral communities had no notion of stories or songs as property needing to be protected; for intellectual property to exist, a technology of communication (initially, writing) is necessary. The legal notion of an individual author – creator of original works protected by copyright – is quite recent, emerging only in the eighteenth century. Previously, the great majority of stories and songs had existed free in the public domain, while composers, artists and writers were generally employed by the Church or royalty.

The idea of the individual creator legally supported by copyright arose in Europe during the convergence of a new economic system (capitalism) and a new technology (the printing press). As Ronald Bettig remarks in his book *Copyrighting Culture*, the printing press was crucial to this development; indeed, it was 'among the first inventions to be exploited by capitalists' (1996: 15). The copying of information had previously been the anonymous work of monastery scribes, producing limited copies. The mechanical reproduction of large numbers of pamphlets and books opened up a commercial market for the distribution of knowledge. Copyright became a legal right with the Statute of Queen Anne in 1710 – but even then, this first copyright law resulted from pressure exerted by printers and publishers, not authors. Copyright only gradually came to focus on the rights of the author. This shift of emphasis was supported in the nineteenth century by the Romantic conception of the author as divinely inspired genius, creator of original works. To a large extent, this notion persisted throughout the modernist period, with its 'heroic' conception of the author or artist. Modernism was in many ways married to the rise of industrial capitalism; where such concepts of the author and industrial capitalism come together, we find the increased significance of intellectual property.

Intellectual property is the ownership of particular items of knowledge, ideas or cultural production. This includes songs, texts, films, recordings, software, even chemical compounds or blocks of genetic material. The ownership of intellectual property, legally protected by copyright and patents, has profound economic significance; intellectual property is one of the foundations of the 'new economy' of information-based societies. Intellectual property is especially lucrative because unlike conventional property (such as housing) it is not affected by its reproduction. It can be duplicated many times and in different forms without being exhausted (a film, for example, may exist for many years in cinema, video, DVD, cable, pay-for-view, webcast or other formats). Authors generally transfer their rights to publishers, institutions or corporations in exchange for royalties; the exercising of those rights constitutes a major source of wealth in capitalist societies. This explains the continuous pressure exerted through trade agreements by the West on non-Western nations, which have not shared the intellectual property regime of industrialized capitalist nations.

Technological change has provoked challenges to both the intellectual property regime and accepted notions of authorship. As Lawrence Lessig notes, 'copyright has always been at war with technology' (1999: 124). Each new technology of reproduction – such as the photocopier or video cassette – has made copying easier, threatening the ability of copyright holders to control the copying and distribution of their work. Copyright law has continually expanded to meet this threat, protecting intellectual property – contained in any form or technology – from unlawful reproduction. Digital technology has brought the greatest threat to copyright, because works in digital form are remarkably easy to copy and distribute (via the Internet) – and this process is difficult to detect and even more difficult to police. Lessig states that:

For the holder of the copyright, cyberspace appears to be the worst of both worlds – a place where the ability to copy could not be better, and where the protection of law could not be worse (1999: 125).

This situation has engendered two types of response: one of near panic, as copyright holders have scrambled to protect their rights with recourse to the law; another of celebration, by those welcoming a digital 'public domain' free of the excessive restrictions of copyright.

The latter response has corresponded to the challenge, evident since at least the 1980s, to the Romantic/modernist notion of the author. The postmodern aesthetic, outlined in Chapter 2, elevates eclecticism and multiplicity over any dominant or 'original' style. Appropriation of other artists' works or styles became an accepted practice within postmodernism. At its most extreme, postmodernism asserts that originality is no longer possible, that all possible styles have been done, and that art now consists of the inventive arrangement of diverse styles. The idea of the artist as original genius has certainly eroded in the postmodern era; the artist is more likely to be thought of as a processor of information, or manipulator of found material. The digital technologies of the scanner and sampler, available since the early 1980s, have been used for postmodern ends. They are appropriation devices: any recorded image or sound is available as data to be manipulated. For many artists and musicians, the digital data bank is there to be plundered.

This new approach to creativity and intellectual property became widely apparent in 1980s pop music, most notably hip hop and electronic dance music. As Andrew Goodwin noted in his essay 'Sample and Hold', this sample-based music culture represented a postmodern dream come true:

> . . . postmodernists and devotees of Walter Benjamin's cultural analysis could be forgiven for patting themselves on their theoretical backs and ruminating on the strange prescience of these two bodies of theory (1990: 258).

As Benjamin had predicted, the 'aura' of the original had given way to a culture of copying and a 'hands-on' approach. Musical works were composed of appropriated fragments, recontextualized into a 'tissue of quotations', to use Roland Barthes's phrase. New criteria of creativity emerged: DJs and musicians could be assessed not on their 'originality', but on their skill and judgement in assembling collages of found materials. In some cases, as with the hip hop group Public Enemy, the sampler was deployed as a guerrilla instrument, appropriating fragments of culture for political ends. Other groups such as De La Soul delighted in a gleeful plundering of music sources, creating 'new' works through the innovative juxtaposition of disparate elements. It seemed as if the sampler and other digital music technologies had permitted a new do-it-yourself form of creativity, with the databank of recorded sounds constituting a vast public domain.

There was only one problem with this new concept of authorship: the law of copyright. In the eyes of the law, unlicensed sampling constituted a flagrant breach of copyright. Many musicians and DJs, including De La Soul, were sued heavily for damages, as intellectual property law clashed directly with the freewheeling postmodern aesthetic and its use of digital technology. The welter of lawsuits generated from this enforcement of intellectual property law eventually resulted in compromise arrangements for the sampling of copyright works. Such material is now usually licensed from the copyright owners, at the cost of a share of royalties; in this way, the music industry has accommodated sampling by making it legal – for a fee.

But there are many musicians, artists and theorists who want an end to copyright law, or at least its modification. The organization Musicians Against Copyright of Samples (MACOS) – whose motto is 'Sampling Is the 21st Century' – allows the public to sample freely from MACOS material, with no legal ramifications. Musician John Oswald based his Plunderphonics project on audio piracy as 'a compositional prerogative'. The musician DJ Spooky typifies this cavalier attitude to intellectual property:

> Nothing is sacred. . . . Everything is 'public domain'. Download, remix, edit, sequence, splice this into your memory bank . . . information moves through us with the speed of thought, and basically any attempt to control it always backfires (1999: 47).

The 'do-it-yourself' ethos associated with digital pop music works to redefine notions of authorship in several ways. As Robin Mackay notes, sonic material flows freely in the circuits of electronica; sounds 'come from anywhere . . . potentially go anywhere, mutating as they pass . . .' (1997: 253). The practice of remixing de-emphasizes the importance of the original author, elevating instead the process by which the song mutates as it moves through different remixes.

The conviction of many artists and theorists is that digital technology has made copyright – and the conventional notion of authorship – obsolete. If copyright arose in the wake of an industrial technology (the printing press), then the post-industrial technologies of digital media call for a new concept of intellectual property. The flow of digital information across the Internet – easily downloaded, effortlessly crossing national borders and jurisdictions – not only makes copyright impossible to enforce, but also problematizes the concept of information as a commodity. 'Information Wants to be Free' is the rallying-cry of those who celebrate digital convergence and the distribution of information on the Net. John Perry Barlow has been one of the leading proponents of this view. His 1994 essay published in *Wired* magazine put the case emphatically, as evident in its title: 'The Economy of Ideas (Everything You Know about Intellectual Property Is Wrong)'. Barlow argues that information is experienced, not possessed, and that the fluidity of information makes copyright law outmoded.

Certain developments in software and the distribution of information have operated on the principles articulated by Barlow and others. The Free Software Foundation, founded in 1985, has developed alternatives to proprietary software. Shareware and open source software partake of a collectivist notion, rather than a commitment to intellectual property as commodity. The Open Source movement argues that basic software should be freely available to all, and should be developed freely within a network of benevolent programmers, constituting something like the 'collective intelligence' advocated by Pierre Levy. An open source software such as the Linux operating system makes the source code available to be modified by any user; any modifications are in turn redistributed to other users. The GNU project, a component of Linux, openly declares that 'Software should not have owners'. These and other schemes are supported by Copyleft, an organization that supports the free use and distribution of open source software. This network of non-proprietary and endlessly mutable software systems has established in effect a new public domain for information. The far-reaching consequences of this development have been recognized by the electronic arts community. The 1999 Prix Ars Electronica awarded its top prize in the *.net* category to Linux, for its encouragement of interactivity and collaboration, drawing on thousands of volunteer programmers:

... the community that has assembled around this anarchic effort demonstrates how strong an aesthetic can be in bringing a community, assets, ideas and attention together (*Cyberarts99* 1999: 16–17).

One of the most publicized examples of the digital public domain has been the sharing of music on the Net through MP3 technology. This practice was brought to public attention in 2000 when Napster, one of many file-swapping networks, was sued by the major record companies for breach of copyright. Specifically, the rock band Metallica demanded that Napster disconnect over 300,000 users who had downloaded Metallica songs for free. But as Metallica and the music industry discovered, their legal right to protect their intellectual property did not necessarily give them the moral high ground on this issue. Indeed, their heavy-handed litigious approach signalled to many Net users that they were out of touch with both the new technology and the attitude of music fans. The realization that many young fans had only ever downloaded music for free – that is, had never paid for music – was regarded as a grave threat by the music industry establishment. Yet other parties, including some musicians, have accepted the file-sharing ethos, using networks to make their music freely available, or as a promotional service.

File-swapping networks have emerged as a major source of activity on the Net. Their democratic nature – in logging on to a network, users make their own files available while accessing other files – is staunchly defended by their proponents in open defiance of copyright. 'We strongly believe that information – like ideas – should be freely available', is the declaration of the Filetopia network. Some networks have no host databases, leaving them less dependent on the central control of Internet service providers, governmental control or commercial gateways, hence less vulnerable to prosecution or shutting down. The Freenet network, for example, aims to 'rewire the Internet' by avoiding centralized control or administration. For these and other Net anarchists, the enforcement of copyright is a form of censorship, something to be violated. Such peer-to-peer (P2P) networking, enabling the free exchange of information, is an increasingly popular use of the decentralized structure of the Internet. The distribution of information through P2P, using instant-messaging or other distribution technologies, has enormous consequences, not only for cultural transmission but for business. Seen by its opponents as a violation of intellectual property rights, it is regarded by its supporters as a cultural stimulus, built on the principles of free expression, sharing and decentralization.

Net culture, Net art

The theorist Sean Cubitt regards sharing – of information, of the creative process – as the major social benefit of Internet technology. Cubitt is critical of conventional Net use, with its emphasis on 'sovereign individuals' imperiously clicking their way around the Net, 'assimilating the alien into the longed for stability of the same' (1998: 110). Networked activity, by contrast, partakes of 'the very purpose of making: to share' (p. 143). These networks, 'formed outside the managed webs of globalization', may take on many forms. A group like Culture Jammers may transcend its geographical base by connecting to other groups and individuals who share an antipathy to commodity culture. A new 'grassroots' political activism has emerged, composed of small locally based groups connected to like groups through the Net. The international campaign against aspects of globalization has mobilized in this manner.

The collaborative spirit is evident in numerous areas of contemporary art practice. Many websites encourage multiple authorship of texts, in the form of Netwriting, digital audio/music, or multimedia ventures. Jane Prophet's *Technosphere* was an early interactive website, allowing users to create artificial life forms which then 'lived' on the site. *Technosphere* evolved as a site by responding to users' suggestions and ideas. Melinda Rackham's site *carrier* exists as both a multimedia artwork on the theme of viruses, and a base for users to register their own experience of biological viruses. The trAce Online Writing Community operates as a site for collaborative projects (see Figure 3.1), 'radically refiguring the writer into a kind of Internet artist', in the words of Net-writer Mark Amerika. The writer-artists contributing to trAce projects 'are busying themselves by reinventing writerly practice – particularly our accepted notions of "authorship", "text" and "publishing"' (2000: 3). Amerika's own Net-based works include *Grammatron*, conceived as 'a public domain narrative environment'. The 'hypertextual consciousness' he advocates has as its motto 'I link therefore I am'. Many Net-based collaborative sites involve works in continuous progress, developing by the accretion of multiple inputs. Most multimedia works – whether websites or CD-ROMs – comprise the work of several artists, providing text, image, sound, design and programming.

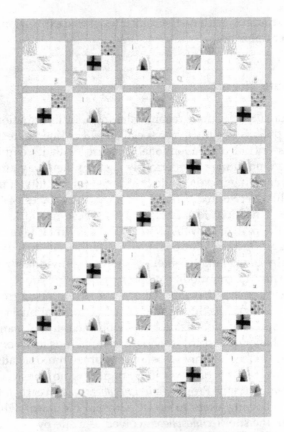

Figure 3.1 The trAce Online Writing Community, *The Noon Quilt*, edited by Teri Hoskin and Sue Thomas, 1998

Such 'collective creativity' is examined by Woodmansee and Jaszi (along with other contributors) in *The Construction of Authorship*. Net-writing sites – as well as the everyday bulletin boards and discussion groups of the Net – are 'dynamic texts', in which individual identities are de-emphasized, while 'useful contributions [are] effectively merged' (1994: 55). Woodmansee and Jaszi argue that writing is increasingly a collaborative practice, and that this constitutes a return to the way writing was understood before the Romantic 'myth' of the author was instated. The tension between evolving notions of authorship, expressed through the means of digital technology, and the legal definition of the author has become marked:

It would seem that as creative production becomes more corporate, collective and collaborative, the law invokes the Romantic author all the more insistently (1994: 28).

While intellectual property law engages with new media technologies and their threat to copyright, net.art continues to evolve in unpredictable ways. According to Alex Galloway, net art is all about 'conversions', as each medium or form mutates into another in a process of 'digital alchemy'. In Amerika's words, the digital works of Net artists

... defy categorization while maintaining an allegiance to the suppleness of nervous words, sonorous syntax, vocal microparticulars, animated imagetexts, and unsung e-motions (2000: 3).

The digital image

The cultural impact ensuing from digital image-making concerns epistemology – that is, the theory of knowledge. How do we know the world? How do we represent it, and what are the consequences when the technologies of representation change? Any socially recognized form of representation rests on a 'reality effect' or 'truth effect', an accepted fit between the world of things and the signs used to represent them. Photography enjoyed such a truth effect in the nineteenth century and for much of the twentieth; this authentic fit between things and photographs has been undermined by the potential for manipulation residing in digital image-making. Digital photography challenges accepted notions of representation in ways which some find disturbing, yet others find liberating.

An invention of the nineteenth century, photography was installed in that decade into a specific system of representation. Photographs were used by police and other authorities to identify citizens, particularly criminals. Journalism incorporated photography into newspapers and magazines. The law accepted photos as evidence in court. All these practices depended on a central assumption: that photography represented the world in a truthful, objective manner. The photographic negative was held as an assurance of this truth effect: tampering may be possible in the developing process, but not with the negative itself. In art, the aesthetic code of realism emphasized the desirability of an objective depiction of reality, most fully achieved by photography.

This reality effect endured throughout the twentieth century, underpinning the proliferation of images generated by mass media and surveillance technologies. But the availability in the 1980s of digital technology – primarily image scanners and software programs enabling the easy manipulation of digitized images – threatened to unsettle this epistemological model. The widespread use in the 1990s of digital cameras in journalism removed the guarantee of truth held in the photographic negative. Some magazines and newspapers were caught manipulating photos for sensationalist effect. Other sections of media seemed to revel in digital fakery: dead celebrities were regenerated in TV advertising campaigns. Many commentators and journalists worried at length on the consequences of digital manipulation. If forgery was now a matter simply of rearranging pixels in a computer – in an almost undetectable process – what was to prevent a faked photograph being accepted in court? Or a news story being based on an untrue photograph? Several theorists announced the 'death of photography' as a practice with privileged access to truth in representation. Bill Jay, for example, predicted that digital photography would remove the truth effect even from family snaps:

> Closed eyes magically open, frowns are converted into smiles, relatives included in the group (or eliminated) . . . wrinkles washed away. . . . Wishful thinking and fantasy will be the factual evidence of the future (cited in Cameron 1991: 4).

Other theorists have been more circumspect, resisting such absolute pronouncements on truth in representation. Andy Cameron prefers an assessment based on probability. All photographs, whether digital or analogue, are judged, he asserts,

> . . . according to what we *want* to believe, what we *already* believe, what we believe is *likely*, and above all, according to the channels of authority through which they circulate (1991: 4–5).

The potential of digital image-making for manipulation calls for a heightened scepticism, or at least alertness, regarding the persuasive strategies deploying this technology, whether they be in advertising, entertainment or journalism.

Martha Rosler points out that manipulation has always been part of photography, whether for purposes of political propaganda, or in the routine editorial process (cropping, placement, captioning) of journalism. Rosler does not agree that digitized images mean the end of meaning or evidence in photography; indeed she finds that there are 'productive aspects to the adoption of a sceptical relation to information provided by authorities' (1991: 63). A critical orientation to the digital image involves a cultural materialist approach – as we outlined in Chapter 1. Such an approach, in Cameron's terms,

> ... refuses a technological determinism which finds evil in the machine, locating the question of image manipulation within the generalized and older study of persuasive discourse (1991: 5).

Several other theorists have highlighted the 'productive aspects' of digital photography identified by Rosler, while countering claims of 'the death of photography'. Many other critics have asserted that photographs have never been 'true': digital images simply make this overt. The famous case of 'the fairies at the bottom of the garden', photographed by two young girls in the early twentieth century, has inspired at least two films. Robert Capa's photograph of a Spanish civil war victim at the point of being shot was discovered, much later, to have been faked. As Hubertus Amelunxen notes, one thing that digital photography has emphasized is that analogue photography was never as reliable as we thought (if indeed we ever did). In short, 'the history of photography is the history of forged testimonies' (1995: 116).

How, then, can we describe the cultural impact made by digital photography? First, as we have seen, the digital image has made the problems with photography as a 'true' representation of the world much more evident. Second, digital photography has raised serious problems with the nature of the originality of a photographic work. Third, the digital manipulation of stored imagery opens up the possibility of a massive amount of variation and combinations of images. Technically this is possible because, as with all digital media, the user works with digital code not on imprints. An artist can work endlessly on an image (or a sound or text) in the digital realm, because digital information suffers no degradation in copying (unlike the rapid degradation in analogue media). Working with code also means that the numbers do the 'hack' work for the artist, enabling swift editing or alteration within the computer. A fourth aspect of digital image-making results from the convergence of media and media roles within digital information. An individual adept at information technology skills may perform many roles in one: photographer, artist, designer, marketer, distributor. As Amelunxen puts it, there is 'not a wealth of different media but the media correspondences "implicit in the computer" – where everything is converted into the same numeric code' (1995: 118).

The communication and exchange between the different arts and different media in the digital realm have had another effect on art photography: it has become more painterly. Photography has had a chequered past as an art practice, derided by some critics as a mere recording technology. Its emergence in the nineteenth century was initially regarded as a threat to the dominant mode of visual representation – painting – leading to declarations of 'the death of painting'. Of course, photography did not kill painting; in one sense it liberated it from the duties of faithfully portraying the objective world, allowing the depiction of interior psychological states in Expressionism and modernism. Now digital convergence, heralded by some as 'the death of photography', has brought a paint-like dimension to photography as an art medium. Various software programs allow for the importation and superimposition of any number of graphic designs, effects, colours and patterns, to be melded with scanned or computer-generated imagery. The photographic artwork becomes a painterly amalgam of visual techniques, achieved by digital means. Many artists have responded positively to the challenges offered by this technology. Phillip George has composed a series of *Headlands* (Figure 3.2), expressing the state of his consciousness over a period of time. Photographic images are overlapped by scanned mythical symbols, coalescing into patterns as memories alter and consciousness shifts.

Artists working in digital media have brought interesting perspectives to the representation of nature. This is partly due to the fluidity of digital imagery, and partly due to broader cultural concerns. The digital/biological distinction has become increasingly blurred: viruses, for example, are said to live in both computers and humans. In the age of the Human Genome Project, we are encouraged to think of the human – indeed all nature – as genetic code. Digital code and DNA appear to fuse in Rosemary Laing's work *Greenwork: Aerial Wall* (Figure 3.3). An idyllic green landscape is divided by a pixilated section forming a digital 'wall'; in this way digital code literally cuts into the naturescape. We are reminded by this intrusion of the technologies and technological language (code) involved in the depiction of nature. A different approach is taken by Char Davies in her virtual reality work *Osmose*, one of the

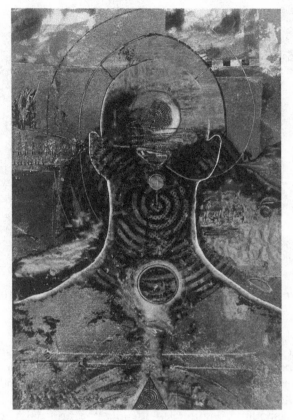

Figure 3.2 Phillip George – *Headlands*, 1993

most successful artistic expressions using interactive convergent technology. The user is immersed into a lyrical evocation of nature, navigating through a virtual world composed of painterly digital images. The effect on the user, once the experience is completed, is to create a heightened awareness of nature.

The theorist Peter Lunenfeld is a staunch critic of the use of the digital to 'return' to nature, which he calls the 'edenic' fallacy. In practice, as we have already seen, there can be quite different attitudes to the relation between nature and technology. Some artists use digital technology to draw attention to the beauty of nature. Others use similar images to undermine the desire to return to nature. Others still use digital imagery to question our prior conceptions of nature, or to reflect on the mediating role of technology.

Figure 3.3   Rosemary Laing, *Greenwork: Aerial Wall*, 1995

Patricia Piccinini uses computer-generated photographs to refer to the programming of code in both media imagery and genetic engineering. Her works such as *Mutant Genome Project* and *Protein Lattice Red* (featuring genetically altered mice perched on a female model's shoulder, Figure 3.4) identify the artificial within the natural. Robyn Stacey's densely layered representations of flowers blur the boundaries between photography and painting, as well as those between technology and nature. Stacey's use of digital manipulation endows the flowers with machinic qualities, so that at times they are suggestive of both technology and nature. Works such as these reveal that in the age of digital information, nature is not an innocent category. It is, rather, a cultural construction in all senses – in the way we think of it, relate to it, and represent it.

A positive appraisal of 'postphotography' entails a viewpoint far removed from Plato's philosophy of pure Ideas and their imperfect copies (which have been called simulacra). Postphotography incorporates a different function for art: it manufactures new relations to the world, and new relations with the world. The components of these new relations are simulacra – digital images conceived not as betrayals of originals but as productive simulacra. In this view of the world, as Amelunxen notes, 'The artificial is at the centre of

Figure 3.4   Patricia Piccinini, *Protein Lattice Red*, 1997

reality' (1995: 120). In the digital realm, the world is something to be constantly created.

Timothy Druckrey argues that in undergoing this transition we are changing what Walter Benjamin called 'the optical unconscious' or 'the collective vision' (1996: 84). He claims that we think differently due to digital photography, primarily because we can no longer fool ourselves into thinking that an image gives us the full picture: the 'trope of totality has been eroded' (p. 85). There is now a multiplicity assigned to images: fragmented viewpoints not of the world as a whole, but composite images made of bits and pieces. Druckrey also claims that digital media, as a form of collage, raise issues to do with narrative as a cultural given. The 'semiotic constitution of the image' is foregrounded as never before in the new 'space' of electronics.

This means that the production and reception of the digital image are much more contingent upon circumstances. For Druckrey, postphotography highlights its origins, its processes of manufacture, or the way it distorts or mutates given images and signs. The digital image is now 'rooted in an "ecosystemic" approach of contextually current processes of production' (1996: 86). Images may be appropriated, displaced from their original contexts, given new meanings by their association with other appropriated images. This recontextualization process may have a temporal dimension. The photographic artist Anne Zahalka scanned reproductions of Renaissance paintings for her *Gestures* series (Figure 3.5), blacking out all but the details of hands holding manuscripts. This temporal dislocation creates an enigmatic effect, as the Renaissance details float in the artificial blackness of digitally created space.

The digital manipulation of photographs may be done with an expressly political intention. Esther Parada, for example, scanned photographs held in the California Museum of a Christopher Columbus monument in the Dominican Republic. The camera angle in these photos conveyed a racist rhetoric, 'showing the dominant Columbus paternalistically towering above the *native*'

Figure 3.5   Anne Zahalka, *Gestures*, 1994

(on the monument) and a black woman walking past. Parada's sequence of digital manipulations of this image reinstates the two figures marginalized in the original photos, placing them at the centre, thus partially obscuring the Columbus figure. For Parada, this computer-assisted alteration is part of the process of questioning official history's colonial bias:

> Perhaps we will be better able to discover alternative realities in the past *and* to understand the basis of certain contemporary relationships and situations. (*Ten 8* 1991a: 70)

There are many projects of this nature in digital photographic practice. They are interventions into the orthodoxy of official history as recorded in photographs and paintings. By deliberately altering images, while foregrounding the act of manipulation, artists modify the symbolic codes of representation operating in their culture. Other artists have focused on personal identity or family histories, as contained in snapshots and other family records. The act of falsification that so concerned Bill Jay (frowns converted into smiles, relatives included or eliminated from shots) has been put to productive use by many artists. Eva Sutton has subverted nostalgia by fabricating old photos, deliberately 'betraying' the viewer's trust (*Ten 8* 1991b: 74). In wilfully manipulating the photographic record, artists may be less interested in an objective correlation with reality than in the highly subjective process of memory. Cultural memory may blend with personal memory, as in the painterly digital photographic art of Cynthia Beth Rubin. Her works often draw on images from Eastern European Jewish culture, creating an 'imagined history' of places that she never knew, but which form part of her cultural legacy.

In this way, digital artists have exploited the potential of digitized imagery. The ease of manipulation creates the possibility of 'alternative realities' – of the present and of the past. Artists emphasize the constructed nature of history, of the narratives through which a culture defines itself. Just as the digital image need not correspond 'truthfully' to objective reality, so there is no one 'true' history, no one true definition of a nation. These concepts become as fluid as the mutating and multiplying digital images. The very facets of digital imagery that led to claims of the 'death of photography' – the loss of a truth effect, the possibility of manipulation – have been used in a creative way by artists, reshaping, in the process, notions of cultural identity.

Digital aesthetics: new labels for the new aesthetic

Having considered specific art practices such as digital photography, net art and music, we now move on to the various attempts
to conceptualize digital art practice in general terms. There has
been much recent discussion of digital aesthetics – the most important question being whether there is anything that is particular to
the digital when it comes to art and sense perception. One cannot
after all perceive the digital itself via the senses, but only its transformations of the analog world. As Steven Johnson reminds us, we
do not engage with the zeros and ones of digital code; we relate to
the computer via the interface, which Johnson defines as 'a kind of
translator, mediating between the two parties, making one sensible
to the other' (1997: 14). So the question of digital aesthetics can
perhaps be more precisely posed in terms of the transformation
of our sense perceptions by (the 'hidden') digital, through various
interfaces. Here, for example, we are talking about web design,
interactivity, immersive environments such as those of virtual
reality technologies, film special effects, hypertext, sampling and
sequencing in music, digital cinema, and the new cultural forms
that are brought into the world through computers.

Indeed, whatever the digital aesthetic is or is not, there seems to
be a lot of it around, and it is tremendously diverse. This diversity
and the constant divergence into new forms – and ever newer
media technologies – might be one of the digital aesthetic's defining features. The digital aesthetic focuses not upon an eternal idea
of art or beauty, but upon an endless transformation of our sense
perceptions through digital technologies (we can see its inheritance
of the drive of mainstream modernity here). Yet we should begin
by saying that there is certainly no definitive approach to the digital
aesthetic. Some even think that the digital is now too pervasive
to offer much as a theoretical term; it is useful to look at some of
the alternatives in order to understand what is going in art and
technology today.

'Interactive' has been proposed as a better term than 'digital' –
but it too is overly general, and indeed many older aesthetic forms
and practices, such as the theatre, are interactive. Chris Chesher
(1996) describes an 'invocational aesthetic', referring to the older
magical nature of art that is present in the way we are 'invoked' by
computer software. Another approach would be a 'differential aesthetic'. This refers to cultures and technologies that are based upon
the in-between, that is difference *in itself* (though not preformed

differences). It is also meant to imply the end of media as clearly bound forms (film, TV, websites). Media also tend constantly to differentiate themselves in a constant, ongoing process. The very basis of new media aesthetics is that there seems always to be new variations on the aesthetic. This is an extension of the media ecology argument (mentioned in Chapter 1). The differential aesthetic, then, implies that things are constantly changing. Lev Manovich (2001) refers to a cultural 'transcoding' – where computers and culture constantly change one another. The concept of a differential aesthetic would suggest that cultural transcoding leads to a speeding up of this process – and to the instability of both computer media and cultural forms and processes.

Bolter and Grusin employ the term 'remediation' to mean a 'double logic' that arises from

> ... our culture's contradictory imperatives for immediacy and hypermediacy ... our culture wants to multiply its media and erase all traces of mediation: ideally, it wants to erase its media in the very act of multiplying them (1999: 5).

Crucially here, remediation applies to both older and newer media in contemporary culture. One example they give is the way that television is 'remediated' through reality television (more and more cameras in more and more situations). But we could also say that painting is 'remediated' through photoshop, or that film is remediated through computer graphic animation and special effects. We would add here that the double logic of remediation means that older media are constantly mutating into new media – an idea proposed by McLuhan in the 1960s.

When we add non-media forms to this equation (as in cyborg performance art in which the body is linked with media technologies), it is possible to claim that the world becomes more and more a matter of art. The work of art is not something unique, or something that resides in a particular place that we have to travel an appropriate distance in order to experience. Instead art becomes something in which we are immersed every day. Thus, as we have seen, the work of art loses what Walter Benjamin terms its 'aura'. Let us briefly recall some crucial points from Benjamin's work. The loss of the aura is also about the collapse of distance. This has many aspects. There is the obvious one of the distribution of the artwork through a network (rather than the 'ritual' involved in going to the work in its unique context). But there is more than this. Other distances are collapsed, distances in time and space, as happens for example in the montage of the film. Much of the 'digital aesthetic' is about enhancing and speeding up this loss of distance. Manovich remarks on both Benjamin and the more contemporary theorist, Paul Virilio:

> Film, telecommunication, telepresence. Benjamin's and Virilio's analyses make it possible for us to understand the historical effect of these technologies in terms of progressive diminishing, and finally, the complete elimination of something both writers see as a fundamental condition of human perception – spatial distance, the distance between the subject who is seeing and the object being seen (2001: 174).

The collapsing of distance not only erodes our sense of subject and object, sense and world. It also converts the world from something we contemplate (as in a painting) to 'an immense and unexpected field of action'. The world seems more dynamic, and with the insertion of the camera and other media technologies into the world, we also seem more dynamically involved with the world.

Steven Johnson uses the term 'interface culture', generalizing from the interaction between user and computer. He argues that this form of interaction marks a break in the way Western culture has conceptualized its use of technology. For centuries, technology has been thought of 'in *prosthetic* terms, as a supplement to the body' (1997: 23). This notion persisted well into the twentieth century: it is expressed by, among many others, Marinetti, Freud and McLuhan. Interface with computers, however, produces a new concept:

> For the first time, a machine was imagined not as an attachment to our bodies, but as an environment, a space to be explored. You could project yourself into this world, lose your bearings, stumble across things (p. 24).

For Johnson, the advent of cyberspace brings with it a highly significant transformation of our spatial imagination, with ramifications across culture.

In this respect, another important term would be 'affective'. Computer media enhance the engagement between world and senses, and in a way make the general question of aesthetics even more important in the contemporary world. New media are no longer to be seen as carriers of information (messages) that we either receive, act upon or both. Rather media do things to us. In turn, we do things with them. They are about affect – how things are affected. We could say that this is about our 'feelings and emotions', but with affect we are also talking about something more basic than this, the very engagement between body and world from which these feelings arise. If computer interfaces engage our senses, they also engage our bodies – a theme frequently explored by cyberartists. The body/machine interface provokes notions of the 'machinic', as theorized by Deleuze and Guattari, whereby distinctions between natural and technological processes are challenged. Machinism implies dynamism, in a series of assembled processes (technological, biological, cultural) that form what Deleuze and Guattari call a 'mechanosphere' (1987: 514).

Perhaps many of these issues are summed up in MIDI, which stands for musical instrument digital interface. When a digital musical instrument is played, a MIDI interface converts the analog playing into digital code – numeric codes for the note played, the length of the note, and so on. Many people think of it simply being used for linking computers and MIDI-controlled instruments (keyboards, sequencers, synthesizers and so on). But MIDI has found many other applications in a much wider world. It quickly became a format for a broad interplay between the digital and the analog not only in sounds, but also lighting effects in large theatre and music events, laser shows, even events in theme park rides. In other words, MIDI both translates and coordinates various digital and analog components of complex multimedia events, allowing many different parts of the world to 'speak' to each other, and for one medium to trigger events in another. An extreme example of this is the performance artist Stelarc's *Movotar* project. In this he is harnessed into a robotic framework that controls his body's movements. Stelarc's own input into this is partly through MIDI switches he can control with his feet, which allow him to input into the circuits controlling his movements. MIDI provides a good example of the translatability, not just of data, but between data and 'the rest of the world' in digital aesthetics. So MIDI makes us realize quite clearly that when we are talking about digital aesthetics we are really talking about the digital and analog in relation.

New media and digital aesthetics

Lev Manovich's *The Language of New Media* is perhaps the most comprehensive account so far of these issues, although Manovich writes of new media rather than digital aesthetics. One of his fundamental points is that many of the things attributed to new media are in fact already present in older media, especially film. For example, film already combined a number of media into 'multimedia'. Yet Manovich thinks there is much that is new to new media.

Of course, everything is driven, technically at least, by the computer and computer-mediated production and communications. He writes that:

> ... the computer media revolution affects all stages of communication, including acquisition, manipulation, storage, and distribution; it also affects all types of media – texts, still images, moving images, sound, and spatial constructions (2001: 19).

Yet we have to be careful here. Manovich points out that new media are not just computer-driven but are in fact a convergence of two different histories – 'computing and media technologies' (p. 20) that begin at around the same time in the first half of the nineteenth century, with Babbage's invention of the computer and Daguerre's invention of the 'photograph'. Put simply, new media are 'graphics, moving images, sounds, shapes, spaces and texts that have become computable'. He points out that 'this meeting changes the identity of both media and the computer itself' (p. 25).

Manovich, though he is not the first to realize most of these points, sums up five principles to new media. First, there is 'numerical representation'. This means that 'media becomes programmable'. Second, there is 'modularity', which is 'the fractal structure of new media' (p. 30). Like fractals, 'a new media object has the same modular structure throughout'. This means that all new media elements tend to be made up of other elements which keep their independent structures. For example, a multimedia work's elements can all be combined but you can work on just one of them at a time separate from the work of the whole, or you can extract single elements and use them in different works. Manovich points out that HTML (the code basis for the web) and the web itself are completely modular. Both are made up of collections of modules from different kinds of media. Even the smaller units of programming involved in computer programs are modular in this respect. Even within media objects there are other media objects or modules, such as the layers within images in digital manipulation software. So we can see that selection and combination as forms of production are greatly opened up by the modular nature of new media.

The third principle of new media for Manovich is automation. This means that many aspects of both the production of new media modules, and, indeed, their reception, can be automated, from the way a server puts together a web page, to the way that many software packages for media production automate processes. This often results in at least a partial removal of 'human intentionality' from creation. It also means that creation itself becomes a process of selecting automated processes. At the highest level, of course, this means the involvement of artificial intelligence engines, in computer games for example. This also means that by our time, the 'problem was no longer how to create a new media object such as an image . . . [but] how to find an object that already exists somewhere' (2001: 35). The fourth principle of new media for Manovich is 'variability'. This relates to what Brian Eno (Eno and Kelly 1995) has called the 'unfinished' nature of new media art. It means simply that new media are never finished, that, potentially, they are subject to infinite variations. Manovich also calls them 'mutable' or 'liquid' (p. 36). This also means that the same elements, when used from a database, can create different works in different combinations. It also means that media can be tailored for individual users, who, in the process, come closer to being a kind of information themselves.

The fifth and final principle for Manovich is 'cultural transcoding', which we noted earlier. This is the most important. Here what he calls the 'cultural layer' (principles of narrative, pictorial representation, and so on) and the 'computer layer' (coding principles, packets and file size and types, forms of compression, and so on) influence each other to make a profound change. The implications of cultural transcoding are profound for media theory. In fact, it means that 'media' might be the wrong word. Manovich suggests that 'to understand the logic of new media we need to turn to computer science. . . . From media studies, we move to something that can be called "software studies" – from media theory to software theory' (2001: 48).

Peter Lunenfeld is perhaps slightly more critical of the area than Manovich. Two crucial terms for Lunenfeld are 'hyperaesthetics' and the 'digital dialectic'. The first implies that aesthetics itself, as the *theory* of art or sensation, needs to become more dynamic. As he puts it, 'hyperaesthetics requires theorization in real-time' (2000: 173). Theory needs to move with the flow here. The digital dialectic implies something similar. Lunenfeld thinks we need to 'ground the insights of theory in the constraints of practice' (p. 171). It is because of this that many of the fundamentals of aesthetics are challenged by the digital dialectic. Lunenfeld writes, for example, of a 'camera rasa', almost the opposite to the camera as we usually think of it as confronted by pre-existing reality. By this he means a kind of empty space that pre-exists our creation of digital imagery. In virtual reality, for example, there is something like a 3-D empty space that we begin to fill with art. More generally, Lunenfeld points to these kinds of different preconditions in digital art that result from the fact that computers, as opposed to a canvas for painting perhaps, possess a 'dynamic non-conscious' which is a crucial part of the human–machine interface. In other words, there is a dynamic computer side to the relation between human (conscious and unconscious) and machine. This applies to the engagement with computer art as much as to making it.

The digital, the future and the past

Yet, as valuable as the insights of Manovich and Lunenfeld may be, it is perhaps to other critics that we should turn for a less technical view of the digital aesthetic. Timothy Murray, for example, is one of the more subtle theorists of digital art. Murray (2000) writes about 'digital incompossibility', in which media elements 'stand in paradoxical relation to one another as divergent and coexistent, as incompossible' (Ballard 1975: 9). This refers to the way in which the digital seems to contain within it the potential for differences to arise in any combination, differences that coexist as potential experiences of the artwork before the work is 'used' or viewed. These are different, 'virtual' experiences of the digital artwork that only cancel each other out in their actualization, which is to say that only in one actual working through of the work are other possibilities within the work eliminated. Moreover, in the digital the sense is that these other possibilities are not entirely eliminated. One can always go back and start again.

The broader implication is about memory and cultural history. Digital art gives us the opportunity to explore the infinite virtual potential held in the past as it dynamizes the present. Any series of experiences that one has within digital art is therefore a series of events which is not impossible with regard to others, but incompossible – this time it happened this way, but it could have happened differently. In short, the digital highlights the many alternatives within one situation. Unlike classic film narrative, for example, which must resolve and move on, with the digital you get the sense that every repetition would be different and any situation has an infinity of 'opportunities' buried within it. This aspect of digital aesthetics has fed back into film, in films such as *Sliding Doors* or *Run Lola Run*. It is also the aesthetic, to some extent, of the computer game.

Many theorists from the Futurists on have suggested that technology-focused art is also focused on the future. Murray suggests something different for the digital. He suggests that, far from completely disregarding the past and leaping into a utopian future, many digital artists are concerned to rework the past through the digital, to see what infinite opportunities it might hold. This is a working with the past, with memory, that is only made possible through the digital aesthetic (its ability to combine and recombine, to select, mutate, and so on). For Murray, the past is in the present in a very real sense and the digital aesthetic is concerned with revealing this to us. Only an understanding of the richness of the past in the present will lead us to understand the full potential of the new in the future.

Murray, then, emphasizes the importance of the past, of memory, of cultural events, without losing sight of the fact that the digital aesthetic's reworking of the past allows for unique effects within new media. He shows, for example, the political potential of the reworking of past film narratives and methods in digital media – as we saw with examples from digital photography earlier in this chapter. He also shows how artists often use new codes to play with the old. The cultural effect of this is found in the 'role played by new interactive art in addressing the challenges of lost memories, traumas, and their counter-narratives of vision and utopia'.

We could think of this in simple terms as the complexity of layering where an image in a digital manipulation software package or other program can have a lot of layers, or a digital music package can provide a lot of tracks which can be mixed and remixed. Murray remarks that:

Such enfolding opens the discourse of memory to multiple registers of time, space, and national identity which are simultaneously present on the screen of representation, perhaps for the first time.

In aesthetic terms this leads to 'an electronic haze of the sensible'. Yet, for Paul Virilio, this haze is dangerous. Along with the interactivity of the networked aesthetic, it leads to a 'kind of connectionism whose effects on the world are allegedly as pernicious as those of computers . . .' (1990: 91). Here Virilio poses the notion of a society where we are in constant contact with images which are not so much representations, but 'presentation in real time of things themselves'. At this point we are no longer dealing with art as something that reflects upon the world at all. It is the world. In what sense, then, is this still art?

Perhaps the answer to this is found in the digital/analog relation itself giving new life to art rather than bleeding the analog dry. An example would be the digital art/theatre/installation work *Verdensuret*, performed in Copenhagen in 1996, and devised by the iconoclastic Danish film director Lars Von Trier. Video images of the movement of ants in an ants' nest in the United States were relayed via satellite in real time to the gallery in Copenhagen. A computer in the gallery took these images and imposed a grid over the top of them. It then 'counted' the number of ants crossing any sector of the grid. A number of events in any sector were programmed to become a trigger for events in the gallery. In the gallery were many actors with loosely defined scripts for an ongoing series of related performances in various rooms of the several storey space. Each room contained props for the scenes performed – and somewhere a row of four, differently coloured lights. When the ants triggered an event via the computer, these lights would flash in different combinations. This in turn initiated prearranged codes for movements of actors from one scene to another and so on. It was of course, both chaotic, arbitrary and highly organized.

In this light we can perhaps understand what Virilio means when he writes that the characteristics of the new art work will be participation in the 'latent thus omnipresent image' (1990: 92). There is a kind of 'failure of facts' in this situation leaving us with what Virilio calls only the 'persistence of the witness' as 'the only element of stability at the centre of an environment at once perpetually mobile . . .'. Yet Virilio likes video installations because they are to do with people negotiating how images work space, and because the 'gaze' structured by the camera lens 'surrenders its power of identification' to the movement through the space of 'an observer confronted with the mass of images'. In the video installation, the 'image', the observer, and we could say with regard to *Verdensuret*, the performers, become, as Virilio says, partners. Indeed, Virilio in general sees the role of art, especially video installation and dance, as guiding us through the transformation of culture into digital culture, or at least drawing attention to its contradictions.

It is perhaps Gregory Ulmer, one of the first major theorists of the new aesthetics, who takes these ideas furthest in their relation to the negotiation of the new culture. Ulmer does not see electronic media as the latest in a line of progress beginning with oral culture and moving through the advance of writing. Instead he sees electronic media as media occurring 'between' print and oral aspects of culture (1994: xi). For him electronic media have also absorbed other aspects of cultural communication and his early work deals with the practices of early Soviet film-maker Sergei Eisenstein and others in order to discuss a kind of combinatory media practice which he calls a 'picto-ideo-phonographic' writing. For Ulmer, therefore, television is something that is now teaching us about teaching rather than frustrating it (1989: vii). Moreover, 'writing' – in the broadest possible sense that includes writing electronically – becomes the new model of education rather than just reading. This notion has similarities with the 'superlanguage' of the future envisioned by Pierre Levy, which would explore the new 'sophisticated possibilities of thought and expression opened up by virtual worlds, multi-modal simulations, the dynamic techniques of writing' (1994: 14).

Ulmer invents a new genre that he calls 'mystory', which 'takes into account the new discursive and conceptual ecology interrelating orality, literacy, and videocy'. It combines high and low cultural explorations and works among 'science, popular culture, everyday life, and private experience'. It is 'always specific to its composer'. It results in a kind of temporary hieroglyphics – an idea extremely useful in the understanding of new media. Education should use the new media to invent and explore rather than to absorb what is already known (although Ulmer is obviously not rejecting reading or knowledge in any literal sense).

This also implies a new series of practices in art – or a new poetics (1994: xiii) or theory of art and culture. Gone is the Greek philosopher Aristotle's idea of neat beginnings, middle and ends. Instead we are always in a network, always in the middle, or 'in-between'. Gone are prescriptive formulas that any member of a culture is supposed to follow, such as the idea of the three-act play which still informs most Hollywood film production. Instead we have 'chorography' – a transitory method that always seeks the 'impossible possibility' (p. 26) that lies between genres, between conflicting notions of nation and self, between imagination and given knowledge, between choreography and geography (p. 39). It is a concept that Ulmer invents to suggest the process of invention itself in response to the complexity of culture and new media. Gone even is the idea that we all just read the theory of our 'betters'. Instead it is reinvented. Artists and students 'become producers as well as consumers of theory'. Behind all these 'chorographic' inventions is a powerful political impulse to redirect many of the colonial notions of frontier and so on (p. 31) towards a curiosity with an exploration of the 'chora' – that undefinable place of ambiguity from which we are constantly given birth. Ulmer simultaneously draws on the past and reinvents the future. He treats memory as a reservoir for creative invention – each act of remembering is a reordering and exploration of the hieroglyphics of memory and aided by new media technologies, we can learn to write this reordering and exploration. As he puts it, 'teletheory' allows us to want to 'learn how to remember' (1989: 175) in a different way.

The various theorists surveyed in this chapter propose different ways of formulating a digital aesthetic. They are all grappling with transformations in technology that have generated new forms of art practice, new forms of communication and new configurations of thought. We have moved from prostheses to interfaces, from substance to data, from objects to flows.

CHAPTER 4

Science Fictions

Science fiction (SF) is the genre most directly concerned with science and technology. Although it is sometimes heralded for its scientific credibility or its predictions of technological developments, for us SF is more interesting as a cultural expression of attitudes to technology. We shall consider SF in this chapter not as a projection into the future, or into outer space, but as a reflection of contemporary cultural values attributed to technology.

Those values have changed markedly over the two centuries in which SF has existed as a distinctive fictional genre. The novels of Jules Verne in the second half of the nineteenth century expressed an optimism regarding technological progress that endured through much of the twentieth century. Later a more pessimistic world view emerged, particularly in the SF cinema of the later decades of the twentieth century, in which technological development is often to be feared. As we would expect from something as complex as the relation between technology and culture, many SF works embody both positive and negative values in their representation of technology. Science fiction has oscillated between hope and despair, between celebration and warning, in its depiction of technological change; these dichotomous attitudes are often mingled in the one SF work.

The status of SF as a discourse has changed over two centuries as well. At times it has been marginalized as a species of fantasy, or as an insignificant, if lurid, popular fiction. More recently, it has assumed an increasingly influential cultural position, in part due to its long-standing ethical probing of the social consequences of new technologies. In an age in which cloning and genetic engineering have become realities, one of the strongest reference points for the media, and for the popular imagination, has been SF. The long tradition of fictional works about scientists 'meddling with nature', or 'playing at God', stretches back to Mary Shelley's

Frankenstein, published in 1818. This novel, pre-dating the classical SF works of Verne, H.G. Wells and others by decades, instigated the 'moral warning' tradition of SF. The impact of this narrative tradition is so powerful that the term 'Frankenstein foods' has been readily applied in recent media discourse to genetically modified foods.

Beginning with *Frankenstein*, SF has channelled society's fears and anxieties concerning rapid technological change. Science fiction narratives have played out the ethical problems associated with the implementation of new technologies, especially those with major transformative powers. Should we accept the findings of science on faith? Do we accept technological progress as the means of making a better world? Or must we place limits on that progress? Are there dangers in unchecked scientific research? Can science, enamoured of its own powers, even be trusted? Have we made ourselves too dependent on technological systems? Will technology alter what it means to be human? Will technology be our doom rather than our saviour?

By exploring these themes in fictional narratives, often projected into the near future, SF is the leading cultural forum for ideas about technology's role in social change. It not only reflects social attitudes to technology, it influences them as well. Leading scientists, particularly genetic scientists, often publicly lament the negative representation of scientists in many SF narratives. We have absorbed so many fictional depictions of mad scientists, scientists drunk with power, scientists obsessed with 'pure research', lacking ethical values or even human compassion, that actual scientists feel the need to present a more positive professional image. Science fiction has also taught us to be suspicious of government (*The X Files*), corporations (the *Alien* films) and the military (the *Terminator* films), all of whom should not be trusted with destructive or intrusive technologies. On the other hand, SF retains the ability to thrill us with visions of future technologies: even dark versions of the future such as *Blade Runner* offer us technological marvels like flying cars and super-responsive computerized devices.

The imaginary constructions of SF have provided several vivid metaphors for the role of technology in culture. The robot emerged as a fictional figure in 1920, reflecting the obsessions of the industrial era. The robot is a mechanical person, a worker-machine, born at the same time as the actual workplace was becoming increasingly mechanized. The post-industrial equivalent of the robot is the cyborg, a figure with wide-ranging cultural presence. We call this chapter 'Science Fictions' in part because the ideas we shall discuss range across diverse discursive forms, not all of them fictional in the generally accepted sense. The cyborg, for instance, exists as an ambiguous figure – part reality, part fiction, part metaphor – in the crossover between science, technology, SF and cultural theory.

Before we continue, we need to make a couple of points. First, our survey of SF deals primarily with cinema, although of course other media forms are considered as well. Many of our examples are the big budget SF films (mostly from Hollywood) that are well known to millions of viewers. The recent cultural impact of SF proceeds largely from films such as these, hence our interest in them. Our focus on cinema, however, has several consequences. Enthusiasts of SF will point to general differences between SF cinema and literature. It could justifiably be argued that SF literature is more likely to be thoughtful, speculative, and engaged with ideas concerning technology, than its cinematic counterpart. A reader of SF is also more likely to find a positive outlook on new technology than a film-goer, at least when recent SF cinema is considered. Science fiction films tend to be conceptually simpler than novels; and since the 1970s, the tone of big-budget SF cinema is most often alarmist, or 'Frankensteinian', to a degree not matched in SF literature.

The second proviso concerning our coverage of SF also follows from our emphasis of cinema. Most of our examples are Western, indeed American, although we also consider briefly recent Japanese SF. Again, this bias in our selection results from our interest in these major films as cultural artefacts: what do they say about Western attitudes to technology and science? It is important to remember, however, that SF, like all cultural forms, will vary in different national contexts. As well, a particular approach or set of concerns found in the SF of one region of the world may exert a major influence elsewhere. One example, among many, is the film *Solaris*, made in 1971 by the Russian director Andrei Tarkovsy, based on the novel by Polish writer Stanislaw Lem. The complex psychological insights of Lem's writing, coupled with the mystical vision of Tarkovsky, produced an SF work whose influence has been widely felt. Certainly, the many SF narratives exploring a psychological approach to the genre – in which characters' inner thoughts or emotions are externalized in some form – owe a significant debt to this non-Western SF work.

The beginnings of science fiction: *Frankenstein*

Science fiction has absorbed many influences, including various traditions of fantasy and utopian literature. Francis Bacon's *New Atlantis*, published in 1627, was a utopian work in which the ideal society was founded on the principles of science. The citizens of this imagined society enjoy the benefits of technological inventions including telephones and flying machines. Folkloric tales of wonder and horror, as well as ancient myths and legends, also fed into SF. The Jewish legend of the golem, a clay figure magically brought to life, was an early version of the automaton. Traditional narrative patterns also found their way into SF: *Star Wars* is based on the medieval quest romance, while *Star Trek* was founded on the western genre, in which a civilizing force travels into the wilderness.

Science fiction emerged as a literary genre in the nineteenth century when writers created tales of wonder or horror in the context of science and its practical extension, technology. In SF, the wondrous act is achieved not by magic, as in traditional narratives, but by the application of scientific method. The SF narrative usually contains fantastic elements, projections into the future or a parallel world. But these elements of fantasy are extrapolations from principles of science or existing technologies. We can define SF, then, as a genre that expresses itself through a discourse of science; technology will always be a key element in this expression.

Mary Shelley's Dr Frankenstein is an amalgam of alchemist and modern man of science. Through a series of rationally controlled experiments, he uncovers the secrets of life, and the means of creating life itself. His creature is a technological double of humanity, produced in a laboratory. Shelley redefines the mystical quest for the secrets of life in the context of scientific inquiry. The experiments described in the novel are an extrapolation from contemporary experiments with electricity, which carried the promise of uncovering the spark of life. Yet *Frankenstein* typifies the Romantic reaction against the Enlightenment's faith in reason and progress. Dr Frankenstein's creation is an abomination rather than a paragon of technology; it is a monster of science that becomes a destructive force, ultimately killing its own creator.

The narrative of Frankenstein and his monster, with its overtones of alchemy and horror, has become the most potent myth of technology. It represents the dark underside of the doctrine of progress. Retold countless times, this narrative pattern is the staple of

SF, or at least of that type of SF that carries a moral warning. Frankenstein's monster stands for technology that runs out of control, that destroys its human creator. There are many variations on the basic pattern, not least in the film versions of *Frankenstein*. At times the scientist is a philanthropist, at others a megalomaniac (at times a mixture of both). Sometimes his great experiment is cursed by his own arrogance, at others it is ruined by bad luck, as in David Cronenberg's version of *The Fly*. The scientist's creation is normally depicted sympathetically, as in James Whale's 1931 film version of *Frankenstein*, yet it is also capable of great destruction. One aspect of this narrative pattern, however, is that the monster's violence is generally directed against its creator. As the product of a scientific project gone horribly wrong, the monster punishes the scientist who has so drastically overstepped his limits. The *Frankenstein* narrative has remained so compelling because it dramatizes the fear, as strong today as in Shelley's time, of science going too far.

Frankenstein's legacy

Patricia Warrick's study of the cybernetic imagination in SF isolates four main themes stemming from *Frankenstein* that flow through much of SF. The first is the Promethean theme (Shelley subtitled her novel *The Modern Prometheus*). In Greek mythology, Prometheus was a Titan, a master craftsman who stole fire from the gods as a gift to humanity. Both Prometheus and mankind are punished by the gods for this act. Dr Frankenstein is the modern Prometheus because 'he goes beyond what has been done before and, entering forbidden territory, steals knowledge from the gods' (Warrick 1980: 37). Whereas earlier such transgressive characters in literature had been magicians or alchemists like Dr Faustus, Frankenstein has acquired his Promethean ability through acquisition of scientific knowledge. Dr Frankenstein is the first of many Promethean sci-fi scientists, 'full of curiosity, pushing the limits, doing what previously only the gods had done' (p. 37).

The second theme discussed by Warrick is the ambiguity of technology. Dr Frankenstein's creature is at first gentle and benevolent, apparently justifying Frankenstein's high hopes for his scientific project. Frankenstein's original inspiration is philanthropic: he believes that he can use scientific knowledge to benefit humanity. This Enlightenment spirit is at first upheld, as Frankenstein's experiment in creating life is a success; the creature represents the miraculous achievement of technology. Only later does this achievement turn to disaster. The creature becomes a destructive monster as a result of its rejection by its creator. *Frankenstein* represents technology in dual terms: as the proud outcome of scientific breakthroughs, and as a calamitous force causing more harm than good.

Frankenstein's rejection of his own creation points to a third theme expressed in the novel: the irresponsibility of science. Warrick remarks that Frankenstein resembles another figure of Greek mythology: Epimetheus, a Titan who lacked the ability of foresight. Frankenstein is so consumed by the spirit of scientific experiment, and so excited by his success, that he fails to foresee the consequences of his achievement. He fails to take full responsibility for his creation, abandoning his creature like a neglectful father. He even comes to condemn his own scientific creation. 'Having loosed the monster on the world, Frankenstein after much reflection comes to regard his act of creation as an unforgivable evil' (1980: 38). The lack of foresight and ethical concern initially displayed by Frankenstein is a key element of the narrative. In SF, disaster usually occurs when a new technology, or artificially produced life form, is loosed on the world without sufficient foresight as to its consequences. In *Jurassic Park*, the villain is the short-sighted entrepreneur responsible for reinventing dinosaurs as amusement-park entertainment (the character blessed with foresight in this film is, for a change, a scientist – armed with chaos theory). In *Terminator 2*, apocalypse is only averted by the actions of Sarah Connor who, having knowledge of the future enslavement of humanity by its own technology, intervenes to prevent that technology being implemented.

Finally, Warrick refers to the shifting of roles of master and servant found in *Frankenstein*. At the beginning of the narrative, the creature is dependent on Dr Frankenstein, who has brought it into being. But as Frankenstein 'becomes obsessed with destroying the technology he has created, he becomes enslaved by it' (1980: 38). The scientist loses his independent will; his life is taken over by the monster as he obeys its instructions to follow him into the Arctic. As Warrick comments, much SF depicts this reversal of the master–servant role between inventor and invention. The technology created to serve humanity instead becomes its master, whether that technology is a robot, a computer, a mutant or some other variation.

One of the most resonant instances of this process occurs in Stanley Kubrick's 1968 film *2001: A Space Odyssey*, based on an Arthur C. Clarke story. The onboard supercomputer HAL is meant to serve the astronauts in every way. Instead it turns on them, refusing to obey their instructions, using its mastery of the spacecraft to eliminate all but one of the humans onboard. At first the astronauts can barely believe that HAL, which has never previously malfunctioned, could let them down. When they realize that the computer is actively malevolent, their situation seems almost hopeless. The astronauts' plight is a metaphor for our own: having put so much faith in complex technological systems, we are seemingly at their mercy when those systems break down. Science fiction often extrapolates from this situation by granting malignant agency to technology itself, thus dramatizing the inverted master–servant relationship.

The other inversion practised in some SF, including *2001*, is that the technological servant may be depicted more sympathetically than the human master. With its warm, friendly voice, HAL seems more human than the cold, dispassionate astronauts. When HAL is finally disabled, its memory banks deactivated one by one, we feel sympathy for this proud computer, reduced to its 'childhood' state. Science fiction is full of likeable robots or artificial intelligence systems, anthropomorphized to such an extent that they are in fact more agreeable than many humans. This process is taken to its furthest extent in *Blade Runner*, in which the replicants, designed to be 'more human than human', are also in many cases more likeable than the heartless humans in Los Angeles, 2019.

Blade Runner in fact partakes of all the themes deriving from *Frankenstein* mentioned above. Dr Tyrell is the Frankenstein figure, a brilliant scientist who has created the replicants to serve humanity. Marvels of genetic engineering, they perform all manner of tasks for the benefit of their human masters. But Tyrell has Frankenstein's flaw: he lacks the moral vision to take full responsibility for his creations, whom he has designed with limited lifespans. Resenting their fate, the replicants become destructive elements. Their leader kills Tyrell, crushing the eyes of the morally blind scientist. In the Philip K. Dick novel on which the film is based – *Do Androids Dream of Electric Sheep?* – it is suggested that Deckard, the only 'person' capable of destroying the renegade replicants, is himself a replicant. As in *Frankenstein*, the technology invented to benefit humanity has instead come to terrorize it.

Robots

The term 'robot' was first used by the Czech writer Karl Capek in his 1920 play *R.U.R.* Derived from the Czech word for forced labour, the fictional robot of Capek's play is a mechanical servant; the company Rossum's Universal Robots sells them as cheap labour. The father and son inventors of the robots, Old and Young Rossum (the name derives from the Czech word for intellect), represent the transition from alchemist-science to scientist-engineer. As Peter Wollen remarks, Old Rossum had the metaphysical goal of proving God unnecessary by creating an artificial man. '[He] is both a scientist and a magus, a creator of golems' (1989: 14) (the play is set in Prague, home of the golem legend). Young Rossum, on the other hand, has no metaphysical dreams. An engineer and industrialist, his goal is entirely pragmatic: a cheap and single-minded mechanical workforce. For Wollen, Young Rossum is the perfect Fordist, his robots mass-manufactured like Model T Fords.

The narrative development of *R.U.R.* is one that recurs in countless SF works. Young Rossum has designed the robots without emotions, but over time they develop sensitivity, coming to resent their oppressive human masters. As Patricia Warrick points out, the robots of Capek's play are made from organic materials, which makes them less robots than androids or, as in *Blade Runner*, replicants. Like the replicants, they are almost indistinguishable from humans; with the addition of an emotional register they are no longer content to be slaves. They develop a rebellious attitude that culminates in conflict between human and robot. Robots specially trained as soldiers turn their skills against their human masters, with such vengeance and such efficiency that only one man is spared. At the end of the play, this sole surviving human is the robots' servant, kept alive to rediscover the formula for making robots. While the order of robots will most likely survive, humanity is doomed to extinction.

This narrative of rebellious robots is based squarely on the *Frankenstein* pattern, yet it extends the notion of technology-out-of-control beyond the story of one errant scientist. When an entire workforce of robots turns against its masters, humanity is faced with its own destruction. The unprecedented destructive force of nuclear weaponry made such extinction a real possibility after the Second World War; humanity had finally developed a technology capable of destroying all life on earth, including itself. The film *The Day the Earth Stood Still*, released in 1951, delivered a trenchant moral warning about the irresponsible use of destructive technologies. This film featured Gort, an alien robot with powers far in advance of human military forces, yet Gort's masters have come to earth preaching peace. The alien species is portrayed as morally superior to our own, having developed a civilization in which advanced technologies – including robots – are put to constructive rather than destructive use.

Perhaps the most chilling vision of humanity undone by its own technology is found in the *Terminator* films. As in *R.U.R.*, the machines have taken over, bent on the elimination of humanity altogether. Technology designed by humans for the waging of war, in this instance a computerized complex called SkyNet, has turned against its creators. The cyborgs sent by the machines to kill key humans are the fictional descendants of Capek's robots; they are just as 'robotic' in their single-minded destructive programming. The *Terminator* films, the *Matrix* films and other SF works depicting an embattled humanity on the verge of extinction, are the dramatic expression of the admonition running through Paul Virilio's work. In designing and implementing technological systems whose capacities far exceed human capacities, we have, Virilio warns, 'programmed our own disappearance'.

As we have seen, robots and other automata such as androids and cyborgs frequently menace their human creators in SF. But there is also a strong tradition of benevolent robots. Isaac Asimov is the SF author most associated with robots: indeed, he coined the term 'robotics'. Beginning in 1940, his many stories depict robots as useful servants of humanity. The robots described in his fiction are far in advance of the actual industrial robots of his time, which were deployed from the 1960s to perform repetitive industrial tasks. Asimov's optimistic fiction projects a future in which social problems are solved using sophisticated technologies including robots; his work exhibits a degree of faith in technological progress. Robots are our faithful servants, programmed with the Three Laws of Robotics, an ethical code for machine intelligence. Asimov's Three Laws prevent the outbreak in his stories of what he calls 'the Frankenstein complex'. His robots are programmed to obey human instructions, and forbidden to injure humans or to allow a human to be harmed.

Popular SF has numerous servant-robots in the Asimov mould. These include Robby the Robot from the 1956 film *Forbidden Planet*, the Robot of the 1960s TV show *Lost in Space* and *Star Wars'* R2D2, all loyal to their human masters, often performing a comical role in the narrative. The 2000 film *Bicentennial Man* was based on an Asimov story, centred on a likeable robot. Yet SF also has a long line of robots unfamiliar with Asimov's Three Laws, or at least unwilling to obey them. At times, as in Fritz Lang's 1926 film *Metropolis*, the robot is invented for malevolent purposes. The robot Maria in this film is created by the owner of the vast industrial complex, for the purposes of subduing a worker uprising. Decades later, the android of *Alien* (1979) is programmed by 'the Company' to sabotage the humans onboard a spacecraft. *Westworld* (1973) follows the narrative laid down in *R.U.R.*: robots conduct a violent attack on the humans they once served. In SF works of this type there is often no explanation given for the robots' sudden about-turn; in other works it is the development of consciousness in the robots' AI that is the determining factor. As this brief survey suggests, the ambivalent figure of the robot plays out a tension in SF – between the optimistic vision found in Asimov and the apprehension at the core of the *Frankenstein* story.

Utopias and dystopias

One of the earliest utopias, Plato's *Republic*, described the organization of an ideal city-state. As Janet Staiger outlines in her study of SF's 'visionary cities', SF has updated Plato by situating the perfect society within highly technologized cities of the future. The great historian of technology, Lewis Mumford, wrote in 1922 that 'modern utopias were inseparable from the rise of technology' (cited in Staiger 1999: 103). Edward Bellamy's *Looking Backward*, published in 1888, was an early and influential SF work in this mould, fusing utopia with technological progress. The novel's narrator awakes in Boston in 2000, to find the social problems of the late nineteenth century eradicated. Crime, war and poverty have disappeared in a technologically advanced society – featuring credit cards and music-by-telephone – functioning as a highly organized 'industrial army'.

This alignment of technology, social control and utopia was most vigorously articulated in SF by H.G. Wells. Wells was a socialist who dreamed of the perfect planned welfare society. Technological progress and education were for him essential in achieving this aim; the enemies of his political vision were nationalism, which pandered to regressive emotional impulses, and overpopulation, which threatened social progress. Wells published his *A Modern*

Utopia in 1905, featuring a world government regulating its citizens from a central base in Paris. Of his many utopian works, perhaps the best known is the film *Things to Come* (1936), scripted by Wells and based on his earlier novel *The Shape of Things to Come* (1934). In this work, humanity descends into barbarism after an apocalyptic war, but rebuilds society with the aid of advanced technology in 2036. The utopian state of the future – Everytown – is a technological paradise, sealed off and climate-controlled, with audio-visual mass communications.

Staiger remarks that the blueprint for Wells's technological utopia was the modernist architecture and social planning espoused by Le Corbusier (described in Chapter 2). Le Corbusier's model of the Radiant City – modern, ordered and technocratic – found its fictional expression in Wells's Everytown and Fritz Lang's *Metropolis*. Everytown has a harmonious social order, but one presided over by an elite dedicated to continual technological progress. In *Things to Come*, a subversive citizen calls for a halt to progress, threatening the elite's new project: a 'space-gun' to the moon. Wells's narrative casts this rebellious figure as the villain, able to whip up regressive emotion in the populace. The elite barely succeeds in firing its astronauts into space, but the film closes with a resounding speech by its leader, upholding unrestrained progress as the key to human happiness.

If we now find such a narrative development somewhat unusual, that is probably because we have become accustomed to its inversion in dystopian SF. The narratives of these works usually involve a rebellious figure, asserting individual freedom against an oppressive political system. Dystopian SF in fact developed partly in response to the optimism of Wells's vision. Mark Hillegas's study of the early 'anti-utopians' documents their explicit opposition to Wells's faith in a system built on technology and rationalization. E.M. Forster's 1909 story 'The Machine Stops' depicts a future mechanized society, designed as a utopia but turned into a nightmare. Individuals live in underground cells, connected by a global communications network (a fictional precursor of the Internet). There is no direct contact or experience of nature; the Machine regulates the network and meets all needs. But when the Machine breaks down, society breaks with it, and its citizens die, unable to adapt to nature. As Hillegas points out, Forster drew on Wells's imagery of future cities, but for him a society built on reason and technology was a tomb, not a paradise.

Hillegas identifies a similar pattern in the three great dystopian fictions of the first half of the twentieth century: Yevgeny Zamiatin's *We* (1924), Aldous Huxley's *Brave New World* (1932) and George Orwell's *1984* (1949). All three authors found Wells's highly organized utopias objectionable. Beneath the social ideals and gleaming technologies, they detected the potential for a repressive apparatus, in which citizens are

> ... conditioned to obedience, freedom is eliminated, and individuality crushed; ... the past is systematically destroyed and men are isolated from nature; ... science and technology are employed, not to enrich human life, but to maintain the state's surveillance and control of its slave citizens (cited in Staiger 1999: 105).

In Zamiatin's *We*, the machine has become God, while individuals have become depersonalized, given numbers instead of names. The stability of this techno-utopia is disrupted when two 'Numbers' fall in love, learning to value emotion and imagination. When a small group of like-minded dissidents assert their right to individual freedom and creative imagination, they are lobotomized by the authorities. Many SF works, including George Lucas's 1971 film *THX 1138*, have followed this narrative pattern, depicting future societies as closed technological systems, more prison state than ideal state. Orwell's *1984* portrayed an authoritarian state ruthlessly enforcing its rule with the aid of TV and surveillance technologies. Terry Gilliam's 1985 film *Brazil* depicts a similar world, with more intrusive surveillance technologies. Janet Staiger comments that *Brazil* ironically visualizes Le Corbusier's metaphor for the modernist house as 'a machine for living in'. The pulsating tubes running through buildings are 'the intestines of the social system', carrying food, air conditioning, information, waste – and people.

Perhaps the most prescient of the major dystopian works is Huxley's *Brave New World*. Certainly its concerns have re-emerged forcefully in the twenty-first century, in the wake of developments in genetic engineering. Huxley imagined a highly rationalized future based on Fordist principles ('Our Ford' has replaced God as the figurehead of a global political system). Social stability is enforced by indoctrination, a pacifying drug called soma, and mass entertainment ('feelies', an extension of cinema). A strict social hierarchy is maintained on genetic lines: individuals are assigned a social category at birth. But 'birth' is now a function of the state: everyone is a test-tube baby, genetically designed with specific characteristics and social responsibilities. Huxley's genetically determined dystopia was revisited in the 1997 film *Gattaca* (the letters A, C, G, T, used to form the film's title, are the 'letters' of the human genome). The possibilities opened up by genetic science, including the 'programming' of offspring with socially desirable qualities, have generated widespread debate in recent years. Ethical concerns have arisen over 'genetic screening' of individuals for employment and insurance purposes. There is a fear that a new social order may develop, based on a genetic 'fate'. All these concerns were vividly articulated in Huxley's dystopia, written in 1932.

There is no doubt that dystopia overshadows utopia, at least in Western SF cinema, from the 1970s onwards. A sub-genre of 'nature strikes back' SF/horror films emerged early in the 1970s, in response to social fears over environmental degradation. Films such as *Squirm, Frogs, Piranha* and *Alligator* featured a contaminated and vengeful nature; the villains of these films were greedy corporations and/or irresponsible scientists. Natural forces mutate and become monstrous as a result of radiation or pollution (a theme established in the Japanese *Godzilla* films commencing in 1954). The negative consequences of science and technology portrayed in these films were projected into the future in a wave of bleak SF cinema. *Soylent Green, Logan's Run* and *Escape from New York* all conveyed foreboding rather than hope about future developments in civilization. Post-apocalyptic films such as *Planet of the Apes* and the *Mad Max* series depict a grim world in which survival itself is an achievement.

From the early 1980s, much dystopian SF focused its vision of the future within an urban environment. *Blade Runner, Robocop, Strange Days, The Fifth Element* and *Dark City* are all set in alienating and confusing cityscapes. Vivian Sobchack describes these urban environments as 'cities on the edge of time': groundless and lacking spatial stability. Such a city, she notes, is 'virtually "bottomed out" and literally fathomless: its inhabitants suffer from giddiness or vertigo and, rootless, they "free fall" in both space and time' (1999: 138). Because these films borrow from the visual style and mood of 1940s *film noir*, they have been referred to as examples of 'future noir' or 'tech noir' cinema. *Blade Runner* has attracted the most critical attention, including a book-length study by Scott Bukatman, and an influential essay by Giulian Bruno, 'Ramble City: Postmodernism and *Blade Runner*'. Bruno connects the film's vision of urban decay and simulation with developments in postmodern theory. The *Terminator*, *Alien(s)* and *Robocop* films were more successful commercially, however, all contributing to a 'techno-fear' theme in SF cinema. One interesting aspect of these films is that the role of villain is filled not by an Orwellian state apparatus, but by huge Corporations. In *Robocop*, law and order in Detroit has been taken over by the Omni-Consumer Products Corporation, with disastrous results. The economic and political power of transnational corporations was increasingly evident in the 1980s; this power was projected into a dystopian future overseen by the likes of *Blade Runner*'s Tyrell Corporation, or the sinister 'Company' of the *Alien* series.

It should be remembered that the distinction between utopia and dystopia is not always clear-cut in SF. H.G. Wells was capable of nightmarish visions of the future (*The Time Machine*), or a pessimistic slant on the super city-state (*When the Sleeper Wakes*). Fritz Lang's *Metropolis* has a narrative resolution between the masses and their industrial ruler which prompts some commentators to interpret the film as utopian; yet the enduring imagery of the film is perhaps more likely to be that of oppressed workers toiling in the future metropolis. As well, although this section has emphasized the techno-fear aspect of recent SF, one of the most popular SF projects – *Star Trek* – has a persistently positive conception of the future. *Star Trek* projects Enlightenment values of reason and progress into the twenty-third century and beyond: social problems including poverty have been overcome, leaving the *Enterprise* and its successors to spread goodwill throughout the universe. If we were looking for examples of utopia in SF, we need look no further than the social order displayed in *Star Trek: The Next Generation*, as well as other *Star Trek* spin-offs. The harmonious order on board the Federation spaceships features an equal opportunity hierarchy and the service of faithful androids: a thoroughly optimistic version of a high-tech future.

Our survey of utopias and dystopias has concentrated on Western SF; non-Western SF expresses a different mix of cultural attitudes to technology. Japanese SF often portrays the bond between humans and machines with less pessimism and fear than is found in Western SF. Japanese culture is perhaps less prone than the West to techno-fear, as reflected in the tradition of friendly robots and androids in animation (including *Astro Boy*, *Gigantor* and *Prince Planet*). While animated features like *Akira* depict a dystopian urban future of the *Blade Runner* type, other films chart the future with less dread. Animated films such as *Ghost in the Shell* depict a symbiosis between human and machine, hinting at a 'spirit' within advanced technologies that need not be malevolent in the Frankenstein manner.

Flesh and machine

We shall discuss the figure of the cyborg in detail in Chapter 5; here we shall limit our study to the representation of cyborgs in SF. Cybernetics emerged as a field of science in the late 1940s, incorporating information theory, systems theory and developments in communication and computer technology. Norbert Wiener's 1948 book *Cybernetics: or Control and Communication in the Animal and the Machine*, established cybernetics as the study of all systems, mechanical and biological. A mechanical system equipped with feedback techniques to control its operations would be cybernetic, that is, self-regulating, without need of human monitoring. But humans and animals are of course also self-regulating in this sense; cybernetics sought to isolate the common elements in automatic machines and the human nervous system. Cybernetic theory rendered all complex systems – whether human, machine or social – in terms of information flow and control. The term 'cyborg' (cybernetic organism) was coined in 1960 to describe 'self-regulating man-machine systems'. As David Tomas remarks, the cyborg was envisioned by scientists as a technological superman, capable of withstanding the rigours of space travel (1995: 36).

The appeal of this concept to SF should be readily apparent. Robert Rawdon Wilson points to the initial optimism surrounding the idea of the cyborg, in the wake of the successful use of prostheses and transplants. Popular 1970s TV shows *The Six Million Dollar Man* and *The Bionic Woman* captured 'the eye-bulging, mouth-gaping yearning for cyborgian evolution' (1995: 243). Less desirable consequences of cybernetics soon appeared in SF. The 1977 film *Demon Seed* featured a computer-controlled house that imprisons, then rapes, its female occupant. The resultant offspring is part human, part computer: a horrific cyborg. Perhaps the best-known fictional cyborgs are *Star Trek's* the Borg. These beings dramatize the conceptual sweep within cybernetics: they are part biological, part mechanical, and operate as part of an information flow. In the humanistic sci-fi tradition of which *Star Trek* is a part, however, these collectivist cyborgs are distinctly malevolent to other life forms.

A more sympathetic cyborg was found in Paul Verhoeven's 1987 film *Robocop*. A near-dead policeman is reborn as a superhuman cyborg, programmed with law-enforcing instructions. Memories of his former life haunt his programming, however: traces of his humanity live on in his new mechanical self. Fictions such as *Robocop* literalize not only the concepts of cybernetic theory, but also more widespread attitudes concerning technology and society. Several commentators, including Samantha Holland, interpret cyborg films as a reaction against the collapsing of conceptual categories such as human and machine, brain and mind (Holland 1995: 170). The cyborg operates as an ambiguous metaphor for our increasing dependence on technology.

The enmeshing of the human in technology, especially information technology, has been most thoroughly explored in cyberpunk fiction. Cyberpunk emerged as a sub-genre of SF in 1983, incorporating a number of writers including Bruce Bethke, William Gibson and Bruce Sterling. Gibson's 1984 novel *Neuromancer* is the most celebrated and most influential cyberpunk work. Included in its rich prose is a definition of cyberspace, a term coined by Gibson. Cyberspace is a 'graphic representation of data abstracted from the bank of every computer in the human system' (1984: 51). In *Neuromancer*, Gibson projected the cybernetic sensibility into a future where humans are neurologically modified to 'jack in' to the 'matrix' of networked data systems. The matrix is a virtual city of information, containing 'lines of light ranged in the non-space of the mind, clusters and constellations of data. Like city lights, receding . . .'. R.L. Rutsky has commented on the major significance of this 'matrix' as envisaged by Gibson:

> Gibson condenses the two most popular figurations of postmodern, techno-cultural space: the city and the computer (or computer network). . . . In the matrix, then, the analogy between the urban grid and the circuitry of the microchip, between the space of the city and the interior space of the computer, is no longer metaphoric at all (1999: 116).

The matrix is an ambiguous zone, both real and virtual, into which cyberpunk characters immerse themselves. Several theorists have remarked on the biological models on which the matrix seems to be based. Nicola Nixon sees the cyberpunk matrix as 'feminine space' into which 'console cowboys "jack in"': this space is both exhilarating and threatening to its male invaders (cited in Rutsky 1999: 122). Claudia Springer has pointed out that the word 'matrix' derives from the Latin for both mother and womb (1996: 59); as Rutsky comments, in cyberpunk SF the womb-like space of the matrix often generates complex technology, such as artificial intelligence, that 'comes to have a fluid and mysterious life of its own' (1999: 122).

The other significant aspect of cyberpunk SF is that the human/machine interface is taken for granted, without the spectre of techno-fear. Instead, the pressing concern is control of information. Cyberpunk heroes like Case in *Neuromancer* are hacker outlaws, resisting the corporatization of the datasphere, subverting the authorized flow of information. This depiction of the hacker as rebel hero is part of the subcultural appeal of cyberpunk, as examined by Mark Dery in his study of cyberculture, *Escape Velocity*. Cyberpunk writing became a discursive site for the role of technology in culture, crossing the boundaries between fiction and theory. Scott Bukatman, David Tomas and Allucquere Roseanne Stone have all celebrated the potential opened up by cyberpunk. Tomas sees fictional cyberspace as a mythological space within which new technological forms may be accommodated. Bukatman argues that social and conceptual problems within urban space are negotiated within cyberpunk fiction. Stone claims that the socially disenfranchised could find within cyberpunk a 'refigured discursive community', allowing the possibility of both an 'imaginal public sphere' and new forms of social interaction (cited in Bukatman 1993: 145).

Certain SF films concerned with technology and the body have attracted intense critical and theoretical interest. The films of David Cronenberg and the *Alien* series are foremost in this category. Cronenberg's SF/horror films all feature human bodies undergoing some form of mutation or hybridity with technology. *Scanners*, *Videodrome*, *The Fly*, *Existenz* and others depict bodies taken over and transformed by information technologies or scientific experiment. Mark Dery remarks that Cronenberg's cinema expresses a perverse version of McLuhan's theory of media as 'extensions of man'. Cronenberg's vision is of a techno-evolution of the human species, 'a sort of unnatural selection catalysed by technology' (1996: 294). This is a 'dark twin' of McLuhan's theories: electronic media and other technologies become the agents of mutation, with disturbing consequences. Of the many other theorists to consider Cronenberg's cinema, Scott Bukatman's analysis in his book *Terminal Identity* is the most extensive. For Bukatman, the transforming powers of technology on the body are so paramount in Cronenberg's films that in them 'the apparent mind/body dichotomy is superseded by the *tri*-chotomy of mind/body/machine'

(1993: 82). Bukatman connects Cronenberg's obsessions not only with McLuhan, but also the paranoid viral metaphor found in William Burroughs's fiction. The contamination by video signal in *Videodrome* represents for Bukatman not just the mutation of human flesh by technological means, but the dissolution of subjectivity. Cronenberg's films convey a general anxiety, concerning 'the breakdown of human hegemony through the deployment of new technologies' (1990: 202).

The *Alien* films have provoked even more theoretical attention. A number of essays examining Ridley Scott's 1979 film *Alien* were collected in the anthology *Alien Zone*, edited by Annette Kuhn. The most influential of these was Barbara Creed's '*Alien* and the Monstrous-Feminine', in which Creed draws on Julia Kristeva's theory of abjection to analyse the representation of the alien in this film. The visceral horror associated with the alien, Creed argues, is part of a 'complex representation of the monstrous-feminine in terms of the maternal figure as perceived within a patriarchal ideology' (1990: 128). The themes of *Alien* were elaborated in the succeeding films of the series. Conceptual oppositions – nature and technology, male and female, rational and irrational, human and alien – become confounded in these films. The aliens seem to be both organic and machine-like; traditional gender roles are continually overturned. Ripley is both science officer and maternal, and by the fourth film, 'Ripley' is a clone possessing alien DNA. Accordingly theorists have analysed the *Alien* films with the aid of cultural theory, feminist theory and psychoanalytical theory. Catherine Constable (1999) discusses the first four films in these terms in the anthology *Alien Zone 2*. As she notes, the scene in *Alien Resurrection* – in which the clone Ripley discovers the monstrous failed clone attempts – is that film's most eerie scene; it is also a haunting vision of genetic science's dark side. Maternity is a recurring theme within the series, represented as 'clean'– the metaphorical rebirth of the crew as they awake from science-controlled hypersleep – or monstrous – the alien queen. The climactic fight at the end of *Aliens* between Ripley, augmented by a technological apparatus, and the alien queen, seems to pit these two versions of maternity against each other.

Hyperreal science fiction

We shall conclude our discussion of SF with a brief mention of those works concerned with simulacra and the hyperreal, or to use

Bukatman's phrase, 'the science fiction of the spectacle'. It should be no surprise that Jean Baudrillard has expressed an interest in SF of this type. Indeed, Philip K. Dick's 1964 novel *The Simulacra*, in which political leaders are replaced by simulations, predates Baudrillard's 'The Precession of Simulacra' by some years. In his essay 'Simulacra and Science Fiction', Baudrillard posits three categories of simulacra. The first is naturalist or utopian (the Garden of Eden would be an example). The second category is productivist, based on the machine, energy and expansion (classical SF, from Jules Verne to *Star Trek*, belongs in this category). The third category is simulation, founded on 'information, the model, the cybernetic game – total operationality, hyperreality, aim of total control' (1994: 121).

Baudrillard finds this third category representative of contemporary society, saturated with images and models of the real, characterized by implosion and information instead of production and expansion. For Baudrillard, SF corresponding to this third order of simulacra merely reflects the contemporary status of reality and representation. Thus Philip K. Dick's works create a world in which the real and the unreal have dissolved into the hyperreal, mirroring the 'hallucination of the real' conducted by everyday media. For Baudrillard, Dick's SF differs from classical SF in that it does not project a double or imaginary world; it depicts instead a space with no other side or exteriority. The films *Blade Runner* and *Total Recall*, both based on Dick books, confound the real/artificial distinction. *Total Recall*, in particular, based on the notion of virtual tourism, delights in erasing the difference between lived experience and its technologically mediated hallucination.

Which other SF works exist in this territory? The films *Videodrome* and *Existenz*, already mentioned, perform a similar 'slippage of reality'; *Strange Days* explores simulation and perception. Bukatman nominates the 1985 film *20 Minutes into the Future*, featuring Max Headroom – a computer-generated newsreader – as a trenchant comment on the colonization of reality by TV spectacle. The *Matrix* films incorporate many of the thematics we have discussed in this chapter, including cyberpunk and the hyperreal. The outlaw heroes of *The Matrix* are in the tradition of Case in *Neuromancer*: data pirates jacking in to the information system in the hope of subverting it. *The Matrix* also contains explicit references to Baudrillard's work, including the phrase 'the desert of the real': the world of this dystopian future is one presided over by simulation in the Baudrillardian sense.

Baudrillard reserves his greatest praise for the work of J.G. Ballard. Ballard's novels, including *High Rise* and *Crash*, and collections of stories such as *Myths of the Near Future*, barely seem like SF at all, so rooted are they in contemporary urban experience. For Baudrillard, *Crash* 'is *our* world, nothing in it is "invented" ... [in] *Crash*, there is neither fiction nor reality anymore – hyperreality abolishes both' (1994: 125). The perverse fascination for car crashes held by the book's characters expresses contemporary culture's obsession with cars, sex and death, as refracted through the mass media. Bukatman points to Arthur Croker and David Cook's use of the term 'mediascape' to describe the saturation of contemporary life by media; as Bukatman points out, Ballard's fiction has consistently charted the cultural effects of this mediascape. The world of Ballard's fiction is dominated by technology, especially media technology – as is ours. 'We live in quantified non-linear terms,' Ballard has said, 'we switch on television sets, switch them off half an hour later, speak on the telephone, read magazines, dream and so forth. We don't live our lives in linear terms in the sense that Victorians did' (cited in Bukatman 1993: 45). In 1974, Ballard wrote an introduction to the French edition of *Crash*, outlining his intention in writing the novel:

> ... the ultimate role of *Crash!* is cautionary, a warning against that brutal, erotic and overlit realm that beckons more and more persistently to us from the margins of the technological landscape.

This introduction is an eloquent defence of SF as the best means of representing, and understanding, our 'technological landscape'. For Ballard, the contemporary world is already like 'an enormous novel', ruled by 'fictions of every kind' generated through the mass media. Ballard's works confront this technologized world with 'extreme metaphors' drawn from the mediascape. We end this chapter on SF with Ballard's exhortation:

> Science and technology multiply around us. To an increasing extent they dictate the languages in which we speak and think. Either we use those languages, or we remain mute (1975: 7).

CHAPTER 5

Cyborgs: the Body, Information and Technology

Science fiction makes it clear that the body is not what it used to be. The contemporary intersection of the body, information and technology gives us a different body from the somewhat fixed and frail, if valiant, body we were used to. One example of the changing cultural conception of the body is the notion of physical 'disability'. Not so very long ago there was debate whether people whose bodies did not conform to the 'norm' should be labelled 'disabled' or 'differently abled' or even, of course, whether they should be labelled at all. The latter has won out. It is now clear that we are all 'differently abled'. All of us require technical assistance and a society that adapts to the different needs of our bodies. In the old terms, we are all perhaps 'disabled' in the sense that we all rely on technological assistance in different ways, yet such reliance is obviously enabling as well. Chris Gray makes this clear in his extensive book covering these issues, *Cyborg Citizen*. Gray writes that '(dis)abled cyborgs' are also 'enabled cyborgs' (p. 99). They

> . . . certainly have their own political priorities, but on closer examination we see that they are not that different from the priorities of the rest of us. Almost all of us are cyborged in some way . . . (pp. 1–2).

Old categories and ideas surrounding the body are certainly breaking down and have to be seriously rethought. Yet the current challenges to the body are only the beginning. Much more drastic change is promised and we do not yet know what price we might eventually pay for the merging of body and machine. In short, if it is true that the body has become cyborg, a cyber-organism, this is not so much one dramatic change as a passing of the body through a series of gateways that seem now without end.

Let us start with some definitions. Although the term 'cyborg' was coined in 1960 by Manfred Clynes and Nathan Kline (Gray 2001: 11), we shall jump forward a few decades and begin with Donna Haraway's highly influential conception of the cyborg.

Donna Haraway's cyborg

Haraway is concerned with the future of a lot of things: the body, machines, feminism, socialism, the cultural function of discourses and metaphors, and oppressed women workers. For Haraway, the cyborg is both a 'creature of social reality' and 'a creature of fiction' (1991b: 149). In other words, the cyborg is a series of real connections between bodies and machines, but it is also a series of metaphors, or new ways of telling stories in order to negotiate culture. These bleed into one another, as for Haraway 'the boundary between science fiction and social reality is an optical illusion' (ibid.). Haraway's ability to present both a critical, feminist, and an engaged, approach to the cyborg has made her 'Cyborg Manifesto' perhaps the central essay in the area.

First she argues for the fact that the cyborg cannot be avoided. It is our 'ontology' – or way of being – and also 'gives us our politics' (1991b: 150). She points out that the cyborg blurs many edges and that, in a quote that is now famous, she is presenting 'an argument for pleasure in the confusion of boundaries and for responsibility in their construction'. She uses the cyborg to imagine a world free of current gender demands and categories. She acknowledges that cyborgs are by and large the 'illegitimate offspring of militarism and patriarchal capitalism, not to mention state socialism', but still sees them as potentially very subversive. This is because they undermine many of the oppositions upon which power is based – and the ways in which power disciplines bodies to do what they are told. This includes the opposition between nature and culture.

For Haraway, culture cannot escape biology as simply as it seems to in some arguments (there is no simple cultural determination). Yet nature is itself a culturally defined concept. The cyborg is exactly the kind of monster that appears time and time again in cultural myths about the natural world (and about technology) when the division between culture and nature is breaking down. Frankenstein's monster is created in a storm. The world of the film *Blade Runner* is permeated by constant rain. As such the cyborg represents both the breakdown of the human–machine boundary and also, crucially, the breakdown of the human–animal boundary. Myths, machines, animals and humans are deeply implicated within each other.

There is another boundary broken down here. This is the boundary between the obvious physical world of visible objects and non-physical, or invisible, processual worlds (the latter conceived of as information or perhaps as electricity – or just the invisibility of computer chips which are so different in this respect from the old machines such as locomotives). She writes:

> Our best machines are made of sunshine; they are all light and clean because they are nothing but signals, electromagnetic waves, a section of the spectrum, and these machines are eminently portable, mobile. ... The ubiquity and invisibility of cyborgs is precisely why these sunshine-belt machines are so deadly. They are as hard to see politically as materially (1991b: 153).

Haraway is highly critical of many of the ways in which humans (especially women) are trapped in new machines that move too fast to be seen and are so all-encompassing they take over the world. The ultimate nightmare of the cyborg is C^3I, the military dream of complete control, command, communications and intelligence through global communications and other technologies that we shall discuss in Chapter 7. Nevertheless Haraway also sees the potential for subversion in a life lived 'in which people are not afraid of their joint kinship with animals and machines' (p. 154).

Along the way, Haraway also proposes a new cyborg conception of politics which she labels the 'Informatics of Domination' (p. 161) On the grand scale, this replaces 'White Capitalist Patriarchy' – the rule of wealthy white men. She opposes the 'comfortable old hierarchical dominations to the scary new networks' along the following lines. The comfortable old forms of domination were to do with representation, the bourgeois novel, realism, as against the scary new networks' simulations and postmodern science fictions. The old ways conceived of the organic, a body which was physiologically intact and able to be repaired, as against the body as an assemblage of 'biotic components' which could be rewritten through 'communications engineering'. Organic communal forms are replaced by optimal communications, and small groups become 'subsystems'. Perfection becomes 'optimization'. Stress management replaces hygiene. The lifelong family wage is replaced by immediate 'comparable worth' in the 'integrated circuits' of the market place. Sex is replaced by genetic engineering and reproduction becomes replication. Labour is replaced by robotics, the mind by artificial intelligence.

Haraway points out that nothing on the scary network side of this is recognizably 'natural' (1991b: 162). Instead, the world is now recognized as 'a problem of coding' in which 'communications technologies and biotechnologies are the crucial tools recrafting our bodies' (p. 164). Yet machines can become 'intimate components, friendly selves' (p. 176). Through such 'friendly selves' and such blurring of boundaries we might realize that nothing is total, everything has its limits but is also connected to everything else, and that nothing has ever been pure. It is perhaps at this point that we should retreat to a simpler discussion of the relation between bodies, cybernetics and information before we further develop the implications of the cyborg.

Cyborg basics

A cyborg is a cybernetic organism, and this could mean anything that crosses the borders between cybernetics and the organic. A cyborg, however, is not just a border crossing but a subsequent exchange, mixing and blurring of the cybernetic and the organic. But how, in turn, do we define the cybernetic and the organic?

We shall expand here a little on the preliminary definition of the cybernetic given in Chapter 4. The cybernetic has a very long history, but the most prominent name in that history is that of Norbert Wiener, who in 1948 published *Cybernetics: Communication and Control in Animal and Machine*. This was a significant moment in the history of technology (even if few people talk about cybernetics today, its progeny are more active than ever). The word 'cybernetics' is derived from the Greek for someone steering a ship. Yet in the whole complex operation of steering a ship the person at the helm and the ship form a system whereby a constant feedback loop enables both to find their way. Of course, to this loop you could add the winds, the tides and so on. The feedback loop allows you to adjust to uncharted waters, or to changing conditions. It allows you to participate in complexity. These conditions do not have to have a human as a central component. As Sadie Plant points out, all that is required is that a cybernetic system possesses a feedback loop and 'sense organs' (1997: 157) to deal with the external environment, or with internal changes. Think of lifts, automatic doors, automatic bank tellers or the computer interface (you sense the keyboard but it also senses you).

How then do we define the organism? Obviously there is something reasonably cybernetic about the organism as well. It is full of feedback loops. Yet its feedback and control mechanisms seem more self-controlling than the ship in the wind (the organic is 'autopoietic' or self-generating). This allows an organism more complexity within itself, but it also makes it a little inflexible. An organism cannot change its system configuration too much or it will die – which is why it invents technologies.

There are other ways of differentiating the cybernetic (considered here now as a machine or system) and the organic. Yet many of these create more difficulties than they solve. For example, we could say that an organism feels pleasure and pain in the way that a cybernetic system or machine does not, but what are pleasure and pain if not the most effective of feedback mechanisms? Obviously, all these definitions are about to become even more blurred as machines, as Donna Haraway puts it, become 'disturbingly lively' and we become 'frighteningly inert' (1991b: 152). In what is more and more everyday practice, when we put the cybernetic and the organic together we see that the organism becomes one part of elaborate feedback mechanisms (technologies but also 'systems' as in exercise or dietary regimes). The cybernetic, in turn, gets to incorporate the sophistication of the organism into its systems. The examples of this are astoundingly numerous. There is the complexity of genetic engineering working on the very code for life in order to enter into its feedback loop and control it through technology. There is the simplicity of using a watch, a clock, or time in general as a human system. What a complex series of feedback loops is involved just to catch that train or plane or meet that friend at the café.

There are some that think, understandably, that this means that the end of the body is at hand. They would like to leave the body behind and inhabit a techo-body built to our specifications, or maybe just hang around on the Internet as a kind of ghost in the machine. Yet the very technologies that seem most suggestive of this fantasy, such as virtual reality (VR) systems, rely very heavily on the perceptual mechanisms of the body in order to work. We feel we are in virtual space only because our senses tell us we are – through our eyes, our hands and our ears. Even our haptic senses pick up the internal arrangement of our bodies, subject to things like movement or gravity to tell us where we are in VR. However, it is also true to say that the body will never be *'the* body' again.

Information as the new 'spirit'?

You would think the all-pervasiveness of technology's influence upon the body would have made just about everyone abandon all idea of the spirit in favour of the most thoroughgoing materialism. This is not the case. Many have of course maintained their religious faiths. Strangely enough, some others have found a new and different sense of the spiritual – often this is the spiritual as information. In a supposed 'channelling' one of the new age gods said 'this new information is not additional data that you will act upon. It is, rather, the very reality of your new nature . . . you are to be my information yourselves' (quoted in Davis 1993: 614).

This may be a very astute perception about the effect of information upon who we are and upon what our bodies are. It is saying that we *are* information. It may be information that connects us to our essence – whatever that might be. Information is no longer about something else that it refers to. It is the thing or process in itself. Information seems more and more to take the place of the 'soul', the 'mind' or anything else once considered to be at the core of our existence. For example, where once we had the 'mystery of life', now we have DNA as the information basis for life. Once we had oracles. Now we have telephone companies and news broadcasts. There is then, in information theory, no outside to the world. It is no longer the gods that call to us.

Information does exhibit a materiality, however. This arises in the form of patterns of DNA, in responses to the environment such as goose bumps, hiccups or a sudden intense memory triggered by a unique odour. It is present in bodily transformation, augmentation, decoration and mutilation. All these are bodily expressions that are more than body; they are calls for the body to do something – to act on information: perhaps to grow some more cells in the case of DNA, to run away from (or towards) the thing giving us goose bumps. This also implies that the body thrives on information. If we ask what a body wants, the answer today is that it wants more information. It wants to ride the flow of information. It wants more feedback – to adjust its course in relation to environment: more pain and pleasure, a thermometer, the meeting of eyes across a crowded room.

The great cultural fear about new technologies such as cyber-space has nearly always been that we may lose our bodies. Yet the result of much technological development has been that, rather than losing our bodies, we may in fact be closer to our bodies than at any time in the past, even if these are bodies which crumble as we finally touch them, into fragments of information. This may indicate the emergence of something new which we could broadly call the posthuman, and it perhaps consigns the postmodern to what is left of history.

From postmodern to posthuman

Haraway's conception of the cyborg abandons ideas of progress yet embraces the great potential of complexity that arises in the dissolving of boundaries between human, machine and animal. Many other thinkers have also embraced, for example, Lyotard's postmodern abandonment of the grand linear narratives of human liberation or speculative endeavour but, like Haraway, they have not stopped there. The somewhat 'posthuman' thought that results shall be the subject of the rest of this chapter.

Manuel De Landa takes the posthuman very seriously. In two sweeping books he abandons a human-centred perspective of history in order to totally resituate the human within the circuit between world and machines. In *War in the Age of Intelligent Machines* he takes the point of view of a future robot historian explaining how robots came to be, from a robot, not human, perspective. In both this book and *A Thousand Years of Nonlinear History*, De Landa points out that computers and the new sciences such as chaos theory that accompany them have given us totally new perspectives on nature, and on ourselves. In particular De Landa is interested in self-organization, the process by which ordered, interactive events emerge from apparent chaos, in the regions of the social or technological as much as in those that seem more obviously 'natural'. He suggests questions such as the following. How does agriculture, or the city with its urban culture, arise out of seemingly unrelated streams of history? What forms of self-organization are present in the chaos of the stock market? How do these change when you add computerized trading to the stock market equation? In general, De Landa writes about 'non-organic life' (1991: 6), a concept which suggests a more lively realm outside the organic than we may have first thought existed. Moreover, it once again suggests that the human, and the organic in general, are only participants in much broader forms of self-organization.

Computers have again been crucial to these ideas. Many of the scientific breakthroughs such as chaos theory that form the background to these areas could not have been made without digital machines to do the number crunching (De Landa 1997: 17). In short, computers give us access to the nonlinear, emergent and dissolving orders of complexity and we can afford to abandon generalizing linear narratives without abandoning all understanding of the world. This in turn allows us to conceive of history and indeed the world differently. We can begin to conceive of patterns within complex interactions such as those between collective human life and the other flows of matter and energy in which this life occurs. We can conceive of human history as something precarious or accidental, something as taking place within a complex web of other events. We no longer see human history as a singular series of links between isolated and decisive human actions. We can conceive of history in nonlinear terms, in terms of emergences and dissolutions. History becomes a series of temporary consistencies and radical breaks, occurring when certain critical points are reached in the self-organization of matter and energy.

At such points the city gives birth to itself, a new language forms, certain equilibriums between organisms are broken and we have a new plague, the stock market begins a pronounced nosedive, we fall in love and so on. This is just as, and related to, the way in which whirlpools form in streams, and rainforests attain the consistency which allows them to form their own semi-enclosed ecosystem. In all of these the 'emergent properties' are 'properties of the combination as a whole which are greater than the sum of its parts' (1997: 17). De Landa concludes that 'reality is a single matter-energy undergoing phase transitions of various kinds' (p. 21). Reality is constantly 'enriched' by the new processes these transitions give rise to. For De Landa, 'Rocks and winds, germs and words, are all different manifestations of this dynamic material reality.' They represent the different ways in which this underlying matter-energy is expressed. As Sadie Plant writes, quoting Ada Lovelace, 'All, and everything is naturally related and interconnected' (1997: 11).

Sadie Plant does not at all mourn the end of the grand narratives because these often hid important contributions to history such as those made by women. Sometimes these contributions were literally in footnotes and this obscured their importance. For example,

Ada Lovelace's crucial invention of computer programming in the nineteenth century occurred in a lengthy series of footnotes to a book written about Charles Babbage's plan for an 'analytical engine'. Plant goes on to explain the conceptual importance of the invention of hypertext as a nonlinear form of digital networking. It allows such 'footnotes [as Lovelace's to] begin to walk all over what had once been the bodies of organized texts' (1997: 10). In general, rather than seeking a single line through the grand narratives of history, now 'cross-referencing' becomes crucial. This gives a much more complex view of history.

In *Zeroes + Ones* Plant maps out the complex links between weaving, the development of computer programming and the participation of women in the technology flows of the world. She points to the fact that the cards used for early computers in the twentieth century were similar in design and purpose to those used to automate the Jacquard textile weaving loom in the nineteenth century. In fact, there are number of technologies with which women have been closely involved that have formed the basis for any number of breakthroughs in digital technologies. Women have, for example, been employed to perform the computations involved in artillery in the First World War, and in cryptology (the deciphering and development of codes) during the Second World War. Both of these were of course central to the development of computing. For Plant, this should cause us to rethink the history and social meaning of technology. It was women who operated many of the early modern computers, a woman who developed the concept of computer programming, women who often now assemble the components of the silicon chips used in digital devices (1997: 37).

Plant writes that when the word 'computer' meant 'flesh and blood workers, the bodies which composed them were female'. It is also true that more and more women have been employed in the workforce as it becomes 'the more sophisticated' (p. 39). In 1997 50 per cent of Net users were women, up from 5 per cent in 1990 (p. 112). Plant also looks to telephony and typewriters, to Grace Hopper, who in 1943 'became the second of the first computer programmers' after Ada Lovelace when she programmed one of the first computers in the United States (p. 151). In all, digital machinery and the social changes they bring about also mean more power for women in some circumstances, as men are no longer necessary (or in some cases adaptable) to the new circuits of employment. Likewise the digital revolution, for better or worse, is not just open to the West (pp. 39, 74).

Plant undermines other aspects of the standard history of the rise of technology through the last two centuries. She discusses Alan Turing who, as we shall detail in Chapter 6, invented the first truly modern computer (or at least the mathematics behind it) just before the Second World War. Plant points out that Turing sought not to affirm every kind of logic but to 'undermine the universal claims of symbolic logic' (p. 81). Indeed Turing proved that there would be limits to logic, as much as he broadened the power that logic had.

N. Katherine Hayles, in *How We Became Posthuman*, attacks linear notions of technological progress from a slightly different direction, that of the inconsistencies and contradictions of information theory as regards the body. Information theory tends to see most things, including human life, as part of a processual system, as nearer to transferable and networked 'flow' than a fixed body. For Hayles, this meant that the kind of scientific, technological and conceptual revolutions developed within information theory and cybernetics could not be kept caged within traditional notions of the world or the human place within it. This was especially so with regard to the challenge such developments threw at established notions such as liberal humanism, in which supposedly autonomous individuals are able to give full expression to their 'freedom'. Hayles points out that even Norbert Wiener, who 'tried to craft a version of cybernetics that would enhance rather than subvert human freedom' (1999: 112) failed because 'no person . . . can single-handedly control what cybernetics signifies when it propagates throughout the culture by all manner of promiscuous couplings'.

Hayles reads the anxieties associated with this promiscuity in the way gender often works in science fiction. Gender in science fiction is something that often seems both overdetermined and ambiguous. Prostheses that reinforce gender are prominent in science fiction yet an anxiety accompanies them – an anxiety about the cultural changes technology presents to sexual organs as the mark of gender. Once such foundations are unsettled, all manner of regular conceptions of the body and its 'naturalness' seem less able to be taken for granted.

If gender is now an uncertain basis for the body, and the fixed body an uncertain foundation for culture, where do we go from here? Hayles highlights the work of Humberto Maturana and Francisco Varela who developed a theory of 'autopoiesis' – literally self-creation or self-organization. Their theories, like De Landa's, posit the self-organization not just of individuals but of systems, for example of the systems involved in scientific experiment in which the observer is just one component. Eventually, these theories develop to account not just for a 'relentless repetitive circuitry' but for the 'living organism as a fast, responsive, flexible and self-organizing system capable of constantly reinventing itself, sometimes in new and surprizing ways' (1999: 158). In short, we participate in the circuits of the world rather than attempting to control them. When technology, information and virtuality enter into the circuits of these self-organizing and evolving systems, however, the relations between control and complexity become extremely vexed.

The idea that self-organization belonged only to life was again to be challenged in the development of artificial life (AL). AL can be seen in, for example, computer programs which self-replicate within computer systems and networks. More generally, it involves networked systems that cooperate in order to evolve – and perhaps to produce something like the collective intelligence we shall discuss in Chapter 6. AL treats technological elements such as computers or smaller robots as basic building blocks in a complex system of parallel and connected processing, in much the same way as individual bees are the basis for the more complex behaviour of a hive, or individual neurons the basis for the brain. Such systems are supposed to be able to learn and to pass on knowledge as they self-generate. Each generation of a self-replicating computer program carries a little more knowledge that the last. We shall discuss this in a different context in Chapter 6.

As Hayles points out, much of the drive behind experiments with AL comes from the wish to see life and indeed consciousness as disembodied information. As she puts it, for those involved in such research, their changed perception of the world is dramatic. Many

> . . . put materiality on one side of a divide and information on the other side, making it possible to think of information as a kind of immaterial fluid that circulates effortlessly around the globe . . . (1999: 246).

Hayles is quite critical of this idea, precisely because it denies the complexity and reality of embodiment. What then, would be an appropriate solution to one's specific embodiment in the new flows of the world? It is here that Hayles's crucial point comes in.

Presence and patterns

Hayles points to a possible shift from a culture based upon the presence or absence of bodies to a society based upon patterns or randomness in information. Hayles suggests that Western culture in particular has long been based upon a series of relations between presence and absence, and the experience of living in Western culture has been determined within these relations of presence and absence. Bodies were there (present) or not there (absent). A body felt things or it did not. You could trust something more if it had been said to you 'face to face' than if it was said from a distance – over the phone perhaps. These relations between presence and absence meant that there was some stability to social order. Something was there or it was not. It happened or it did not. Everyone belonged to a certain country in which they lived (were *present* within). People were 'men' or 'women' according to the presence or absence of various parts of the body, and there was not supposed to be much ambiguity to this. There was a given order in time and a given order in space. The sun rose and the sun set. It was light (presence) or dark (absence) and strange things in between (such as the moon at night) were strange things. All of this was underwritten by an order of presence and absence in the way that people conceived of the world and of ourselves. This was generally true of the absence or presence of bodies in general, and of particular bodies in particular (gendered bodies, aged bodies, bodies given racial categories, and sexualities).

Now this has all changed. Presences have become much more precarious. We are less sure of our bodies – perhaps, for example, as distinctively and absolutely male and female. We know less what it means to belong to a country. We have light whenever we want (with electricity) but this only makes the border between light and dark the stranger.

This is not to say that presence and absence have lost all their meaning. Nor is it to say that the patterns and randomness crucial to information have never existed before. It is merely pointing to a radical change in their prominence within culture at large and to a radical change in the way that we conceptualize the world, our bodies and our machines. Information-based technologies are based precisely upon the blurring of presence and absence and a mixing of them into pattern and randomness. In VR or cyberspace, for example, it is the pattern that one can recognize and manipulate that is more important than one's actual presence or absence.

What does this tell us about information? Firstly, information, even if materially 'in' the world, is something conceptually distinct from its carrier. It is true that, to the information carrier (the body, the print on the page), presence or absence may matter a lot. To information itself, however, it is the pattern formed that matters. Hayles suggests that information, the basis of so much in contemporary society, is never really present in itself. The flickering light on the television is present. So is the print on the newspaper, but neither the images on the television nor the actual newsprint on the page are information. Strictly speaking, information is neither the presence of the images nor the newsprint on the page. It is rather something we get out of the patterns formed. If this is still unclear we could consider the English alphabet, which consists of 26 arbitrary shapes combined in different ways on the page. The information found in any particular page is not found in any particular unit, letter, or even word. It is something conceptually distinct, drawn from the patterns in those marks (and crucially from how these patterns relate to other patterns beyond the page). One could think here of looking at the markers on the page of a language you do not understand. It may even use the same 26 or so letters as English. Now if information was present in the markers themselves you would understand it but you do not.

Another important point here is that information is probabilistic – in short, it is about calculated guesswork. Hayles writes that information is defined by 'the probability distribution of the coding elements comprising the message' (1996: 60). Here one could think of the way one can sometimes figure out what a strange word (or strange look or glance from someone) means when one has not been confronted by it before. One judges how this might fit into a context or pattern of the other words on the page, or of other signals the person looking at one in a particular way might be giving to one. It should be noted also that it is an element of randomness that one attempts to draw into the pattern, in accordance with the probability that it connects one way with the pattern and not another way.

Hayles points out that randomness is often a crucial part of the information, despite the fact that 'noninformation should be the absence of pattern' (1999: 260). This is partly because codes – and the patterns they form – seem to constantly change with the movement of the world. The word one does not recognize on the page or the puzzling look someone gives one is the very thing one worries about – it is what structures everything else. In short, within complex systems 'pattern and randomness are . . . comple-ments or supplements to each other'.

For Hayles then, such insights have meant that, at least since the birth of cybernetics after the Second World War, a culture of *manipulable* relations between pattern and randomness has been substi-tuted for the stability of presence or absence. The technocultural difference has been that there is so much more variation possible in the case of pattern and randomness. Pattern and randomness are not as absolute as presence and absence. We can suddenly see pat-terns in the random. And, alternatively, we can suddenly perceive randomness in the pattern.

We can now view bodies as forms of information interacting with other forms of information, or as patterns and randomness interacting with other patterns and randomness, tearing patterns apart, creating or perceiving new patterns. In cyborg terms, cyborgs are not only about people suddenly growing machine legs and arms. Cyborgs are as much based upon information. They indicate a culture in which information has got under our skin. It is with this in mind that we can conceive of the cyborg body as floating on electromagnetic waves, or of cyberspace invading and colonizing us – floating through us like one cloud through another. This also means that our cyborg bodies are more dispersed than we have first thought, more distributed through information networks, more malleable in terms of their form and function within these networks, and more manipulated by these networks.

This also changes the nature of power. Presence and absence seemed so absolute (often they seemed given by some power far beyond us like God, king or country). There seemed very little we could do about it. This was not very cybernetic. It is hard to be part of a cybernetic feedback loop when the system is inflexible and feedback is short-circuited. A culture of pattern and randomness might be more contingent, dynamic and manipulable. Put simply, because patterns are interactive and constantly shifting, once we can see one pattern we can change it slightly to form another (as in genetic engineering or word processing, or dressing according to how you feel today). This is particularly the case where patterns lie within patterns. In DNA, for example, combinations of four basic elements themselves combine to form very complex patterns. These combinations, in turn, are a key to changing the body itself at a higher level. In general terms of control then, the at first sur-prising realization is that controlling the information comes first. Presence and absence come later. When we begin to manipulate, to operate within, this threshold between pattern and randomness, we can rapidly change our bodies, cultures and subjectivities, to the point that we may have to invent new words for what it is that these have become.

The simplest example is writing. Long ago, one spoke, and one's speech was tied to one's bodily presence. This was freed up a little with writing – particularly with the letter, but it was hard work to change something once one had written it – even with a typewriter, let alone a pen or a quill! Now, however, with a stroke of a couple of keys one can change the whole document (into italics, or even now into another language). This is only the beginning – what has happened to writing is also happening to the body, to culture, to subjectivity, to what we used to call 'nature'. We are learning to manipulate with more and more speed the thresholds between pattern and randomness. To find more and more information that we can work with buried within the body – both our bodies and what we might call the body of the earth. It starts with plastic surgery of course, but it quickly moves to drugs, implants and genetic manipulation – all of which can be thought of as the equivalent of hitting a key and changing the whole document to italics. How then can we rethink the body in this light without losing it?

The body as collective

We often think of our bodies as one thing – and as a coherent and unified expression of our very own mind/soul/rationality. In fact, the body is a collective thing – not only of organs, but also of little animals (bacteria, cells, amoeba), chemicals and now technologies and their effects. Deleuze writes, 'our body is a type of world full of an infinity of creatures that are also worthy of life. The animals that I meet outdoors are nothing but an enlargement of the latter' (1993: 109). The body is a network of communication and information within this collective, a constant transfer of organic, electrical and chemical effects and conflicts.

This explains the link between machines and animals we have mentioned several times during the course of this chapter. One of the great paradoxes of really understanding cybernetics and information theory is that this understanding not only makes our bodies seem more machine-like, it also makes them seem more like packs of animals. As Wiener wrote in founding cybernetics, it is about 'communication and control in animal and machine'. Cybernetics is therefore as much about ecology as computers, once we make the notions of feedback, pattern and information broad enough. The body not just a high-tech theme park but a wildlife sanctuary. What machinic and animal insights into the body have in common is precisely that they see the body as a collection of elements of pattern and randomness in dynamic communication. It is for this reason perhaps that Donna Haraway, whose essay 'The Cyborg Manifesto' we have discussed, later qualified her notion of the cyborg. This was a qualification that read us as part-cyborg, but also part-coyote, part-machine but also part-animal (1991a). And strangely enough this is a constant theme in thinking through the relations between technologies and bodies. In order to understand our relation to technologies and what it is doing to our bodies, we very much need to understand our relation to animality. A computer analysis of our DNA tells us as much about the basis of our animal nature as it does about our marriage to the machine.

Something to add to this is that, as the philosopher Spinoza put it several hundred years ago, we do not yet know what a body can do (1952: 396–7). We do not know what the body is capable of, not just as a stable entity, but as an interactive entity, as what it could become. We are only on the threshold of this as we begin to decipher the informational systems and codes which inhabit the body and its relations with the world. For all these reasons, a body is better viewed as an event than as an entity. The way matter such as air, information, other bodies, coffee, energy, thoughts and so on, are moved through this location in space – this constant bodily event – is what determines the 'given power or degree of potential' of the body (Deleuze and Guattari 1987: 260). In fact the body is a *series* of events, of collisions with other bodies that are productive or destructive for either or both. Bodies are constantly mutating, depending upon circumstances and meetings that are always somewhat accidental. Part of the challenge of being a body is turning these random accidents into patterns – of, you might say, turning pain into pleasure.

In sum, the realization that bodies, like information, are as much about relations as they are about fixed forms is one of the most interesting ideas to arise at the junction of culture and technology. This idea implies once again that bodies are never, in this sense, discrete entities. The more interactive they are, the more interactive they can be. The more they can deal with different and changing environments, the more powerful they are. This is certainly where the body relies, at least in part, on technology. It is an unusual artist who perhaps gives such ideas the most clarity.

Stelarc

In the work of artist, and cyborg extraordinaire, Stelarc we have one of the best (and most radical) statements of the utopian scenario in cyborg experimentation. He began by demonstrating the body as prisoner of gravity in a series of 'suspensions' where he would suspend his own body from large hooks over the ocean, hundreds of feet over Copenhagen or in lift wells. Soon he moved from the negation of the body to its positive augmentation through technology. He developed a 'third arm', a virtual arm, and began hooking up his muscles to computers, allowing signals from computers to stimulate his muscles and control his movements. Recently he has been wired up to the Internet and allowed a collective stimulation of his body from all over the world. He has developed laser eyes. He 'dances' on stage with industrial robots which sometimes have arms which give live 'machine eye' views of his performances. He wants a third ear. As discussed in Chapter 3, in his *Movotar* project his body is subjected to a harness that controls its movement through feedback loops that he himself can feed into through foot switches. In 1983 he said:

> I see technology as an evolutionary energizer. . . . The first phase of technology contained the body, whereas now miniaturized technology can be imparted into the body . . . the end of evolution is at hand (McCarthy 1983: 18–19).

Stelarc sees technology as enabling the body to overcome the 'problems' it faces when stuck within a gravitational field (such as not being able to fly – not being able to leave the planet). He would like to see the body as freed from its gravitation restrictions and in a more serious confrontation with the expanding information environment (see Figure 5.1).

For Stelarc the skin could be critical to this project. He has suggested that a reformulation of the skin through technology, by which, for example, the skin could both breathe and absorb nutrients, would fundamentally change the requirements of the inside of the human body (Overall 1991). There would no longer

Figure 5.1   Stelarc, *EXOSKELETON: Event for Extended Body and
Walking Machine*, 1999

be a need for the lungs or digestive organs, and, as Stelarc sees it,
the entire cavity of the chest and abdomen would have space for
re-equipment. The 'depths' of the body would become a massive
potential series of 'surfaces'. Here he reverses some of the notions
of robotics. Instead of humans uploading themselves into – in a
sense being consumed by – robots, Stelarc is promoting the human
consumption of robotics.

In fact, despite proclaiming it obsolete at the beginning of his
work, Stelarc is not really 'against' the body. Rather he performs
what we might call its contemporary problematic:

> ... instead of seeing the Net/Web as a means of fulfilling outmoded
> metaphysical desires of disembodiment, it offers on the contrary, pow-
> erful and unexpected individual and collective strategies for amplify-

ing body functions and extruding body awareness. The Internet does not hasten the disappearance of the body and the dissolution of the self – rather it generates new collective couplings and a telematic scaling of subjectivity (1996: 12).

He is actually not that far from Paul Virilio here, as both acknowledge that 'the information thrust is a more significant pressure than the gravitational pull' (Overall 1991). And while Virilio mourns the passing of the body we have known, Stelarc is asking what the body might be tomorrow. In this, his work is remarkably free of concepts of the body, such as the psychoanalytic, that are based on what the body did in the past.

Stelarc has many critics and their criticisms sum up many of the criticisms of a more utopian approach to the cyborg. Some see his project as continuing the age-old (and masculine) denial of the body in favour of technical reason. Richard Restak sees 'Stelarc's fantasies as pathological . . . extreme, narcissistic fantasies of complete isolation' (cited in Dery 1996: 164). Virilio, despite their common understanding of information, has been scathing in his attack upon Stelarc. He has called him 'a kind of prophet of bad news' (Zurbrugg 1995: 10), involved in 'the third technological revolution' where 'technology now aspires to occupy the body, to transplant itself within the last remaining territory – that of the body' (pp. 10–11). In *L'art du moteur* (1993), Virilio sees Stelarc, in a parody of the philosopher Nietzsche's 'overman', as a contemporary 'overexcited man' (p. 147), technological progress as a way of evading moral responsibility. He mourns the loss of the spiritual here and suggests that all that is left to be colonized in Stelarc's work, in the name of extraterrestrial escape, is the 'body-without-soul'.

Stelarc's art and the arguments that surround it capture the central issues that lie within the coming technological challenge to the body. This challenge will be founded upon the potential, radical transformation of culture by genetic engineering, nanotechnology, robotics and the possibility of 'mind uploading'. We have only just begun to adjust to the information age, if we really have at all, when its more startling progeny are beginning to emerge.

Material immortality and 'genethics'

It was one thing for humankind to believe in immortality in a spiritual realm. It is quite another, as is now possible, to consider the possibility of a material immortality. Many recent events suggest a very radical rewriting of what it could be to live life. Lifespans in the first world, already extended through the medical and nutritional breakthroughs of the twentieth century, now look to be on the increase again. There is the possible alteration of the genes for ageing, the regrowth of organs through cloning and the control of stem cells to produce any kind of cell we require. There is, as detailed in Chris Gray's *Cyborg Citizen*, the possible use of cloned and genetically altered animals, fetuses, neomorts (brain-dead bodies with hearts still beating) (2001: 109), or even commercially produced headless humans – all to become factories for those whose cyborg bodies are granted the privilege of citizenship in the new technopolitical environment. There are tiny nanotechnologies that could repair our bodies without the current trauma of surgery. Of course there are the massive advances in medical science and biology in general. There is, for example, the promise of vaccines and other cures for cancer, for multiple sclerosis, for Alzheimer's disease and many others. Then there are the solutions that bypass our bodies as we know them. There is the possibility of 'uploading' our minds into computer systems or robots and leaving our human bodies behind. As Gray points out, in the face of all this the question of cyborg citizenship – and of the politics of 'life' itself – becomes more than urgent.

There are also many related nightmare scenarios. There is the possible outmoding of the human body by more 'evolved' machines. Our tampering with our DNA, or the DNA of the organisms we rely upon, could cause sudden genetic disasters. There could be new self-replicating viruses, or new forms of biological weapons. Or perhaps the increased transfer of genes and organs between species will lead to new epidemics of viruses that, for example, may not trouble pigs, but are deadly to humans. Even without such disasters, intelligent machines could dismiss us as no longer useful. Nanobots might invade our bodies and multiply to the point of suffocating them from within, or simply attack vital organs, or lead to unspeakably devastating forms of warfare. All these suggest a radical rethinking of what death could mean in the future.

In sum, the last decade of the twentieth century may have seen more change than the world has ever witnessed, but this may pale in comparison to the changes coming. Yet this does not mean that the basic issues involved are complex. When computers were first invented it was unsure how they would be used. It would be decades before they would become a consumer item. Many of the developments in biotechnology, nanotechnology and robotics are, in contrast, responses to age-old demands: to eliminate illness, even death, to maximize health and happiness, to extend power, to accumulate wealth. Many are being developed as consumer items from the start. Moreover, technically, what has been achieved is often easily understood. The cloning of Dolly the sheep and other animals are indeed amazing advances, for example. Yet cloning merely gives us control over the process of producing identical twins, something we have been long used to. The word 'control' is perhaps the important part of the whole process.

On the other hand, the ethical and general cultural problems such breakthroughs present to us are perhaps unable to be resolved within our current frameworks. Increased technical control often creates more problems than it solves. It may, for example, be age-old desires for children and family that drive some of the push within biotechnology, but what, for example, does it do to the fundamental cultural notions of family when your parent is also your twin? Or when, perhaps, some clones are sacrificed for the well-being of other clones? Moreover, how much does the manipulation of the age-old desire to increase fertility, to have healthy children and to form a family mask the commercial interests that profit from biotechnology developments in unforeseen ways? Ethics may be as much a question of invention as reflection here – and for some this is precisely the danger.

There are broader, immediately technical, dangers. Far from liberating us from biology, genetic engineering, in giving us the illusion of control over the biological world, may instead lead to overconfidence. Many have pointed to the fact that we do not know what the consequences may be of engineering crops for particular qualities. When tied into the commercial desire for one company's trademarked seed to dominate (or even for five or six companies to dominate), genetic engineering could in fact threaten biodiversity rather than enhance it. For example, if hundreds, or thousands, of varieties of wheat are replaced by just a few, what will happen if those few suddenly fail one year? In addition, we are mixing up the genetic make-up of the planet as a whole – mixing up the genes of animals and plants, for example. We simply do not know where this will lead. Law-making is also heading into unknown territory. Should one company be able to gain rights of intellectual property over the human genome, or individual genes, for example? In short, who will attain immortality and who will pay for it?

David Suzuki and Peter Knudston have proposed a number of

'genethics', or ethical principles for engineering life. In emphasizing the limitations of scientific knowledge, they wish to safeguard
against ecological calamity as well as the discriminatory use of
knowledge gained from genetic research. Genetic screening for
employment and insurance, for example, has the potential for a
divisive social impact, consigning some individuals to a preor-
dained fate (early fatal illness, undesirable traits such as addictive
or criminal personality). Of course, many of the suppositions concerning personality and identity drawn from genetic research are
highly suspect. Yet its spectacular public profile – evident in the
2000 announcement of the Genome Project's completion – worries
many scientists and cultural critics. If an individual were to be
'branded', as a result of genetic screening, as a 'born criminal' or a
high-risk health proposition, genetics would become a new form
of fate, with oppressive social consequences. Accordingly, Suzuki
and Knudston propose that:

> Information about an individual's genetic constitution ought to be used
> to inform his or her personal decisions rather than to impose them
> (1989: 142)

R. C. Lewontin has been an outspoken and articulate critic of
genetic determinism. He has regularly attacked the simplistic
model of causality implicit in the proposition that genes cause
certain types of behaviour, or indeed diseases. Lewontin sees
genetic determinism as a form of mystification, seeking unitary
causes by removing individuals from their society, their environment and more complex causal factors (such as industrial pollution). For Lewontin, behind the Human Genome Project is the idea
that

> . . . in knowing the molecular configuration of our genes, we know
> everything that is worth knowing about us. It regards the gene as
> determining the individual, and the individual as determining society
> (1993: 51).

Lewontin is a staunch critic of the arrogant claims made in the
name of genetic science; his essays remind us that some aspects of
biology will never be measured or known, let alone controlled. 'I
have tried to give an impression', he writes, 'of the limitations on
the possibility of our knowledge' (2000: xxi). Lewontin's cultural
materialist critique also reaches beyond the glamour and mystique

of 'the doctrine of DNA' to the huge profits being made in the biotech industry:

> What appears to us in the mystical guise of pure science and objective knowledge about nature turns out, underneath, to be political, economic and social ideology (1993: 57).

This critical approach is shared by many commentators on recent developments in biotechnology. Watchdog groups such as Human Genetics Alert are concerned with the ethical ramifications of genetic engineering. Hindmarsh and Lawrence, editors of the collection *Altered Genes II*, urge a 'thorough public debate' of gene science and its social consequences: 'If we are to realise an ecologically sustainable future, we must decide if and where biotechnology "fits"' (2001: 29).

Cultural studies theorist Andrew Ross also engages with the ideological assumptions behind 'the sweeping new world view engineered by biotechnology and genetic medicine' (1994: 15). His book *The Chicago Gangster Theory of Life* takes its title from the Darwinian biologist Richard Dawkins's comparison (in *The Selfish Gene*) of the human gene to a 'successful Chicago gangster'. Ross disputes this view of social behaviour as determined by genes, that is, rooted in nature – 'We are in dialogue with the natural world, it is not our supreme court' (1994: 15).

Radical futures and 'gray goo'

Some suggest that we might be able to avoid these problems, perhaps avoid nature altogether, by 'uploading' our minds onto computers or networks. We shall deal with the philosophical problems involved in this question in Chapter 6, but there are many who suggest that these problems have already become irrelevant, and that we are on the verge of becoming absolutely one with machines. The transhumanist movement in general, and the Extropians in particular (the most prominent of these is appropriately named Max More), follow Stelarc in believing in maximizing human potential to the point that we cease to be human as we have known it. For many, it is just a matter of technical competence – building machines that are able to take us there – and this is just a matter of time. One version of this fantasy involves the total uploading of minds into mobile robots – robots of course that would be more powerful than us in every way. Science fiction is, of course, full of the conflict that may arise when we place ourselves within the same space as machines.

The second version of the uploading fantasy involves the uploading of minds directly into computers and computer networks. Here one could choose to lead a totally simulated life. This would be a technical realization of Baudrillard and Virilio's worst nightmares. Yet for some, a consciousness that can change its form at will, even if this form is a simulated form, is a free consciousness indeed. Perhaps the best examination of the philosophical implications of uploading is in Greg Egan's science fiction novel, *Diaspora*. In this novel uploaded 'human' minds travel to the end of the universe in computers placed on spacecraft. In the end they 'switch themselves off'. Having attained material immortality, the question becomes whether they really want to know everything there is to know.

Many say this is all simply impossible. We shall chart a middle course in this chapter and the next and suggest (with many others) that it is partially possible, but not necessarily in the way that some think it is. There can be no doubt that computers do not only augment the mind, but to some extent, house parts of our 'mind'. Then again, so do diaries and notepaper. On the other hand, the way we mediate the world changes the world – even email is a different way of being from snail mail. Different forms of material embodiment are difference itself. The idea that 'we' will simply transfer our minds elsewhere without our bodies is a nonsense. As we shall see in Chapter 6, Andy Clark has written of the way developments in cognitive science have suggested that the embodiment and world that the brain finds itself within are just as important as the brain in determining which thoughts emerge. In short, the brain is a link in a circuit within the world, not just a container. To put it simply, if you had a tiger's body – or a slug's – would you still really be you? Why, then, would a machine just contain a mind without changing it? (Of course, for those who believe that the mind is something quite distinct from the brain these technical issues are moot – at this point we are talking of the transfer of the soul, which is a matter for religion or mysticism and outside our scope.)

Similar issues involving the difficult relations between control and complexity emerge in discussions of nanotechology. The blueprint for nanotechnology first emerged into popular culture with Eric Drexler's *Engines of Creation* in 1986. Nanotechnology involves the developing of tiny machines built of atoms or molecules. These machines are smaller than body cells for example. They are essentially miniature robots ('nano' means either just very small or, more precisely, 10^{-9} of a given measure – as in nanometre, or one-billionth of a metre). Of course, nano has also come to mean any development of very small machinery, even if in many cases, these machines are, strictly speaking, larger than nano. Mihail Roco defines them in this way:

> ... they have at least one dimension of about one to 100 nanometers, they are designed through processes that exhibit fundamental control over the physical and chemical attributes of molecular-scale structures, and they can be combined to form larger structures (Stix 2001: 28).

Nanomachines would work en masse. In the air, for example, they would form a cloud. Nanotechnologies could also be machines for building other machines ('assemblers'). They could theoretically self-replicate and would in fact often need to in order to meet the claims made on their behalf. They could be injected into the body in their thousands or millions. They could repair the body (or other machines) from the ground up. They could perhaps seek out and destroy aberrant cells. They could carry oxygen or food where needed, or repair organs and damage to arteries by forming micro-factories within the body. Some hope that they will be able to reconstruct living beings from their cryonically frozen dead bodies. They could potentially 'computerize' the internal workings of the body with nanocomputers tinier than cells. They could even form powerful artificial mitochondria (which are inside all cells and which turn food such as glucose into energy). They could turn us into plants, enabling us to live off the sunshine and air absorbed at our skin – giving material form to some of Stelarc's fantasies about the body. In general, think here not just of being able to alter your DNA structure but of being able to build it from the ground up!

In theory nanomachines could create anything. They could turn lead into gold, or repair environmental damage by literally rebuilding the molecules and atoms involved. Coupled with quantum computing, they would pose perhaps the greatest creative challenge to the world ever seen. They could also lend themselves to the most dystopian scenarios imaginable. Vast clouds of self-replicating, and perhaps mutating, nanomachines could just as easily tear the world apart molecule by molecule as repair it. They could turn the entire universe into 'gray goo' (Regis 1995: 121). As

Mark Miller puts it, the 'reason gray goo is gray is because it could take over and eat the whole universe, but never become anything interesting' (quoted in Regis 1995: 121).

Nanotechnology seems more fantastical than the concept of mind uploading, but it is not. It is real and it is arriving, though to what extent is still unsure. It is also heavily funded. The Clinton administration in the US established a National Nanotechnology Initiative in 2000 and between 1997 and 2001 funding in the area quadrupled (*Scientific American* 2001). Nanomachines have already been created, though not at the level envisaged by Drexler and others. They are already used in disk drives for data storage, in the microscopic seeing, and touching of atoms (Stix 2001: 28–30). They could have important future applications in the building of tiny transistors and computing chips, in wireless information transmission, in gene production technologies and thus in genetic engineering as a whole, in disease detection, and the creation of new materials that are, for example, both superlight and superstrong.

Yet, as Gary Stix writes, 'distinguishing between what's real and what's not in nano throughout this period of extended exploration will remain no small task' (p. 31) and there are many sceptics. Nobel prize-winning chemist Richard E. Smalley, for example, suggests that there is simply not enough space at the nano level for the required manipulations of molecules. Drexler responds to such criticisms by replying that such arguments do not understand the new 'systems engineering' (2001: 67) at the molecular level that will make advanced nanotechnologies possible. Indeed, the jury is out on the broader cultural implications of nano until there is more development (the same could be said about quantum computing). Again the best discussion of the possibilities of nanotechnology, apart from Drexler's, is that conducted by a science fiction writer, Neal Stephenson. In his book *The Diamond Age* (1995), clouds of nanomachines go to war, there are assemblers in even the poorest of houses to create material needs from scratch, and nanotoxins are used to control those whose bodies are invaded by them (or to execute criminals).

Bill Joy gave a surprising and prominent assessment of all these developments in *Wired* magazine in 2000. It was not surprising because it was so dystopian. It was surprising because Bill Joy is not an anti-technology radical but a scientist. Moreover he is not just any scientist but the co-founder and chief scientist for Sun Microsystems (among other things he was instrumental in the development of the Java scripting language – vital to the workings of the Internet).

Joy met Ray Kurzweil in 1998 and it was the latter's *The Age of Spiritual Machines,* along with the ideas of Hans Moravec on robotics, that began to worry him. Citing the way in which the overuse of antibiotics has led to a dangerous antibiotic resistance among bacteria, Joy writes of the complexity of the 'interaction' and 'feedback' involved in the real world (2000: 239). For him 'any changes to such a system will cascade in ways that are difficult to predict; this is especially true when human actions are involved'. Joy points out that species in general do not survive superior environmental competitors and that, of course, in many ways, robots would be superior competitors. He quotes Drexler with dread, when he writes that nano-enabled ' "Plants" with "leaves" no more efficient than today's solar cells could out-compete real plants, crowding the biosphere with an inedible foliage' (p. 246). Joy notes the urgency to the consideration of such possibilities, despite the fact that 'we seem hardly to have noticed' (p. 256), quoting Thoreau's dictum that 'we do not ride on the railroad; it rides on us' after giving a long history of the cultural failures involved in the technological development of nuclear weapons.

As Joy points out, finding a path between the utopian and dystopian scenarios in the area of the cyborg may indeed be difficult. Our cultures seem so dependent upon seeing the body as the site of our salvation or damnation. Yet perhaps theorists such as Haraway and scientists such as Joy begin to show the way forward to an engaged, critical stance to the potentially – and perhaps literally – mind-blowing developments with which we are currently involved.

CHAPTER 6

Technology, Thought and Consciousness

In May 1997 Deep Blue, the chess-playing IBM computer, beat world chess champion Gary Kasparov in something of a technology freak show. This was a major first-time victory for machines. Shortly after this, Ray Kurzweil wrote a book titled *The Age of Spiritual Machines, When Computers Exceed Human Intelligence*. In this he suggested that the equivalent of a 1000-dollar personal computer would attain the processing power of the human brain by the year 2019 (1999: 278). In 2029 such a computer would possess the power of 1000 human brains. More staggering even than this was Kurzweil's observation that in 100 years, a 'penny' would buy you a computer that would possess a billion times the 'brain' power of all the humans on earth (p. 105). Of course by then the computers might be buying us – if they bother. Or, as Kurzweil writes, at the very least, there will be 'no clear distinction between humans and computers' (p. 280) and no one will be buying anything. Kurzweil does not, however, consider the fact that intelligence (and certainly consciousness) may not be the same as computational 'power'.

Obviously computers are getting faster and maybe even smarter but what does this mean? They can beat us in chess but could they ever 'think' without us programming their 'thoughts', even with all their increased processing ability? Is intelligence the same as consciousness or spirit? If technology *could* think, would this mean that other objects, even the entire world, has always in a certain sense 'thought'? Have we misunderstood the nature of thought all along, buoyed by faulty metaphors and creaky beliefs? Some critics think we have.

The relation between technology and thought is full of paradox. Humans have long assumed themselves to be at the top of the tree of 'creation'. Accompanying this is the belief that since humanity is so clever, and, in particular, so adept at solving technical problems, that it will create better and better technologies to solve any problem the world can come up with – eventually. In the area of computing, of course, this seems to mean better and better machines for thinking. The paradox arises when we begin to ponder the possibility that the machines we create will become both cleverer than us, or more powerful or, as in films from Fritz Lang's *Metropolis* in 1927 to the *Terminator* or *Matrix* films, a whole lot meaner and nastier. Much of this, however, depends upon machines becoming conscious. This is a very uncertain proposition.

Consciousness

'Consciousness' is one of those terms, like 'culture', which is almost impossible to define. Beyond the normal difficulties of definition, the case of consciousness is further complicated by the wide range of disciplines that now focus themselves on consciousness studies. Once the province of philosophy – concerned with questions of mind and being – consciousness has become, in the last few decades, an interdisciplinary subject heavily influenced by the neurosciences. The emphasis has in large part shifted from mind to brain, or at least the relationship between mind and the functions of the brain as revealed by new generations of technology. This development is one reason for our interest in this chapter in the relation between technology and consciousness. Another is the way that everyday discourse about the mind and behaviour is informed by technological metaphors: we speak of being 'hard-wired' or 'programmed' to act in a certain manner, of our minds 'processing information'. These recent additions to the popular vocabulary point to the pervasive influence of computer-based technologies, which have come to stand as models for aspects of consciousness. Behind this common metaphorical use lies a vast and elaborate network of competing theories of mind.

What then is consciousness? For some theorists it is simply the state of being aware; for others it entails self-awareness. At even the simplest level, however, there is much disagreement. Are animals conscious in the same way we are? Are there different levels of consciousness that could accommodate differences between humans and animals? For a long time, discussions of consciousness centred on rationality, but some recent theories have emphasized the role of emotion. Perception and cognition have long been foregrounded in studies of consciousness, but an expanded definition also includes creativity, memory and the sense of the self. Why did consciousness evolve, and what is its purpose? How do the workings of the conscious mind fit with non-conscious activities, or those of the unconscious? Is one's consciousness affected by technologies of perception, including media?

Every one of these issues has been debated at length. Consciousness studies are pursued by specialists of philosophy, cognitive science, psychology, psychiatry, neurology, evolutionary biology, computer science, mathematics, artificial intelligence, physics, chaos and complexity theory, artificial life and parapsychology. Technology has played a key role in neuroscience research. Positron emission tomography (PET), magnetic resonance imaging (MRI) and other technologies have been used to study the brain's responses to various stimuli. Genetic research attempts to trace the influence of genetic patterns on brain function and behaviour. The neuroscience industry is huge, prestigious, high-tech and well funded. It hopes to solve the enigmas of consciousness in the same way that biology and physics have achieved their successes – using empirical methods of research and observation.

But there are many sceptics. Science writer John Horgan, for example, favours the 'mysterian' position, which doubts that consciousness will ever be explained by conventional scientific methods. As Horgan remarks in his book *The Undiscovered Mind*, mysterians take inspiration from linguist Noam Chomsky's distinction between problems, which seem solvable in principle by scientific methods, and mysteries, which seem insolvable even in principle. Horgan notes that neuroscientists and philosophers are unable to agree on what consciousness is, let alone how it can be explained. Psychologist Stuart Sutherland has offered the following comments by way of non-definition:

> Consciousness is a fascinating but elusive phenomenon; it is impossible to specify what it is, what it does, or why it evolved. Nothing worth reading has been written about it (cited in Horgan 1999: 228).

That blanket dismissal writes off hundreds of thousands of pages devoted to consciousness; needless to say, the authors of those pages do not agree with such a dismissal of their work. The philosopher Daniel Dennett admits that consciousness is 'just about the last surviving mystery', but devotes a book – *Consciousness Explained* (1991) – to solving that mystery. The neuroscientist

Susan Greenfield (1997) concedes that no overarching framework exists to unite the many fragments of knowledge gleaned from the various branches of brain science – but that should not deter work in the area.

One of the boldest attempts at explaining the mystery has emanated from the field of evolutionary psychology, most notably in Steven Pinker's book *How The Mind Works* (1997). This approach is of interest to us here because it draws in part on mechanistic models of the mind, and has been highly influential in moulding contemporary attitudes to mind and behaviour. Pinker helpfully summarizes his thesis in one sentence:

> The mind is a system of organs of computation, designed by natural selection to solve the kinds of problems our ancestors faced in their foraging way of life, in particular, understanding and outmanoeuvring objects, animals, plants and other people (1997: 21).

The evolutionary psychology approach encapsulated here is a fusion of two disciplines: the cognitive science developed in the 1950s and 1960s, and the neo-Darwinian evolutionary biology developed in the 1970s. The former, pioneered by mathematicians (such as Alan Turing), computer scientists (Marvin Minsky) and philosophers (Jerry Fodor), proposes a computational theory of the mind. Thoughts, beliefs and desires are information, or 'configurations of symbols'. The computational model enables a concise definition of mind: 'The mind is what the brain does; specifically, the brain processes information, and thinking is a kind of computation' (Pinker 1997: 21). The evolutionary biology component of this theory springs from the updating of Darwin's evolutionary theory with genetic science, a feat most famously achieved in Richard Dawkins's *The Selfish Gene* (1976). Dawkins's argument is almost brutal in its reduction of the human condition to the 'gene's eye view':

> We are survival machines – robot vehicles blindly programmed to preserve the selfish molecules known as genes (p. v).

The work of Pinker and many others is based on the ready alliance of these two approaches (one thing the approaches share is a fondness for machine metaphors). Evolutionary psychology depends on a technique known as 'reverse engineering', in which aspects of human behaviour are explained by proposing the adaptive purpose they must once have served. Since the mind is a product of evolution, each of its capacities must, according to the theory, have arisen according to the dictates of natural selection. This technique has been used to explain the purpose not only of cognitive and physical attributes but also cultural phenomena such as art, music and religion. But it is the scale of this ambition – proposing an evolutionary explanation for almost everything – that has attracted criticism.

Noam Chomsky has criticized it as a speculative project masquerading as a scientific one, in which any number of plausible-sounding explanations may be offered with little or no supporting evidence. For its many critics, evolutionary psychology does not justify its high media profile because it 'explains' too much through little more than guesswork. A range of critical responses to evolutionary psychology – from scientists, anthropologists and cultural critics – is assembled by Hilary Rose and Steven Rose in the collection *Alas, Poor Darwin*. For Rose and Rose, evolutionary psychology – 'the most pervasive of present-day intellectual myths' (2001: 1) – is founded on loose assumptions and false premises, which are obscured by the 'ideological zeal' with which the project is pursued (p. 247).

A major criticism of evolutionary psychology relates to the reductionist nature of the computational theory of mind. Although Pinker is careful to distance his argument from a crude reduction of consciousness to the workings of a computer, his work is characteristic of evolutionary psychology and cognitive science in its use of mechanistic metaphors and models. For Pinker, the mind is composed of 'modules' whose processing function is determined by a genetic 'program'. Dennett's philosophy of mind is more complex, but it reduces consciousness, at base, to the product of 'algorithmic' processes of evolutionary development. Dawkins's concept of the 'meme' is taken up by Dennett and by many other theorists. The meme is the cultural equivalent of a gene – an idea, a tune, technique or fashion – which replicates throughout the cultural sphere in a way analogous to genetic replication in biology. The notion of the meme has proven popular in some quarters, including consciousness studies, but it typifies the weaknesses of reductionism. In this instance it imposes a biological model onto the cultural plane; in terms of sociology or cultural studies it is a simplistic notion indeed. As we argued in Chapter 1, culture is a complex of myriad influences; the meme concept is a severe simplification. To argue that minds and cultures are determined by such replicating units as memes is to transfer the 'gene's eye view' in a way that does violence to the richness, contradictions and multiplicity of culture.

Reductionism is a near-constant factor in neuroscience (which is one reason we wish to concentrate on the philosophy of mind for much of the rest of this chapter). As Horgan remarks, mind-scientists proceed from the assumption that the mind is nothing more than 'a pack of neurons'; the question is whether their research into those neurons can reveal anything satisfying by way of explanation. Typical of the neuroscience reductionism is the claim by Francis Crick (who was earlier co-discoverer of the structure of DNA) in his book *The Astonishing Hypothesis* (1994). In attempting to explain the 'binding problem' – how different brain activities bind into the unified perception of consciousness – Crick observed that neurons in different parts of the brain sometimes oscillate at the same frequency – about 40 times per second. That consciousness can be reduced to the figure of 40 Hz dangerously approaches an astonishing reduction! One neuroscientist who opposes reductionism of this kind is Gerald Edelman. His theory of 'neural Darwinism' proposes that consciousness is a perpetual adaptation of mind to environment; he suggests that an apt metaphor for this process is not the computer, or any kind of machine, but a rainforest – continually evolving in an organic process. Edelman's theory, rooted in biology, is a rare exception to the mechanistic rule of neuroscience. The biologist and neuroscientist Steven Rose remarks that the crucial omission in modular theories of mind – with their vocabularies of 'architecture' and 'processing' – is emotion. For Rose, 'the key feature which distinguishes brains/minds from computers is their/our capacity to experience emotion' (2001: 261).

We shall go into recent discussions in cognitive science and related areas a little more presently. For now, let us begin by drawing a very scanty sketch of some of the history of ideas behind computing as a form of machine-based thinking.

Computers as universal machines

It was the philosopher Gottfried Leibniz (1646–1716) who first tried to systematize his belief in the possibility of a *universal* machine (Leibniz also developed an amazing *systemic* rationalist philosophy, made a major contribution to logic and invented the calculus, without which our technologies would never be where they are today).

The universal machine is a machine that can perform many different tasks – ideally all possible technical tasks. Its function will vary depending upon the instructions it is given. The problem is finding a language for these instructions. Leibniz believed that all the world's problems could be solved if a universal language were developed through which to communicate. This language would use a common set of symbols that would allow the expression of all common human notions (including the technical). In modern-day terms the idea is that you could use this set of symbols to install new software, get your car to drive you across the country, repair a damaged relationship or perhaps write a poem. Leibniz can thus also be said to be the origin of the idea that a machine could be built to *manipulate signs as a way of 'thinking'* (Heim 1993: 93).

For Leibniz (as for many before him) mathematics could play the role of this universal 'language' through which other languages and practices could meet. So Leibniz's thought paved the way for the development of computer languages – the simplest of which is the development of the universal binary series of 1s and 0s that enables everything else to be coded by the computer. (In the computer there is literally a meeting of languages with other practices and objects such as graphics, games, word processing, direct operational controls and so on.) In a broader sense, Leibniz's idea of a realm of communication that was universal paved the way for hypertext and for the communications revolution in general. He did build a computer prototype, the Stepped Reckoner (Plant 1997: 18), which used rotating wheels to add and subtract. It was a kind of complex abacus.

It is hard to understand the success of the computer, or its future, without understanding the nature of the universal machine. Alan Turing developed the mathematics that became the basis for such a machine by 1936. Turing's great discovery was that any machine could be reduced to a table of behaviour – states of on and off, differences between these states, combinations of behaviours and so on (De Landa 1991: 130). This would enable you to record the 'machine' as an abstract record (on paper for example). If this record could then be made active in the 'universal machine' it would then operate to simulate the machine's behaviours that had been recorded. Thus a computer can become a virtual typewriter (De Landa). It can just as easily become a missile guidance system. Or a powerful code-breaker.

Even more than this, as De Landa goes on to point out, since the 'universal machine' itself can be abstracted as a table of behaviours, it can simulate itself. A computer is portable in more senses than is the physical computer laptop. It can be transferred wherever you like through any system that will allow the transport of the instructions for behaviours, from a piece of paper to a global communications network. The only problem is one of converting these instructions into 'embodied', contextual actions when needed. These are problems that can be solved in many different ways. Solutions can come in the computer interface through which we can implement certain 'actions'. Or, the solution could be robots, or simple automation, as in the many computer systems that the contemporary car is fitted with to adjust steerage and so on. Another solution might be networked software packages that allow for temporary contextualization in particular machines.

Yet none of this tells us whether we can extend the universality of the universal machine's manipulation of symbols to the realm of thought, or, more particularly, to embodied thought. This is a question that has concerned computer specialists at least since Turing. Michael Heim, for example, uses the work of Walter Ong who points out that the whole notion of a universal language involves a shift from site-specific oral communication to a more generalist and transportable symbolic form (that is, a language you can write). Ong criticizes this movement in thought as 'binary, visualist and monological' (Heim 1993: 44). This is to say that such thought is based upon unchangeable binary oppositions (such as the 1s and 0s of the computer but also other more directly cultural oppositions such as 'good' and 'bad'). Such thought is also visualist in that it seems to privilege what can be seen when framed by these oppositions. It is, thirdly, monological in that, being universal, it has a lot of trouble accepting the idea of more than one point of view. For the universalist, the binary and the visualist feed into the monological in that, by categorizing everything into binary oppositions and then making these categories visible to all in the culture, you attempt to give the impression that you are making progress towards a kind of ultimate comprehension of the world. This perhaps reached its peak in the nineteenth century with its magnificent attempts to categorize the world in its entirety, to put everything in its place within a universal system.

The danger here is that the very idea of universal thought could lead to a mistaken instrumental view of the world: the world becomes something that we think we know fully and that we operate on as if it were just another of our instruments. The German philosopher Martin Heidegger questioned this when he asked 'whether thinking, too, will end in the business of information processing' (Heim 1993: 56).

Ada Lovelace, who outlined the blueprint for modern software, did not think so. She worked with Charles Babbage, who in 1822 developed the 'difference engine', a prototype for another machine he planned but never built – the analytical engine. It is these machines which many consider to have laid the cornerstones for computing, and the analytical engine in particular caused Ada Lovelace to ponder the issues of intelligence and machines. She concluded that these early machines, at least, could only do what they were ordered to do. They could not originate anything. They had no agency. In other words, they could not seek out and work towards goals in and of themselves (Turing 1990: 56). In short, computers might assist intelligence but they would never be truly intelligent themselves. True thought was a non-technical process that lay elsewhere. The universal machine had its limits.

At what point, however, would assisting intelligence cross some kind of border into intelligence itself? There have been many technologies developed that raised exactly this kind of question. For example, there was the 'Memex'. Vannevar Bush's 1945 idea of the 'Memex' was for an associative information 'memory' retrieval machine that was the prototype for hypertext. It was based upon the way it was thought that the human mind worked (by links and associations developed through habit). It was designed to assist human memory. In one sense it externalized our memory processes, if they had not been so before. It would be as if you could open a book in a library, find a topic that interested you, push a button and instantly be standing in another place in another library with another book in your hands devoted to that topic. The subsequent full realization of the idea of the Memex (by Theodor Nelson in the 1960s who brought hypertext into reality) has complicated matters, because in many ways hypertext is more efficient than our memories. For a start, being a technology, hypertext does not forget (at least, not in principle).

If we could begin to externalize memory in systems, and had already shown that we could externalize other thought processes such as calculation in systems, would it then be possible to create an entire intelligence that was external to the human brain? Furthermore, if we could, could we externalize our own intelligence (and consciousness, personality, dreams and so on)? In other words, could we 'upload' the contents of our brains onto a computer, perhaps located in the new body of a robot?

There are many problems that arise in thinking through these questions. The basis of most of them is this: can the brain be said to 'contain' consciousness – or thought in general (which cannot be restricted to conscious thought)? It is perhaps time for a brief consideration of artificial intelligence.

How artificial is intelligence?

First, it should be pointed out with Hans Moravec (1988), one of the great pioneers of robotics, that artificial intelligence (AI) may require the addition of robots to pure computing. Intelligence is always placed and sensed intelligence, and needs senses and motors to operate in the world.

Taking this as a given to which we shall return shortly, we can move on. We shall ignore, for the moment, the question of whether a computer system and a robot body could ever 'carry' human intelligence and bodily awareness without changing it into something else entirely. Instead we shall retreat a few steps and ask a simple question. How would we know if a computer – or a robot – were intelligent?

Here we turn again to Alan Turing. In 1950 Turing developed an idea for a test. In this he suggested that if a computer could, through an interface, fool a person into thinking they were communicating with another person, then it could be deemed to be intelligent. Intelligence in this case basically meant being able to carry your side of the conversation, with all the complexities that that implies.

In 1980 John Searle, a major philosopher in the area, argued against this being a satisfactory test. He distinguishes between what he calls 'strong' AI and 'weak' or 'cautious' AI. The 'weak' version, in accordance with Ada Lovelace, merely proposes AI as a useful tool to assist our own intelligence (no matter how fast the processors and powerful the computer generally). 'Strong' AI claims are much larger, leading into areas of agency and consciousness. Now while Searle has no problems with weak AI he does not believe in strong AI. He therefore rejects the idea that computers will ever be fully intelligent. He also rejects the idea that computers will ever provide adequate models for human consciousness. He proposes a kind of counter-model to Turing's test.

In this, he suggests a person alone in what he calls 'The Chinese Room'. In this room there is a person who understands the English language but knows nothing of written or spoken 'Chinese', yet they are given instructions, in English, about how to manipulate the flow of 'Chinese' symbols through the room. Under these conditions this person could, from outside the room, appear to communicate in Chinese once they had used their English instructions to put their Chinese symbols in the right places. Of course, they would not know 'Chinese' at all. Many others have mounted similar arguments. Most of these objections amount to the same thing – processing information is not the same as awareness or consciousness. In short, computers can process as much as they like and as fast as they like, but they will never become conscious, which is another matter entirely.

For behaviourists, however, Searle's argument would not be troubling. As far as they would be concerned, since the 'room' that Searle proposes was *behaving* as if it understood 'Chinese' then that would be enough. There is a sense in which behaving as if it understood 'Chinese' is, to all intents and purposes, understanding 'Chinese'. That is, it does not matter quite *how* things operate in themselves in the end – what matters are the operations themselves. For such theorists, there may never ultimately be anything behind these operations (and to a large extent consciousness is a series of necessary, functional illusions). Daniel Dennett, although not a behaviourist, also thinks that to look for something outside of the whole process that 'understands Chinese' is to miss the point. We may, he argues, have a model of consciousness as something a little like a spectator watching, at a distance, a performance (the world) on a stage, but this is just a convenient illusion. It is just one mental process among other processes, the function of which is perhaps just to enhance the operational nature of the system. The processes become more important than the 'components' which carry them. Even consciousness – for many the crowning glory of the human – is not as important as what brain, body and world together allow us to do. Indeed, there are many scientists and philosophers (such as Benjamin Libet) who have suggested that consciousness plays a much lesser role in our cultural life than we like to think (as opposed to habit, instinctual bodily reactions, the unconscious and so on).

Related to all this is the assumption of information theory and many other areas in the research and development of machine intelligence. This is the idea that the carrier of information does not matter nearly as much as the patterns of information that are carried. This is a crucial idea because it suggests that two very different material objects – a brain and a computer – can carry the same patterns and processes in their materially different ways. Others point to the specificities of particular embodiments as crucial. That is, you could never upload your mind onto a computer because you would lose the body and its situation in the world that was so important to consciousness. We discussed this in the previous chapter.

These arguments are as yet unresolved, but that has not stopped other questions being addressed. How the brain actually works is the next stage of the debate. For some the brain is more like a traditional, unified, hierarchically designed factory, where information (and all thoughts, if you are a believer) is processed within a system which is given from the beginning. When applied to computing, this leads to a top-down approach to AI, an approach which informed many of AI's early developments. It attempts to model the entire process of thought in machines upon a notion of human thought as a coherent, ordered, complex and more or less unchanging program. The problem is that, to mimic the brain with these assumptions, you have to build the entire system before it can do any thinking at all. Attempts to build such 'thought factories' have by and large failed.

More recent work has followed the idea that the brain actually works from the bottom up, not the top down. To greatly simplify some very complex research, in this work thought is seen to develop a little along the lines of a more associative and low-level series of connections. The neurons in the brain are stimulated by the impressions directed to them by the senses. These impressions, and the responses to them, form patterns in the neural pathways and networks through which they travel. When some pathways through these networks are strengthened we call this learning. At a certain level some of these patterns form what we might call conscious thoughts. Of course, through time, these patterns will change, again perhaps from the bottom up. This 'connectionist' model has been followed in more recent AI research with the technological development of 'neural nets'. In these, the complex parallel processing powers of the brain (that is, the web of neurons) are copied in the construction of small computing elements that work in parallel and in connection. The AI pioneer Marvin Minsky calls some of the most basic of these elements 'perceptrons' (Minsky and Papert 1988). If this bottom-up model of thought is true, then AI is a question of replicating low-level processes, not necessarily of replicating the exact structure of the brain. Of course, if it is true, it also implies that consciousness *will* be attained by machines, given the right connections between low-level components and the right environment in which to learn.

Will neural nets finally give birth to machine consciousness? Well, neural nets already appear to be able to learn. What is more, given that they can learn, that they learn through connection and relation to other elements in a given scenario, and that they transmit this learning, in a certain sense they can be said to reproduce and perhaps even evolve. Many theorists at this point talk about artificial life, as discussed in the previous chapter, rather than artificial intelligence. (This of course, raises exactly the same set of questions in a different context – 'alive in what sense?' and so on.)

Some aspects of human consciousness may in the end be explained in terms of machines and some may not. Machines may take up some aspects of human intelligence and not others. It is too early to answer any of these questions.

N. Katherine Hayles (1999) points to another set of illusions here in applying any possible machine intelligence to an understanding of how the human brain works. For this we need to understand the difference between what are called 'black boxes' and 'white boxes'. 'Black box' is a term used, for example, in the military. It is a component brought into the field which the soldiers do not know much more about than how to switch it on and make it do whatever it does. It is black because we cannot see inside it, figuratively speaking. A 'white box', according to Hayles, is a component we can see inside. Not only do we know what it does, we know how it does it. We are familiar with its mechanism. Currently we could say that computers are white boxes, and that brains, despite all the recent research into cognition, are largely black boxes.

Hayles points out that many researchers and theorists in AI take a piece of human behaviour, make a machine that can imitate this behaviour, and then claim that the way that the machine does it is a model for the mechanical processes of the human brain. In other words, having built a white box to do something, they then assume they know what is happening inside the black box on which the behavioural abilities of the white box was modelled. There are obvious problems here. It may be best, on the one hand, not to divide technology and thought, as if the carrier of thought made no difference. On the other hand, this would suggest that one cannot equate different 'technologies' – such as computers and brains – with regard to thought, and just pass information between them.

In fact, it would seem that the technology with which one thinks makes a difference. Firstly, different technologies suggest different embodied experiences of the world. One assumes, for example, that a robot experiences a different world from a human being. Secondly, different technologies seem to make different kinds of thought – or even information – possible. In short, in one way or another, mind is embodied. Mind is sensitive to, and perhaps even produced by, the bodies involved, and the world within which these bodies find themselves.

Varela, Thompson and Rosch, writing in *The Embodied Mind*, suggest that 'embodied cognition' occurs through 'enaction'. For them cognition 'depends upon the kinds of experience that comes from having a body with various sensorimotor capacities' which are in turn 'embedded in a more encompassing biological, psychological, and cultural context' (1991: 173). Because all are so mutually influencing, there is no easy separation between carriers of information and information, between perceptual systems and perceptions, between agencies of thought and thought. It is suggested that these are all produced in tandem, through the various connections between bodies in what is called 'structural coupling' (p. 151). Here mind is seen as an 'emergent and autonomous network' or 'system', 'constrained by a history of coupling with an appropriate world'. In sum, mind emerges as a certain enaction of the world, and a history (through evolution for example) of the kinds of couplings developed within a certain world. Crucially, for these writers, 'perception and action are fundamentally inseparable in lived cognition' (p. 173). Anything perceived is only done so through 'perceptually guided action'. The 'structures' that support thought, including the basic biological structures (such as certain patterns of colour reception which vary from species to species) emerge from such action over time. In other words, perception has emerged from engagement with the world, and in turn, this perception seems to give us the world as we know it. Thought is not something to be produced in a laboratory, separate from the world. Varela, Thompson and Rosch ask what cognitive scientists should do with 'the fact that lived experience of the world is actually between what we think of as the world and what we think of as mind' (p. 231).

Similarly, Andy Clark (1997) argues that we should be putting 'brain, body and world together again', rather than seeing any one of these – by itself – as the seat of thought. He gives even more credit to interaction with the world. Clark gives the analogy here of some aquatic creatures such as tuna or dolphins. These seem to ride – and sometimes even create in order to ride – turbulence in the water in order to swim faster than their muscle capacity should allow. Likewise, Clark feels that we use our environment to think, and thought exceeds the capacity of our isolated brain, or even our isolated bodies. This is a 'dynamicist' approach to thought, one that obviously emphasizes the dynamism of the emergence of thought within somewhat turbulent systems of interaction within the world. Another dynamicist, Alicia Juarrero, puts it this way: a 'complex dynamical system emerges when . . . components . . . become context-dependent' (1999: 139). How does technology fit into this?

Technology affects thought

Some ask whether this is all, in fact, a much older question than we might think. In Darren Tofts's (Tofts and McKeich 1997) account of Freud's 'Note upon the Mystic Writing Pad', we find the idea that, in a sense, all media technologies, from the ancient invention of writing, have been based upon two things. Firstly, all media technologies have been involved in extending human intelligence (in the case of writing, giving a place to extend the powers of the unconscious as a kind of place for storage and retrieval – what we would call an archive). Secondly, all media technologies (and techniques from the Ancient Greek mnemonics or memory techniques) have explicitly or implicitly modelled technologies and techniques upon our own 'machinery' and vice versa. Tofts puts the contemporary version of it as follows:

> As cultural technology, the computer simulates the workings of the psyche. A screen receives as well as displays latent data as manifest information; multiple drives and processes scramble and unscramble the unintelligible babble of digital code; and the whole process is controlled by the all-powerful central processor, the electronic ego – I navigate therefore I am (1997: 21).

Pierre Levy goes further in this direction than many other theorists and suggests that even 'artificial intelligence' is the wrong term. He moves intelligence out from the context of a brain sitting by itself, or even a body situated in a certain immediate physical context, and radicalizes the notion into what he calls 'collective intelligence'. As he puts it, with the virtualization of culture we pass from 'cogito' (I think) to 'cogitamus' (we think) (1997: 17). Collective intelligence is 'a universally distributed intelligence that is enhanced, coordinated and mobilized in real time'. It is something only made possible by new media technologies. It seems in some ways a greatly enhanced form of connectionism though it is based much more upon social concerns than a direct consideration of the cognitive sciences.

Where does this leave us? Have we arrived at any definitive solution to what seems the very contemporary problem of intelligence? Obviously not, yet we hope it is now obvious that fields such as thought, culture and technology are extremely interconnected, often in ways that we might not have realized. How we think about technology and how technology lets/makes us think may sometimes be more important questions than what the technology itself is at any moment. We think differently about relaxation because of music technologies and media technologies (such as TV and computer games). We think differently about travel, and about time and space in general because of aircraft and cars. We think differently – we can think very differently – about sexual relations and romance because of contraceptive technologies, reproductive technologies, the telephone (or computer chat room), or even the surgical technologies and techniques that enable gender reassignment.

Several theorists have pondered the relation between thought and the technologies through which thought is given expression. The pen, the typewriter and the word processor are all such technologies: how do they affect the way we think, and write? Is an essay or letter different when composed on a word processor rather than written by hand? Heim thinks so: for him, thought and expression take on the attributes of whichever writing technology is being used. 'The word processor is computerizing our language', he claims (1993: 3). Your prose will come out differently as you 'formulate thoughts directly on screen' (p. 5). The benefits of increased efficiency via digital technologies may be outweighed, Heim suggests, by 'mindless productivity', as 'infomania erodes our capacity for significance' (p. 10).

Technology changes thought and vice versa, in every sphere. The result of the current rapid pace of technical change is that workplaces, professions, schools and universities, even family relations and religious institutions, are now, rather painfully, going through perhaps the biggest change in 200 years, if not ever. It is therefore a pity that so much of the discussion in this area often seems so combative. Yet still, for some all these more 'machinic' theories are a danger to who it is we think we are – and to what we have thought that we were for a long time. These people are of course right about that danger – many of the newer models of the mind from Freud to the connectionists have threatened the notion of a stable self, of free will, and of agency in any absolute sense.

The sense of self

It is perhaps time to deal with the impact of technology on individual sense of self, with particular reference to media and other contemporary technologies. Several of the theorists we have already encountered in this book – most notably McLuhan and Virilio – address this issue in a general way. Constant exposure to media, information and urban technologies, they insist, must structure our consciousness – including perception and sense of self – in certain ways. In this section, we consider this proposition in the light of the contributions made by various theorists, as well as the work of artists who have explored the cultural ramifications of this idea.

The neuroscientist Susan Greenfield differentiates between 'mind' and 'brain' by focusing on the subjective experience, the 'private place' of the mind. This involves a continuum, a 'stockpile of memories, prejudices and experiences [which] serve as a counterweight to the flood of everyday sensory experience' (1997: 149). For her, consciousness is 'the actual firsthand, first-person experience of a certain mind, a personalized brain'. Mind has an 'evolving personal aspect', in which the individual sense of self is sustained yet able to develop throughout a lifetime. Greenfield believes that facets of the individual mind – including imagination and attention span – are continually influenced by stimulation from external sources such as media. Media forms such as the book or radio, which encourage users to conjure their own images, are likely to stimulate the brain, and the mind, more actively than media such as television which provide ready-made images.

Theorists of all persuasions agree on the central role of memory in forging the continuum of individual identity known as 'self'.

Steven Rose, in *The Making of Memory*, discusses the great complexity of human memory, much studied but still little understood. Rose contrasts human memory with computer memory: while computers simply retrieve digital information, the mind works with meanings in a creative and imprecise manner:

> ... each time we remember, we in some senses do work on and transform our memories; they are not simply being called up from store, and once consulted, replaced unmodified. Our memories are recreated each time we remember (1992: 91).

This active 're-membering' takes place in the context of other forms of memory, termed by Rose *artificial* memory and *collective* memory. Rose agrees with Walter Ong that artificial memory, beginning with the written word, exercises a profound impact on human consciousness. For Rose, there is a 'powerful interaction of our technology with our biology' (p. 95), one of whose consequences is that 'whereas all living creatures have a past, only humans have a history' (p. 326). Artificial memory from papyrus to computer – and including photography, film and recorded music – is 'profoundly liberatory', freeing the mind to pursue other goals. Artificial memories also make possible that cultural reservoir of shared understandings and beliefs that Rose calls collective memory. This domain of interpretations and ideologies, in which we 're-member the past' is also, of course, a site of conflicting attempts to define collective identity.

Another intriguing aspect of the 'interaction of our technology with our biology' concerns the way artificial memories, such as photos and home videos, may become confounded with our individual memories. At times it may be difficult to disentangle your childhood memories from home movies (artificial memories) of your childhood. The film *Blade Runner* provides a vivid metaphor of our saturation by technological memories in the figure of the replicants, whose memories – and hence their sense of self – are provided by technological implants. Our own memories, Rose insists, are composites of individual and artificial memories, as mediated through the collective memory of culture.

The consequences for individual selfhood of a highly technologized and mediated environment have been analysed at length by Kenneth Gergen in his book *The Saturated Self* (1991), and by Raymond Barglow in *The Crisis of the Self in the Age of Information* (1994). Both theorists contend that the self is a cultural construct, historically determined and susceptible to changing social conditions. The Western emphasis on the individual is the basis for the notion of a sovereign self. The Enlightenment systemized the world by scientific knowledge, connecting the sovereign individual (recognized by law) with the technological mastery of nature. Barglow argues that the post-industrial world, on the other hand, provokes a crisis in this sense of self: individuals feel increasingly 'lost' in an advanced technological society. For Barglow, the huge 'self-help' and therapy industries, with their quest for wholeness and centredness, betray an insecurity regarding the coherence of self. While industrial machines were tools used by a human agent, post-industrial technology comprises 'intelligent' machines. Automation and information systems have dispensed with the human subject, while we have become dependent on such computerized systems. Our everyday vocabulary for human interaction has absorbed terms originally used for information technologies: 'input', 'feedback', 'interface'.

As our lives become more involved with information technologies, and information-processing concepts become culturally as well as technically more influential, we may find these involvements call into question the notions of centred, coherent subjectivity and personal freedom that have traditionally propped up our ideals of selfhood and individuality (1994: 14).

Barglow sees this crisis of self manifested in the language of fragmentation: individuals 'cracking up', 'falling apart', losing coherence. Gergen is particularly concerned with the saturation of the self by media images, a process that generates a 'self-multiplication'. For Gergen, much of our concept of self derives from the Romantic age, with its emphasis on intense feeling and an emotional inner self. The postmodern age engenders a form of overload through its technologies of social saturation, primarily media. Individuals are encouraged to 'live' the heightened emotional experiences of films and TV programmes as if they were real. Yet there are so many different versions of selves on public display – either fictional characters or the lives of celebrities – that identification with one core version of self becomes increasingly difficult. Individual identity becomes a patchwork construction, made of many alternative personae. Gergen calls this form of selfhood a 'pastiche personality'. The *Untitled Film Stills* by Cindy Sherman, discussed in Chapter 2, are a celebrated artistic response to this 'self-multiplication' due to media saturation. The chameleon-like public personae of pop stars David Bowie and, more significantly,

Madonna, have been highly visible pop culture manifestations of this 'pastiche personality'.

Other theorists have discussed the relation between contemporary technologies and aspects of the self. David Harvey (1989) finds the postmodern condition characterized by a 'space-time compression', brought about by technologies of transport, communication and information flow. The speed and fragmentation of media contribute to a shortening of attention spans and a withering of the sense of a lived past. Postmodern space is compressed, confusing and saturated with images. Celeste Olalquiaga expands on the confusion of postmodern urban space in her book *Megalopolis* (1992). She connects the ubiquity of video screens and the dizzying spatial design of shopping centres with contemporary disturbances of the self. Psychasthenia, a psychological disorder in which the self becomes confused with its surroundings, serves as a metaphor for Olalquiaga for the 'induced disorientation' of consumers in shopping malls, seeking 'concreteness' in the act of purchase. Likewise, she regards the nervous disorder obsessive compulsive disorder (OCD) as indicative of a more widespread condition of uncertainty. Defined by the uncontrollable repetition of a single act, OCD is a 'doubting disease' that produces 'an overlapping of the self' onto space and time. This condition entails a loss of confidence so that 'all acts are suspect and self-perception is unreliable' (p. 7); it generates rituals of mechanical repetition that paralyse the individual.

Certain urban spaces are designed to encourage particular forms of behaviour, generally related to consumption. Contemporary casinos have become mini-cities, in which individuals may live for days on end. Casinos are intoxicating spaces (extra oxygen has even been known to be added to the air), designed to overstimulate the gambler. Airports have become standardized spaces, air-conditioned to a uniform temperature, traversed by international travellers. (For Virilio, the airport is the prototype for the future city.) Many artists have explored the psychological and cultural effects of contemporary technologies, particularly those of transport and communication. Rosemary Laing's photographic works often convey the vertiginous condition wrought by technological speed, most notably flight. Robyn Backen's work *Weeping Walls* (Figure 6.1), installed at the departure gate of Sydney International Airport, is a glass case housing tangles of fibre-optic cable that pulse messages in Morse code (including, aptly enough, 'parting is such sweet sorrow'). The airport departure area is at once a

Figure 6.1.   Robyn Backen, *Weeping Walls*, 2000

technologically produced space and an emotional site – it is a public place in which strong emotions are frequently expressed. Fittingly then, Backen's work uses the contemporary fibre-optic technology to transmit an obsolete code, that pulses at the same rate as the human heart.

Finally, of the many theorists who have analysed the impact of computer technology on consciousness and identity, one of the most thorough is Sherry Turkle. Her books *The Second Self* (1984) and *Life on the Screen: Identity in the Age of the Internet* (1995) examine in detail the consequences for individual sense of self ensuing from interface with computers and interactivity on the Net. Her findings are generally positive, particularly concerning the multiplicity and flexibility involved in interactive Net experiences. In multi-user virtual environments, the self may be 're-constructed', and 'the rules of social interaction are built, not received' (1995: 10). Virtual community experiences 'acknowledge the constructed nature of reality, self, and other' (p. 263), so that participants become 'authors of themselves'. For Turkle, this play of identity and interaction represents something valuable – 'This reconstruction is our cultural work in progress' (p. 177). For others the modern deployment of technology in itself is dangerous, whether in the service of the development of a flexible sense of self, or in any other form.

Heidegger and 'The Question Concerning Technology'

Heidegger's essay 'The Question Concerning Technology' is a crucial philosophical essay about thinking and technology – almost the crucial essay. Heidegger was a pessimist. He was concerned with the way in which modern technologies might destroy thinking in the process of tying us into the new machines.

Heidegger was largely concerned with ontological questions. These are questions that relate to the *being* of something. Put simply, they relate to the question of the essence of what something *is*. What it is *in itself*. What is a tree in itself? What is technology in itself? Another way of putting this is to ask what, for example, 'treeness' or 'tableness' is? What more general treeness lies behind all trees? This becomes a little more complicated, however. For Heidegger's major preoccupation was with the ontology of being itself. Which is to ask, *what is being*? What is it to ask 'what is'? What is the Being that lies behind, or within, all beings?

Heidegger, in asking such questions, differentiated between Being (with a capital 'B') and beings (us – with a little 'b'). They have a crucially different relation to time. Being – with a capital B – is continuous through time. It is always there. However, beings – with a little 'b' – you and I, and ants and trees or Beta videotape (for those who remember it) – are obviously discontinuous – we come and go. We emerge and disappear. We are transitory, at best small, momentary expressions of the larger Being through time. Of course, we invent all sorts of excuses to ignore this, from religions, philosophies and humanism to fabulous careers in Silicon Valley. Nevertheless, Heidegger's point here is that these excuses are merely distractions from the fundamental ground of our existence – namely what he calls 'being-before-death'. This 'being-before-death' is simply the facing of the fact that we are temporary, little beings and that there is a more general Being that is grounded in a time that exceeds us, and will always get us in the end. The great cultural and philosophical task for Heidegger is to keep this fact alive, to maintain contact with Being – with a capital 'B' – by facing our own 'being-before death', and the specificity of our 'being-there' only at particular moments in time and in particular places. We must maintain contact with an awareness of the gift of Being to little beings.

Heidegger saw technology as something that could either participate in this massive cultural project or present a great danger to it. His major assertion here was, although technology was inescapable within culture, *that there was nothing technological about technology*. Technology was not about independent mechanisms. In a sense, culture, the world and thought were everything and technology followed. At the very least, technology always had a relationship to other practices, particularly knowledge and art. Here he takes up the Ancient Greek term *techne*, which can be broadly translated as knowledge 'at work' (Lacoue-Labarthe 1990: 53). For Heidegger, following the Greeks, technology, knowledge and art were, and should be, all filtered through each other. For Heidegger, instances of technology should be subordinated to the 'knowledge at work' which makes them possible. The best form of this working knowledge is that which contributes to making the project of preserving the right relation to Being. Technology, art and knowledge come together to reveal this relationship to Being. For Heidegger, the Ancient Greeks had this all just right, with their temples on the hill using *techne* to reveal that there was always something beyond our comprehension.

Heidegger did not, however, celebrate modern technology. Heidegger portrays the modern focus on what he calls 'technicity' – that is, technology in itself, technological determinism or technology as the primary driving force within culture – as an extreme danger both to culture and thought. In particular, technicity leads us into the delusion of thinking we can overcome the world, overcome time. It leads us to think we can know the world. Worse, it leads us to think that we can overcome Being, the world's fragility and our mortality.

Technicity is not, however, just a series of technologies. It is also a way of thinking – a peculiarly technical or instrumental way of thinking. Heidegger sees technicity as a result of the delusions of humanism generally. More specifically, he targets the thought of the seventeenth-century Descartes (who wrote 'I think therefore I am'). For Heidegger, Descartes's emphasis on the power of the thinking human subject led this subject to overestimate its ability to transcend time and the world. It led to the notion of that subject's ability to eventually gain control of the world. In this, ironically, nothing is thought through properly. So through instrumental science, for example, we use science to destroy forests the more quickly before we have even begun to think out the consequences. For Heidegger this delusional thinking only leads to our loss of control to the technological instruments that are used in order, paradoxically, to feed our illusion that we can control the world. For Heidegger this is a violation, a turning away from the fundamental realization that

Being lies beyond the technical knowledge of beings. Being is not just something for beings to use up in order to attain a feeling of omnipotence.

Deforestation, the depletion of the oceans, and so on, are all symptomatic of this faulty instrumental thinking. It is for this reason that we should realize that 'the essence of technology is by no means anything technological' (Heidegger 1977: 4). For Heidegger, the essence of technology is, or should be, something other than technology. Technology should therefore be a way of *revealing* (p. 12) other aspects of life, not of controlling life and the world just to enable more technological development. Just to remind you, this is a revealing relating to what the Ancient Greeks called *techne*. *Techne* – knowledge at work – is in turn related to 'poiesis', or creation, which, as art, is not the creation of the new, but a bringing forth of what is. Ultimately then, for Heidegger, technology needs art as much as it needs science. One needs to perfect the art of finding the sculpture that exists within the stone as much as one needs to be able to sculpt the stone technically. One needs to be able to find the carving in the tree. (Yes – sometimes it does seem that quaint and old fashioned, though it is not always that simple.)

Heidegger opposes the revealing of Being in art to the more instrumental revealing of pure resources for exploitation through modern technology. He calls this a simple challenging-forth of the environment. This is a bit like the bank robber saying 'Give me all the cash!', except that we are saying it to nature, and by implication to Being. 'Give us it all now! Whatever the consequences!' This is a technicity where, instead of running with the environment, we run against it, get as much out of it as we can and trust in a new technology to fix the problems afterwards – a position best summed seen in the nuclear power industry. In this challenging-forth of the environment the essence of technology is once again conceived of only as technological and not as intrinsically related to the disclosure of Being.

You will have noticed, however, that revealing is common to both cases. In both cases, technology 'reveals whatever does not bring itself forth and does not yet lie before us' (1977: 13). *Techne* reveals a relation to Being. Technicity reveals more resources to exploit. On the one hand, the two are produced by different ways of thinking about the issues, and imply an ethical dimension to these ways of thinking. On the other hand, the two are clearly related, and the ethical dimension is complicated by this. Ethically favoured, as everyone will guess by now, are the handcrafts that seem closer to a revelation of Being, not technology for its own sake. We flow with the grain of the wood. We do not put an autobahn or information superhighway through it.

Ethically unfavoured seems to be just about any modern technology, in which art, or craft, is subtracted from *techne*. *Techne* then gets out of control and heads towards technicity – everything becomes technological determined. The harmony with the world and with Being is destroyed. In a sense Being is forced into hiding. The world is treated with a degree of contempt, only as a kind of resource for the furtherance of the technological. Everything – humanity, the world and everything in it – becomes what Heidegger calls a 'standing-reserve' (1977: 18) for technicity. Something is revealed here but this revelation is only a revelation of the opportunity for further exploitation. In short, modern technology conceals its relation to the Being that exceeds the finite life of beings. It does this so it can more efficiently exploit the world.

It is here that thinking comes in. We lose, in technicity, the reflective person preserving a careful relation to thought which had been begun by the Greeks. Instead we have the following situation which forces us to pay a high price. Humans are now themselves 'enframed' (1977: 19) within technicity's treatment of the world as standing-reserve. So is human thought. This has dreadful consequences, not the least of which for Heidegger is that 'In truth . . . precisely nowhere does man today any longer encounter himself, i.e. his essence' (p. 27).

For Heidegger there is luckily a way out of technicity, although part of his greatness as a philosopher is to suggest that we cannot avoid technology. He writes of technology's 'saving power'. This can lead us back to an ethical relation to the world. Yet this saving power is precisely the danger of the situation. The danger of technicity, according to Heidegger, becomes so apparent that, in fright, we realize that we are, in fact, temporary beings and begin again to *think* about it all the right way. We come back to where we started – in that the essence of ethical activity as regards technology begins with thinking about technology and allowing the revealing of Being.

This is a great but, for many critics, troubling set of ideas. Perhaps it is sometimes useful to turn all this on its head. Does technology kill thought, or does it simply activate alternative ways of thinking? In the end, according to Heidegger it seems to do both, though with different ethical consequences.

Outside thought

As Heidegger and many others surveyed in this chapter point out, whatever the ethical consequences, technology is about dealing with that which is outside our own little headspace. Tools, for example, are things that enable us to transform thoughts into action, or that let us move through the world to have more experiences and so think more thoughts. We can here differentiate between two models of thought in culture at large – that which uses figures or images of interiority (as in 'what is going on in your head') and that which uses figures of exteriority (as in 'get out of your head').

This is as much as to ask a question which is important for a lot of obvious reasons, but is particularly important when thinking about the relation between humans, thought and technology. It is a question that has taken many forms throughout this chapter. This is the question of where, in the end, thought occurs. Does it occur 'inside' or 'outside'? Can we think of thought as the property of the soul, the interior consciousness, in short, of the thinking subject, or as an exterior relation between a series of outsides (which we could think of as 'folded' into an only apparent 'inside' like the brain or soul)? To put this another way, when you have a conversation with someone, perhaps on the telephone, or, when you interact with a landscape, and animal, a computer, where are the thoughts involved coming from? Are they all coming from 'inside', or are they created 'between', in the interaction? If it is in between – does that mean that the computer, the animal, the landscape is thinking too? Does it mean that we can *only* think in connection with an animal, another human, a landscape, a city or a machine? If we assume an 'inside' we tend to assume some kind of unity to thought – I think therefore 'I' am. If we assume that it takes place 'outside' we assume that things are much more fluid and a bit more chaotic. Thoughts are perhaps also more interactive, more networked, if they take place 'outside'.

Paul Patton (1984) – writing as so many do in this area on Deleuze and Guattari – shows that this also has a political dimension. Outside thought is the thought of the nomad – of thought that is fundamentally changed by everything it encounters. In this way of thought technology helps us to encounter and change. 'Classical thought' on the other hand, which he also calls 'State' thought, is much more restrictive. It attempts to impose itself on the environment and reduce everything to its way of thinking.

We can here collapse 'inside' thought into 'classical' or 'State' thought. 'Inside thought' suggests a subject who thinks he or she is self-contained and is capable of knowing enough to make them very special. This is the scientist who will save the world or destroy it in the name of the nation, him or herself, the company, humanity as a whole. We can put it another way and say that, in such thought everything comes back to the question of our interior state. The world comes second. Questions of Being only matter because they matter to us. Outside thought, however, is always to do with encountering the world. In this case, 'Before being there is politics' (Deleuze and Guattari, quoted by Patton 1984: 63). You can find both these attitudes very clearly in the rhetoric surrounding technology.

Now we can qualify Heidegger's realization that 'there is nothing technological about technology'. Actually, this qualification is more of a reversal. We could not think any of these thoughts without having thought through the general issue of technology (which is more or less what Heidegger says as well – this is all part of technology revealing things for us). Technology does not merely allow us to manipulate the outside. It makes us confront a fundamental shift in what thought is when we consider how deeply involved thought is with the outside, and with various technologies.

Just as, with Heidegger, technology is nothing without thought, thought itself begins to look like it possesses some surprisingly machinic qualities. Here we will outline three. Firstly, thought relies on techniques and technologies directly, such as writing, communications, even techniques such as mnemonics and other memory-aiding techniques. Secondly, thought relies on systems – previously systems of thought which included both techniques of analysis and discussion – such as the dialectical method, but now systems that are indeed purely technical systems (such as computer operating systems). Thirdly, and more contentiously, thought uses techniques, technologies and systems to give the illusion of something separate from these (the 'I think therefore I am', consciousness).

We can create – and think – the new with machines. We do not have to see them as destroying the old.

CHAPTER 7

Getting Wired: War, Commerce and the Nation-State

Gilles Deleuze once stated that 'we ought to establish the basic sociotechnological principles of control mechanisms as their age dawns . . .' (1995: 182). Is there a dawn today of new 'sociotechnological' principles of control? At the same time, is the movement towards control futile? It may seem so in the face of the increased complexity of the world created by the very same instruments meant to provide control.

This chapter begins with sovereignty – the idea that a nation, community or individual can justify some kind of control over its own destiny. Following this is a brief account of war and technology. Here logistics and networking respond to the conflict between control and complexity. We then look at the fate of the nation-state in the face of the rising tide of networked capital.

Sovereignty

The idea that individuals or states can exercise power autonomously is the idea of *sovereignty*. It may be a fatally flawed ideal. Yet, rightly or wrongly, the pursuit of the ideal of sovereignty has fuelled much of the pursuit of technology. Ironically, this sometimes seems to produce societies that sacrifice a degree of freedom to what we could call 'technosocial' forms of control.

This becomes obvious in war, in which the clash of sovereign nations tends to lead to technological developments to which other forms of social or individual sovereignty are sacrificed. Ironically, the more sovereignty falls apart, the more war is called upon to recreate it anew, in new weapons programmes or perhaps in new wars. It is this that leads to the accelerating technological development of contemporary warfare (Nancy 1993).

Perhaps we should retreat a little from these difficulties and elaborate upon our preliminary definitions of sovereignty. In fact, sovereignty has many definitions, but all of them are to do with the source of power and all them assume that there *is* a source of power (as opposed to those who are powerless). In short, sovereignty is what rules, in theory at least, absolutely and independently. It is sovereignty *over* (even if this is over oneself as in self-control or even personal freedom). As such it can be seen as both a condition and an active process. It is something one 'has' and something that one 'uses'.

Some subsequently seek a more utilitarian definition of sovereignty – purely in terms of the power of the state – not as an ideal, but as it really operates. If this is the case, sovereignty might be in even more trouble today than ever. For several hundred years sovereignty has been tied practically to the rise and fall of the nation-state (Elfstrom 1997: 39). Yet the interplays between nations, and the practical sovereignties they imply, are currently being put out to pasture by the rise of the network society and its real-time, border-hopping communications. This is a world in which even government officials sometimes get their information from the international media during a war (Neuman 1996: 11).

Sovereignty, then, is a flawed, fragmented and complex concept. Moreover, it seems a concept in decline. Many current political problems may indeed stem from the fact that the concept of sovereignty, the basis of so many political and legal concepts and practices, may be out of date. This is, at least in part, due to technological change.

Sovereignty and technical control

In reality, the ideal of sovereignty and the practical technical control it relies upon – and which in turn can subvert it – are closely related. In fact, sovereignty itself can be seen *as* a series of technical procedures when we do not attempt to justify it via religion, 'the will of the people', or the necessity of the rule of law. In fact, this seems to have become more acceptable in more technocratic societies. When, as Giorgio Agamben (1998) points out, there are the technical means to control life at its most basic levels (population controls, genetics, weapons of mass destruction), sovereignty mutates into much more specific and potentially more brutal forms of control that may not feel the need to justify themselves through idealistic concepts.

It is here that Agamben situates globalization. The technologies of globalization involve a series of flexible, but specific controls. These are designed to impose non-localized forms of order on specific locations in the world, as and when needed. Agamben here points to the camp, from the concentration camp to refugee camp, as this kind of technical 'dislocating localization' (1998: 175). For Agamben, sovereignty, not actually being divine, has to be constantly recreated through technical means. It is a technical means of creating the social world in a certain way, and of excluding many from this social world, whether through the camp or genetic engineering. In the contemporary world, many of those excluded from the social world are reduced to 'bare life'. What this implies is that true political struggle will no longer be over control of the state but a 'struggle between the State and the non-State (humanity), an insurmountable disjunction between whatever singularity and the State organization' (p. 181).

Is this kind of brutal sovereignty over bare life recognizable as sovereignty? For many the answer is no. Although, once again, talk about the collapse of sovereignty in the new networks of our times does not always mean the end of control. It could mean the opposite – that there are new forms of social control that no longer need the idea of sovereignty to justify them.

For some, then, the flawed notion of sovereignty is being replaced with the practice of pure technical control. A more theoretical understanding of this is perhaps that given by Michel Foucault. Foucault thought that we could not really even understand the operation of power if we began first from an assumption of juridical sovereignty (1997: 59). In Chapter 1 we discussed Foucault's (1980) depersonalized and somewhat technical notion of power. Foucault rejected the notion of a power held by some against others, instead proposing the diffusion of force throughout the world. In accepting the world as determined by the conflict of forces, Foucault sees no central sovereign control either in existence or possibility.

Here, obviously, we do not assume the truth of sovereignty. At the same time we shall re-emphasize the fact that technology is crucial both to the confused assumption of sovereignty and to the move away from it. Many critics, for example, have pointed to the crucial role of industrial revolutions and communications in the rise of the nation-state, for example in the development of railways.

In the middle of all this complexity for the last 200 years has been the military and its attempt to develop technological control of this complexity. Yet Rochlin (1997) points to the accidents that have bedevilled the use of technology by the military as examples of the fact that, technically speaking, complexity often tends to overwhelm control. Here we shall simply point out once again that if the rise of the network – in the military, in accelerated forms of capitalism, in everyday life – is the child of sovereignty, it is a rebellious one.

We shall now turn to the military's role in the development of logistics and networking.

War, technology and the question of control

The Gulf War of 1991 was the major, recent turning point in the history of war and technology. It still informs much of what has followed. Here was a war premised upon the replacement of direct combat with advanced, networked technologies. It was portrayed as a telepresent war, conducted by technocrats via satellite and brought to the world live via CNN. Yet if this was war, it was not war as we have known it before this. For a start, there was little sense of contest in this war. There could be no clearer example of the social divisions in terms of power and access to networks that can be brought about by globalization. On the other hand, the Gulf War demonstrated that such technical control can easily be overwhelmed by social complexity. Although victory for the US and its allies seemed certain from the beginning, in the end it was not sure what this victory actually meant when it came. Indeed, Saddam Hussein claimed victory at the time, and even Margaret Thatcher remarked after the war that she wondered who had actually won it.

For better or worse, wars such as this seem more like global policing exercises. Yet just as policing may control but not eliminate crime, in this war technical control, and the military victory it provided, proved to be no real guarantee of political victory. It was true that, at the time at least, technology itself seemed to have won many hearts and minds, in part through the many, repeated and in many ways illusory, bloodless images of precision, video-guided missiles. Yet over ten years later, as we write this book, Saddam

Hussein, though forced out of Kuwait, is still in power in Iraq. It also seems that Iraq still possesses weapons of mass destruction. This despite continued bombing after the war 'ended', economic sanctions and the subsequent death of many Iraqi civilians due to the lack of food and basic medical supplies.

Jean Baudrillard (1995) famously wrote at the time that the Gulf War 'did not take place'. By this, Baudrillard did not mean that there was no violence. There was in fact a great deal of suffering. Iraq experienced a great deal of destruction of life and property and some allied troops were killed and injured. For Baudrillard the Gulf War 'did not happen' because the rhetoric of 'war' was a cover for something else. This 'something else' involved a new technology of violence, one which produced a carefully controlled technical event, played out as much in the media as on the ground. This was supposed to bring about what George Bush (senior) at the time called a 'new world order', one which continued in the policing of the situation in Kosovo later in the decade.

Ten years later, on 11 September 2001, the problems of assuming technical control over the world's complexity showed another side. As is well known, while the United States sought to enhance its military, technical control through a reinvigorated missile defence shield costing a fortune to develop, four US planes were hijacked at knifepoint by terrorists. Again played out in what is left of 'real time' in the media, three aircraft flew into the World Trade Center in New York and the Pentagon in Washington. All those repeated images of video-guided missiles from the Gulf War and Kosovo were suddenly cancelled out by the repeated airings of images of aircraft flying into landmarks of Western culture (these images were repeated to the point that viewers had to ask the television networks to stop showing them, such was the *media* fascination with the event). This apparently low-tech terrorist attack was arguably, and sadly, the most successful in history, both because of the devastating loss of life, and because of the symbolism of striking at the core of both US and Western capital and culture. Many argued that it changed the nature of the world, and we should perhaps point out in this regard that this attack was perhaps not as low-tech as it appears. We should not miss the networked nature of this attack, or its use of globalizing technologies such as aircraft, the media, the Internet or the networks of world banking.

In sum, from the Gulf War to the World Trade Center attack, it seems that neither the older notions of war as the conflict of sovereign nations, nor newer notions of technical control, sit well within a complex, networked world. Even the United States government spoke of a 'new kind of war' after the World Trade Center. We could almost characterize this new kind of war as a war between networks in which complexity is a given. Or we could see it as a war of networks *within* other networks, as demonstrated by the Bush government's freezing of bank accounts linked to some of its terrorist opponents.

Such events no doubt change the world and the development of the 'new war' is still being played out in Afghanistan as we write. Yet such events also perhaps arise in response to a changed world. We would therefore like to give a very brief history and analysis of the military contribution to the rise of the networked world. Much of this repeats the dynamic of control and complexity that we have discussed previously.

Riding turbulence

Manuel De Landa (1991) sees the problems involved in warfare as problems of turbulence. The aim of a good war machine is to create turbulence, used against the enemy, but in a controlled form. Firstly, one must know how to use turbulence, and to direct it towards the enemy. For example, the development of the conoidal bullet (a bullet in the shape of a slightly rounded cone instead of a lumpy metal ball) allows a projectile to ride the turbulence of the air with more accuracy. Likewise, the spiralled rifling on the inside of the rifle, perfected in the nineteenth century, changed the nature of warfare almost entirely, precisely because firearms suddenly became so accurate. Such developments, for example, removed the need for massed soldiers all pointing their (inaccurate) weapons in the same direction. As Rochlin puts it, before the rifle, 'for more than four thousand years, military history was dominated by the search for better ways of organizing mass formations for massed fire' (1997: 132). With more accuracy the battlefield began to disperse and it is here perhaps that we begin the see the need for better communications and, ultimately, networking.

The second understanding one needs of turbulence is how to survive it, and there is no turbulence like the turbulence of warfare. In addition to the obvious chaos and destruction involved in war, De Landa points to the *information turbulence* created by the sophistication of many armies. Martin van Creveld points to the turbulence created by both the turnover in new weapons systems and the mix of newer systems with older (1989: 231). In any case, it becomes obvious that soldiers in the field, or command posts in the midst of battle, need to be able to find order in this chaos of men and machines. For De Landa, this does not only involve control. It also involves the seizing of or better, flowing with, complexity.

Here we come to one of the major themes of this chapter. This is that order and complexity need not always be opposed. Here we shall repeat the basic idea that informs the theory of apparently chaotic events such as the formation of clouds, or the turmoil of battle. This is theory of 'chaos theory'. Despite its name, chaos has come to be seen in chaos theory as a form of highly complex self-organization that only looks chaotic because of its complexity. These forms of self-organization emerge at certain 'singularities' or critical points (the boiling point of water for example, which leads the flow of water molecules to reorganization itself). De Landa sees parallels to this in the relations between society and technology in, for example, the way in which social processes reorganize themselves at the outset of war or some other emergency. Certain technological breakthroughs create social or 'historical singularities' (1991: 49) and are in turn created by them. At such points the entire field of self-organization – social and technical – can shift radically and rapidly.

De Landa locates one crucial shift in the emergence of the 'distributed network' (1991: 72). This came with the German 'blitzkrieg' in the Second World War, which for the first time employed two-way radio communications to coordinate air and ground attacks from *within* the field of battle, in real time.

There are other related shifts in military organization. With the invention of aerial bombing for example, 'fortress walls' begin to 'dematerialize' towards 'the electronic walls of radar' (p. 48) which in turn lead to the development of satellite systems for both surveillance and communication. When satellite communications became capable of 'transmitting data in real time' in effect what had once been a defensive fortress wall had evolved into a tactical weapon that could be used in attack (p. 56). This in turn led to the globalization of communications. The US Air Force, for example, developed a worldwide, integrated, real-time communications system in 1962 (van Creveld 1989: 240). The first overall 'fully automatic military communications system' was used in Vietnam in 1964. Effective spy satellites were used from 1965. This all resulted in a confusion of what we might call virtual and actual spaces, and the new forms of self-organizing social and technical complexity that followed. A new paradigm emerged – C^3I or the integration of command, control, communications and intelligence. War now took place – technically speaking – in two types of location. It took place firstly across the entire world (in virtual space – through the networks of spy satellites and planes, more and more sophisticated analyses which could be done in the US and relayed to the sites of conflict, and so on). War took place secondly at specific places – in Vietnam and elsewhere (actual space). In Vietnam this led to confusion in the field (in the Gulf War this led to clarity – at least it seemed to). In the meantime, C^3I has become a business model, from which it flowed to many other areas, as in 'flexible learning' and the virtual university.

The important point here for De Landa was that a new arrangement of machines (communications) 'was made to cut across [other] elements' (1991: 74). This was a way of controlling complexity but in turn it created more complexity of a different order. In this shift the 'flow of information in a system becomes more important than the flow of energy' (p. 158), not that the flow of energy is abandoned. Let us look at this increasing domination of logistics, information, communication and networking in more detail.

Logistics and networking

Van Creveld points to the lesser importance of weapons' development up until the nineteenth century (1989: 226). Rochlin points out that armies before the nineteenth century often tended to import technological changes from civilian life rather than the other way around. The Industrial Revolution changed this reluctance on the part of the military to get involved with the newest technologies, slowly perhaps, but irrevocably.

De Landa writes that it was the military's desire in the early nineteenth century 'to create weapons with perfectly interchangeable parts . . . [that] . . . marked the beginning of the age of the rationalization of labor processes' (1991: 31). In other words, the development of logistics, the methods of supplying an army with the provisions and weapons that it needed, created many of the most advanced forms of production and organization that the planet had seen. These were later 'exported to the civilian sector' as 'scientific management'. De Landa thinks that the management sciences that we currently live with found their origin in the drastically increased complexities of logistics in the Second World War.

The logistics process ultimately aims to encode other processes into a system in which they become standardized (and later made more flexible again through computing). Thus the munitions factory standardizes the local artisan's production of weaponry. More recently, the skills of the office secretary are imported into office software packages. Or computing in general attempts to import and systematize human intelligence. All of these are what are called 'expert systems'. As Hubert Dreyfus (1996) points out, any kind of machine organization such as artificial intelligence will need some kind of expert system in place. And in part what this expert system will always be will be the transfer of the 'expertise' of bodily experience into the system. Without this contextual bodily experience intelligence would remain too abstract to operate in the world.

It was perhaps for this reason that it was never easy to integrate new technologies with old army cultures, tactics and strategies. Rochlin (1997: 136) points to one example in 1942 when an Admiral Callaghan took a fleet into Guadalcanal. His ships, for the first time, had naval radars with a screen display, but he refused to open fire until he could actually see the enemy and the ensuing battle was a very messy affair in which Callaghan's fleet suffered great losses.

Yet slowly, despite or perhaps because of such setbacks, the march of machines over the top of humans to the central place in warfare continued to its inevitable end in the 1990s. Troops in the field now are often technical experts who rely on all kinds of complex relations to other forms of military action and support, and on communications as a weapons system in itself. As van Creveld puts it:

> . . . the most important outcome of technological progress during the decades since World War II has been that, on the modern battlefield, a blizzard of electromagnetic blips is increasingly being superimposed upon – and to some extent substituted for – the storm of steel in which war used to take place (1989: 282).

Control, complexity and computing

As more 'control' leads to higher levels of complexity the need for computers arises. Computing can be viewed as the expert system of expert systems. It provides a series of machines designed to enable the transfer of embodied experience of the world to the system 'universal'. Thus the computer is a 'universal machine'. As discussed in the previous chapter, Alan Turing's abstract mathematical framework for the universal machine had been developed by 1936. Yet before this practical, embodied 'computers' were the human beings, usually women, who calculated the tables used in ballistics – the trajectory of projectiles under different conditions and with different weapons (De Landa 1991: 41). These human computers were more and more supplemented, and then replaced, by machines during and after the Second World War. Their use to the military was initially in coping with the overwhelming flow of information the military now dealt with (van Creveld 1989: 242). Soon, however, they would be useful for a host of other functions: communications, intelligence analysis and even command and control. They also infiltrated operations research – the complex 'science' in which the optimum ways of using people and machines was considered. In this we can see how far logistics has come, and how military problems have influenced the course of general culture.

Moreover, if we feel that culture, for better or worse, is increasingly abstract, increasingly generalized, we can see that this is partly because of the way in which concrete machines have been pushed towards abstraction. This also explains why networks are now more important than any single instantiation of them. It is in the network that the abstract meets, communicates and operates, producing the world after it. We can also understand why logistical control increasingly becomes a question of the control of networks. We can therefore see why De Landa defines logistics in general as 'a matter of network management' (1991: 107). As De Landa puts it, we are still very much indebted to the railways.

> The problems encountered in trying to implement a supply network via railways began to acquire a generic character. In essence they are not different from the problems one faces when trying to organize a complex telephone grid or a network of computers. These are all problems of traffic control . . . (p. 115).

As this traffic moves to what Virilio calls 'terminal velocity', the deep implication of logistics and networking in the complexity of what Virilio describes as a permanent state of 'pure war' (1983) becomes more obvious. Virilio once called the twentieth century the 'century of war machines' (Zurbrugg 1995: 9). In our passion for war, according to Virilio, we suffer from a kind of brutal 'technological fundamentalism' (Madsen 1995: 82).

There is a biographical side to this. To quote Virilio:

> I was formed by war – I was born in 1932, one year before the rise of the Nazi party in Germany, and I spent the war in Nantes, a city with armament factories and a submarine port, which was destroyed by air-raids. I was traumatized by the war. I kept a notebook when I was ten years old (Zurbrugg 1995: 14).

For Virilio, as soon as states began to form, war always came, and always comes, first. War forms the reason for the development of the city and the changes cities go through. It provides the ground for economic activity and of course for technological development. It even pre-exists politics to an extent. It also lies behind most aspects of civilian life. And here, Virilio is basically saying that if a country is not actually at war – then it is preparing for war. The population is always in a state of 'pure war', in that everything is always channelled through the consciousness, technologies and economics of war.

Virilio also ties our perceptual and cultural technologies – the entertainment technologies for example – to war and, points out that such technologies as cinema arise from war and feed back into it. This is partly because so much of war is about perception. For him, '. . . the history of battle is primarily the history of radically changing fields of perception' and the bombs dropped on Hiroshima were examples of an 'information explosion' as much as anything else (1989: 6–7).

For Virilio, especially with the development of nuclear weapons, the state now moves too slowly to keep up. In addition any notion of duration – the time of political discussion, of democracy, of politics in general – is swallowed up in a total war machine which is out of control. When you only have minutes or seconds to respond to a nuclear attack there is no time for a referendum, a meeting of congress, or even advice of any kind. Time in the normal sense of the word, as experienced duration – we think about it, discuss it, then we make a decision – is depleted to the point of exhaustion.

Pure war?

Everything from agriculture to business to 'flexible learning' seems to use military organizational models. Does this mean, for example, that every time we hop onto the Internet we are participating in a

gigantic war machine? Not at all. In fact, technological developments such as the Internet inevitably find uses completely incompatible with military aims and objectives. Thus the network that
can withstand a nuclear attack is also incredibly hard to police. The
tremendous shared database for scientists and technicians sharing
their weapons research becomes the backbone for the biggest
public library we have ever seen. Moreover, the feedback mechanisms necessary to control the virtual battlefield also allow for the
possibility of global community as never before, even for new
notions of democracy.

You could easily find parallels to all this in other areas. In politics media vectors take control along with 'information bombs'.
In business horizontal and portable networks parallel and even
perhaps sometimes exceed the military's. Technical performance is
overdetermined at every level. In education we now have what
is called flexible learning and online education is a developing
battlefield for the educational sovereignties that are still called
universities but now increasingly resemble consortiums. In medicine there is the drive for control by pharmaceutical companies and
their developments and the general patenting of scientific developments by those corporations which have funded them. Gaming
and sports are increasingly dominated by media technologies such
as the video game and the fine-tuning of performance (through
techniques but also through drugs). Sexual reproduction is made
more efficient through cloning and so on. Food is genetically engineered. Crucial to all this has been the shift to communications
intervention in warfare and mediated violence (as shown in the
terms of C^3I) and its subsequent transfer to commerce and capitalism. Yet it is also important to remember that in some ways the
logic of technology and war are opposed, and this means that
the pursuit of technological advance which so obsessed first world
military establishments in the twentieth century, is not always a
guarantee of success (van Creveld 1989: 320).

Yet there is no doubt that the networked technologies the military has helped to create are currently taking a stranglehold on the
globe. Communal structures such as the nation, the corporation
and more local forms of community are undergoing enormous
changes as a result. Nowhere could the questions and perhaps
some answers in this area be clearer than in the fate of the nation-
state when confronted with the new networked economy of the
information age.

The network and the fate of the nation-state

We shall begin with a basic assumption shared by many thinkers. This is that the sovereignty of the nation-state is under threat, if not already seriously undermined (Poole 1999: 144; Khan 1996; Castells 2000b: 13, although see Everard 2000 for some reservations about this idea). When we say, however, that the sovereignty of the nation-state is in decline, what do we mean? We shall begin by considering the relation between the nation and the state.

The first thing that the information age has clarified is that the nation is not the same as the state. It is true that, for the last 200 years, the two have often coincided in the powerful formation of the nation-state but this has not always been the case. We can think of the state as something operational. It has fixed borders. It has laws one must follow. It is an entity to which one belongs, whether one likes it or not. To a large extent the state is then a purely pragmatic entity – a set of functions (borders, laws, armies, police, education systems, taxes, regulation of industry, the protection of copyright and so on). All of these state functions are enabled by technologies, and all of them change with changing technologies. For example, consider the techniques and technologies that enable states to keep a tab on movements of people and goods (from passports and bureaucratic paperwork to networked computing). Or, consider the technologies used to maintain surveillance over their borders (aircraft, satellites, the coastguard or more exact forms of cartography). There are other technologies enabling the state to keep electronic records of the citizens (or immigrants, legal and illegal) within the state, or to communicate with neighbouring states about all these matters. The rise of larger states has often been made easier by the rise of technologies that have enabled the state to rule a particular territory with some consistency: roads, railways, telegraphs, telephones and of course military technologies.

The nation is a different matter. We could say that it is more of an ideal, more of a concept. Benedict Anderson (1991) has famously called it an 'imagined community'. As Ross Poole puts it, the 'the nation is a principle of identity, or – better – it is a number of principles of identity. It collects together a diverse range of peoples and groups, traditions and ways of life, into one' (1991: 95). Put simple, while the state is a collection of functions, the nation is a collection of principles. With regard to sovereignty of the nation-state, it is the state that puts sovereignty into practice (through the rule of law for example), while the nation gives it its underlying concept and justification. One identifies with the nation. One sees oneself as Japanese, Australian, English, American, Chinese or Chilean. Nationalism gives a unified sense of place (the homeland) and a unified sense of time (a common and often 'mythic' history which gives a justification to the future) (p. 96). This shared identity gives the basis for a sense of 'belonging'. One would not willingly sacrifice one's life for the tax department (a state function) but one might do it for the 'nation'. Indeed, as we have seen, the sacrifice of war is something that propels the illusion of the nation, for whether positive or negative, the nation is always, to some extent, an illusion.

Part illusion or not, the very notion of the nation-state has become so commonplace that it is now hard to understand why the nation-state seems under siege by globalization at the moment. In short, the nation-state has formed the fundamental basis for the concept and practice of sovereignty for at least 200 years but is now being seriously eroded. What is eroding it? Manuel Castells, along with many others, points to the demise of the nation-state as the result of two things: the globalization of the world economy due in large part to the rise of information and communications technologies, and the challenge to the state from identity politics. Although this spells the end of the *sovereignty* of the *nation*-state (even as there are still many trying to bring their own nation-states into existence), it does not spell the end of the state itself. Castells suggests here the rise of the 'network state', accompanied by the only form of power that can resist it, 'autonomously defined cultural identities' (Roberts 1999: 36). In short, clashes of sovereignty in the information age are more likely to be between two extremely polarized positions: the local and the global. Poole puts this another way, writing that modern life is 'atomistic' in that one does not always see oneself in connection to broader social entities such as the state (1991: 92). In both accounts, the sovereignty of the nation-state is redirected in two opposite directions: into 'network states' such as the European Union, or into identity groups such as the environmental groups, cults, survivalist movements, virulent forms of nationalism that do not correspond to states, ethnic groups and so on. The state still performs its functions, but more and more of these occur at an international level, enabled by networked communications. We shall briefly follow Poole here.

Poole (1999) gives three reasons for the rise of nationalism. These are, firstly, that new territories could be consolidated as the basis of the nation as 'market relations eroded earlier forms of self-sufficient rural life' (p. 146). Secondly, the state developed the tech-nologies and techniques that enabled it to 'monopolize coercive power within a defined area'. Thirdly, the spread of print and sub-sequent media throughout all levels of a society enabled the 'devel-opment of public spheres'. All three of these factors are increasingly undermined in the modern world. Firstly, market relations are now global as never before, controlled by multinational, not national corporations. Secondly, the resulting global market, upon which the economic health of any individual state depends, undermines that state's ability to refuse increasing international intervention in its affairs (for better or worse). Thus the nation-state today pos-sesses a 'diminishing authority' and is 'hostage to a variety of international agreements' and world bodies (from the World Bank to the UN). Thirdly, there are the cultural shifts brought about by access to international forms of communication.

Poole, however, argues against an 'emerging global culture' here (1999: 148). Instead, he argues that the globalization of culture has given rise to the 'diversification of cultural forms'. We can live in Australia and take up West African drumming. We can participate over the Net in worldwide discussion groups about obscure hobbies or philosophers. Not only can we buy music produced and distributed by the musicians themselves from around the globe, but we can make it and distribute it ourselves. As Poole puts it, 'very few of these cultural forms are organized along national lines, and most resist being subsumed within national cultures'. In addition, the national language that was so important – along with a 'national literature' – in creating the sense of the nation is now undermined by the increasing importance of global electronic visual and oral media (p. 149). Does this all mean the 'end of the affair' with nationalism, Poole asks? The probable answer is yes, and he suggests that part of the move forward shall be through the development of 'cosmopolitanism' (p. 165), although he is sceptical about whether this will actually mean an improvement on the nation-state.

Let us now look in more detail at the way the global and the local are squeezing out the nation-state.

The new economies

The NASDAQ – the technology-weighted stock market index – has recently plummeted and then taken a roller-coaster ride up, down and around, in a major correction to overinflated technology stock values. The ride continues. Yet, as with many changes described in this book, there is no going back. The decisive steps towards the digital economy have been made. Businesses small and large are adapting themselves to the new economic imperatives or going extinct. The successful businesses are those who are dramatically rescripting what they do in the world. Even Sony corporation, for example, in 2000 drastically changed its corporate policies and processes in order to become 'eSony' (McIntyre 2000). It planned on the one hand to integrate the compatibility of its products (in, for example, a memory chip that can be used in all sorts of digital applications, not just computers). At the same time, it is allowing its business enterprises around the world a large degree of independence in order to adapt these products to local markets, or even tailor the processes of manufacturing and services to the idiosyncratic demands of local markets. In this respect Sony is the opposite of McDonald's that attempts to globalize without 'localizing'. As Poole points out, the market *is* global these days, but it is also more and more specifically local – and both at the same time. The old slogan used to be 'think globally, act locally'. This holds true but, at the same time, it is also more and more possible to think locally and act globally.

What are the main forces at work in the new economies? What place do the new economies have within the other techno-cultural issues we have discussed? Of course, we have already written about capitalism in many other chapters but in this section we will take it as one of our central concerns. In particular we will ask whether what is left of sovereignty is now in the 'hands' of capital, and whether all sovereign power over life and death returns to the circuits of the market. Will the power of capital in turn be eroded? Are we witnessing the beginning of the end of capital that Marx predicted – its final triumph being the end of money as Pierre Levy predicts and a world of abundance for all? Or will it be a world of new forms of division and domination?

We perhaps first need to understand the differences between capital and the state as regards their relation to networks and territory. Following Deleuze and Guattari (1987), we can say that they have different relations to deterritorialization and reterritorialization. Which is to say that capital and the state have different relations to the dismantling or creation of territories. This is true whether these are spatial or what we might call our existential territories – territories that are made up of all the processes that define our existence.

Put too simply, we could say that capital has always been about networking, and always felt more comfortable with it. The state, however, is more comfortable about well-defined territory – in fact, the state is often defined in part by the territory which it occupies. Following from this, we could say that capital is interested in deterritorialization. Capital likes to moves things around, and in the process it likes even more to deterritorialize a certain value from this movement – a 'surplus' value over and above the value of the use of an object. This forms the basis of capital itself. Capital does 'reterritorialize' but in a very singular way. To put it simply once again, capital deterritorializes the entire world in order to reterritorialize it on capital (that is, on money). Where is this determining territory of money? In one sense, it is nowhere but in the totality of exchanges it makes possible. It is no wonder that capital embraces the network.

Where at least is the surplus value produced by the operations of capital stored? This once lay in reserves held in identifiable banks (that, for example, you could physically rob if you were bold enough and bad enough). Now it increasingly lies within networks. The result is that the contemporary world is now reterritorialized, as 'surplus value', onto networks by capital. Of course, a network is not quite a territory. In fact, we could say somewhat paradoxically that the new territories are precisely those of massive deterritorialization (another reason for the demise of the territory-fixated state). Increasingly, every activity in the world has a value within the expanding networks of capital flow: goods of all kinds but also cultural products and services, even health and education. When there is talk of 'privatization' what is normally meant is that another service has been put into the flow of the networks.

It is perhaps time, however, to go into issues of business a little more systematically as they are no doubt core issues in any consideration of culture and technology. We shall expand upon the idea that it is business and capital that are eroding many other forms of sovereignty. This is a conclusion that will surprise no one. What is surprising, however, is that critics and proponents of the digital economy alike also seem to agree that forms of sovereignty *within* business and capital themselves seem also to be undermined.

In order to discuss all this in a necessarily short space we shall mainly concern ourselves with some widely disparate theorists. We shall begin with two 'gurus' of the new economy, Kevin Kelly, the editor of *Wired* magazine, and Don Tapscott, an author and consultant whose books sell hundreds of thousands of copies. We shall then head to the ideas of Manuel Castells. He not only has more misgivings about what he calls the 'rise of the network society'. He also provides a much more complete analysis of its global effects.

Both Kelly and Tapscott provide us with systems of rules. At the risk of simplification we shall begin by reiterating these without criticism as these rules do seem to provide a glimpse from within of the thinking of those involved in the higher levels of the new business practices.

Old rules, new rules

Kelly gives us 12 'New Rules for a New Economy' (1997). Tapscott (1996) gives us 'Twelve Themes for a New Economy'. Tapscott writes, as do many others, of both a digital economy, powered by computers, and a knowledge economy, where knowledge itself is commodified. He also emphasizes networking. Kelly goes further. As with all the more astute critics here, Kelly immediately heads us away from the idea of the digital economy to the 'network economy'. Like others, Kelly points out that it is the networked nature of the network economy that presents us with the 'much more profound revolution'.

Kelly wisely points out that the current rate of change in the transformations involved within this network economy may not last for ever (it is well to remember that the Industrial Revolution ceased to look strange after a while – one indication of this has been the very mixed fortunes of technology-based stocks since Kelly wrote his 'new rules'). For the time being, however, we live in an age based upon uncertainty. This leads to a few fundamental assumptions which seem to go against many received wisdoms (at least in boardrooms) of business practice. Best summed up in Kelly's maxim 'wealth is not gained by perfecting the known, but by imperfectly seizing the unknown', these amount to using networks to constantly move away from established practices, processes and products and towards uncertainty. As Tapscott puts it, 'if it ain't broke, break it before your competitors do' (1996: 11). He points out that merely making your enterprise more 'efficient' is not enough. He writes that 'business process reengineering' or BPR (p. 3) (based upon economic rationalism and productivity gains) is 'in trouble' as a business solution (pp. 27–9). You can reorganize your business processes all you like, cut as many jobs as you like and 'encourage' employees to work as 'productively' as they possibly can, to the detriment of every other aspect of their lives, but you will still be completely out of tune with the new economic (dis) orders currently taking over the world. Kelly is even more radical here, suggesting that 'any job that can be measured for productivity probably should be eliminated'. He thinks instead that 'wasting time and being inefficient' are the paths ahead to 'discovery'. Discovery is important because networks are dynamizing change, and depend upon change. The new complexities that networks now bring to any commercial (or cultural) interaction mean that one has to ride this change as one surfs a rather wild wave. What then, are the rules here, if there are any (they could be better called techniques)?

Kelly suggests that we should firstly 'embrace dumb power'. Tapscott writes about 'smart products' (1996: 44). These amount to the same thing. A little computing power and a lot of networking go a long way in transforming the very nature of a product. Both refer to the way in which not only humans but machines and more and more everyday objects are both embedded with cheap, low-level information devices (computer chips) and networked in order to become 'smart'. Cars, for example, carry more and more chips and can now lock into global positioning satellites (GPS). Yet it goes further than this. Tapscott also points to the development of 'smart tyres', 'roads' or even ice hockey 'pucks' (p. 45). As Kelly puts it, soon 'all manufactured objects, from tennis shoes to hammers to lamp shades to cans of soup, will have embedded in them a tiny sliver of thought'. Again, it is not only humans being networked here. It is not even just computers. It is everything. Through all this there is a sense in which everything 'knows' everything else. So when one talks about the knowledge economy it has a wider meaning than one might think. What 'knows' and what is 'known' is a question now posed in economic terms at many levels – higher and lower, from expertise as a commodity to the ability of a door to 'know' who is passing through it. One of the consequences of this is that simple labour is no longer the commodity it was (Tapscott 1996: 47), something emphasized in Castells's more critical analysis as we shall see. Knowledge replaces labour as a commodity, something which, to some optimists such as Kelly, means that those who know live in a sellers' market.

Kelly and Tapscott share two more fundamental approaches. The first is the idea that constant innovation is the key to business in the networked economy. The second is what Tapscott calls 'discordance' (1996: 66) and Kelly calls, somewhat more optimistically, 'the churn'. Both are referring here to the disruption caused by the demands of the new economy. Tapscott is concerned by the 'new world (dis)order' (1996: 4) and the 'dark side of the age of networked intelligence' (p. 31). Kelly makes no excuses and sticks to the task at hand, asking how it is that the new economy itself will manage the 'churn'. His 'rule' here is 'seek sustainable disequilibrium'. He sees the new networked economy as taking on the characteristics of a complex evolving 'ecology', primed by 'perpetual disruption'. He points out that economics has always been about change, but that with the coming of the churn, there is an exponential growth in change to the point that it becomes something else, and 'hovers on the edge of chaos' in a churning whirl of both destruction *and* creation. The faster individual businesses grow and die, the more opportunities there are for business, that is, for *other* businesses and individuals to capitalize on what is created by the churn. The rhetoric here is that it is the destructive edge of the new economy that 'is life-giving renewal and growth'. This is good advice for entrepreneurs. Yet there are obviously problems for those left in the wake of this 'churn'. It is perhaps time to give these ideas a broader, and more critical, context.

Network society

Manuel Castells writes of the 'rise of the network society'. In this society he sees a polarization towards two forms of power – that of the network and that of the self. There is less and less in between (although he does not predict the total demise of the nation-state). Networks are primary and result in flows so complex and powerful that 'the power of flows takes precedence over the flows of power' (2000: 500). In a massive three-volume study, Castells outlines the fundamental and worldwide shifts in every sphere of human life that result. He is careful not to focus purely on the way the network society has arisen in the first world, but also on the uneven consequences of globalization. For example, he sees the rise of fundamentalisms as an attempted if inevitably futile rejection of the society of flows, and the rise of global criminality as in the ex-Soviet Union as an alternative attempt at participation in the society of flows. Old forms of military domination give way to the newer domination of networked capital. Castells writes, 'Power does not lie any more along the barrel of a gun but lies, instead, in the editing programs of the television networks' computers' (1999: 62).

Yet, as regards the self, far from setting up a postmodern fluidity, the rise of the network society leads to a reassertion of identity. While many are now involved in, or affected by, 'global networks of instrumental exchanges' (2000: 3), this is just something that they are involved in because they have little choice. Moreover, the network is confusing and disruptive. Consequently, Castells documents a retreat from this fluidity in which 'people tend to regroup around primary identities: religious, ethnic, territorial, national'. Who they are is increasingly figured in distinction from the networked society. The result is that communication in any traditional sense actually ceases to function in the new hyper-communicative media networks, and social groups fragment into alienated splinters. One of the great powers of Castells's analysis is that he can account for the rise of such diverse groups as the American militia, Japanese sects or the 'development of Falun Gong, the Chinese cult that challenged the Chinese Communist party in 1999' (p. 7), or the rise of global terrorism directed precisely against the network society within the framework of the information age.

How does technology fit into Castells's scheme of things? Firstly, for him society and technology are not separable (p. 5). Yet a society's different relationships to technology will indicate different relationships to its concept of itself as a society. Some societies will attempt – particularly through state controls – to hold back technological development. This is how he explains the stagnation of technological development in China after many inventions well in advance of those in Europe. Why did China not industrialize when it could? Simply because the state was (correctly) afraid that such change would disrupt social stability. This is the dilemma now experienced by governments everywhere (although Castells points to nations such as Japan as more successful in dealing with this dilemma). The unleashing of technological development was a crucial factor in the formation of the nation-state, but now the process continues to expand beyond the nation-state and undermines it in the process. The state becomes just one player, albeit an important one, swept up in the history of social/technological development that has led to a new kind of society. Sometimes *statism* attempts to control informationalism rather than give full rein to its capitalist allegiances. Statism is the attempt by the state, especially the communist state, to feed back surplus value into the reinforcement of the state itself. This has not had much success, although Castells points to modern China as attempting to negotiate the global economy without sacrificing the state. At the end of the day, however, the state is not very flexible with regard to the new society's use of technology to transform itself.

For Castells the new society is both 'capitalist and informational' (p. 13). These two aspects are deeply related and reinforce one another, although there is a difference between the two.

What then is informationalism? For Castells 'informationalism' is a new 'mode of development'. Modes of development, in turn, are 'the technological arrangements through which labor works on matter to generate the product, ultimately determining the level and quality of surplus' (p. 16) above and beyond the specific utility of the product. This surplus will feed back into the health of capitalism *or* the state.

For Castells (and many others in varying forms) there have been three modes of development. There were the agrarian (dependent upon the use of land) and the industrial (energy). The third is the informational. Castells points out that knowledge is important to all modes of development but that in informationalism there is 'the action of knowledge upon knowledge itself as the main source of productivity' (p. 17). The informational mode has different fundamental aims from the 'economic growth' and 'maximizing output' of the industrial mode. It may lead to these indirectly, but the informational modes' fundamental aim is towards 'the accumulation of knowledge and towards higher levels of complexity in information processing'. This is not understood by many even at the centres of capital and government today.

Technologies are now developed to 'act upon information' whereas before information was only there 'to act on technology' (p. 70). For Castells, information technology as the basis of the information age or the network society gives a material support to a more abstract 'networking logic' which, though it can be conceived quite separately from the actual technologies, would be 'too cumbersome to implement' without them (p. 71). This networking logic, quite distinct from the technologies it uses, is a distinct organizational logic (one that informs an international, state-independent shift in the structure and processes of all kinds of organizations, from those involved in scientific research to the new corporations).

The information technology paradigm also provides the material basis for the new 'flexibility' (p. 71) by which components of an organization can be quickly rearranged. It thus provides the basis for much of the dramatic restructuring undertaken by capitalism, and here Castells gives a more complete account of the 'if it's not broken, break it' rule. He writes, 'Turning the rules upside down without destroying the organization has become a possibility because the material basis of the organization can be reprogrammed and retooled.' It is perhaps important to note here that this means that many areas of cultural activity previously divorced from each other are now coming into play together in a way that begins to make them 'indistinguishable'. Notably, there is increasing convergence between the 'biological and microelectronics' (p. 72), something we have discussed in the context of genetic engineering and nanotechnology.

Yet there is even more to it than this. The informational mode of development deals with symbolic communication, the basis of culture. This means that it is the informational mode that strikes directly at the heart of culture itself, although all modes of development obviously change culture.

It is informational capitalism that has led to what could be the most dramatically social restructuring over a short period of time that the world has yet seen. It has provided the drive behind the restructuring efforts of states and corporations. This has involved deregulation and the privatization of public resources. It has involved the dismantling of the welfare state and the erosion of various social contracts between labour and capital. It plays cities, states and even continents against each other. Its virtual, informational nodes apportion the actual world into territories of value (or non-value), even from one small section of a city to another. Any attempt at an independent, state-based financial control becomes unworkable.

Castells suggests that the notions of the struggle between the self and the network, and of communities to define themselves when faced with the network, to a large extent replace the notion of class struggle that informed resistance within the Industrial Revolution. Arthur Kroker and Michael Weinstein (1994) propose here the equally compelling notion of a new kind of privileged class – the 'virtual class' in a world of 'data trash'.

For Castells, what now emerges is a seeking after 'new connectedness' and 'reconstructed identity' (p. 23) separate from the more instrumental connectedness of the network society. He follows Raymond Barglow here on the network society's total war 'upon notions of sovereignty and self-sufficiency that have provided an

ideological anchoring for individual identity since Greek philosophers'. For Castells, this crisis is not just in the West but also in the
East, and is as much based upon *enhanced* notions of identity
becoming so abstract within informationalism (p. 24). Thus European nationalisms and racisms both arise against the backdrop of
the abstraction of the European Union. This is a resistant logic (for
better or worse) which is one of 'excluding the excluders'.

It may seem that Castells is resisting the information age himself
but this is far from the case. He is attempting to see it for what it
is, and, at the same time, gesture towards 'a plural perspective that
brings together cultural identity, global networking, and multidi-
mensional politics' (p. 27). Here he points to a culture of ' "creative
destruction" accelerated to the speed of the opto-electronic circuits
that process its signals' (p. 215).

> It is a culture, indeed, but a culture of the ephemeral, a culture of each
> strategic decision, a patchwork of experiences and interests, rather than
> a charter of rights and obligations. . . . Any attempt at crystallizing the
> position in the network as a cultural code in a particular time and space
> sentences the network to obsolescence . . . (pp. 214–15).

This passage introduces concepts central to Castells's understanding of contemporary relations between culture and technology.
These are the 'culture of real virtuality', the 'space of flows' and
'timeless time'.

The culture of real virtuality is a concept that readers of this book
should be familiar with by now. Castells follows others in claiming
the uniqueness of the current unfinished development of multimedia, hypertext and interactive networks that merge all previously separate forms of human communication. There is a 'new
interaction between the two sides of the brain, machines, and social
contexts'. In this context the mass media lose their hold, and are
replaced by interaction, even if this is within the scope of services
provided by larger and larger corporations. An 'interactive society'
(p. 385) is emerging in which a 'symbolic environment' (p. 394) is
extended into the whole of human existence. For Castells, there is
nothing new about a 'symbolic environment', and there has never
been any separation between reality as we communicate it, and the
'symbolic representation' by which it is communicated. He claims,
however, that what is new about the network society is not 'its
inducement of virtual reality but the construction of real virtuality'. This is basically the idea that media systems totally submerge

us 'in a virtual image setting' (p. 404). 'Make-believe is belief in the making' (p. 406) and this whole process of dwelling within real virtuality gives rise to a new material basis for the experience of space and time.

Space is no longer (for the elite at least) a 'space of places'. It is a 'space of flows'. The 'local' becomes portable and is no longer attached to a specific geography or cultural setting.

This in turn leads to the development of a new mode of collective life – the 'informational city' (p. 429) that is 'not a form, but a process . . . characterized by the structural domination of the space of flows'. This space of flows is more organized, however, than it might seem. It possesses 'nodes and hubs' (p. 443), for example, by which Castells means that the space of flows is not quite as placeless as it might seem. On top of this such nodes and hubs are 'hierarchically organized' and the network is not nearly as egalitarian as some of its proponents would like to think. Castells also refers to the new elites that concurrently live out their cosmopolitan, ahistorical and transnational existence and at the same time preserve their own social cohesion (have their own sense of *place* as people). This is backed up by such things as 'the very material barrier of real-estate pricing' (p. 446).

Castells's notion of 'timeless time' implies the end of history. Past, present and future 'can be programmed to interact with each other in the same message' (p. 406). It is not just that time as traditionally understood is erased, or that things happen at the speed of light, that is, instantaneously, in the new regime of timeless time. It is that this gives time a new flexibility. Timeless time is a time in which one is not longer bound by history in the way that one was – by a personal or cultural history, by the time it takes to deliver a letter or a package, by the working week. It is this 'supersession of time' (p. 467) that is at the heart of the new productivity of the network enterprise. Time, following the seeming end of historical consequence and chronology, becomes infinitely flexible. Time 'is managed as a resource' (p. 468). For Virilio, time is 'compressed'. Castells is pointing to more: time is also 'processed'.

As with the space of flows and space of places, timeless time is only available to some, and there is a sense in which all must live within 'time discipline, biological time, and socially determined sequencing' (p. 495) to a greater or lesser extent, just as we must all return to the space of places every now and again. In these relations lie all the paradoxes of living in the network society.

Castells differentiates between two kinds of labour in the new system. The elites and their self-directed flexibility typify one kind – that which he labels 'self-programmable labor'. Everyone else performs as 'generic labor' (p. 372). Generic labourers, even though they may work for the space of flows, have little flexibility and instead are 'assigned a given task' (this *includes* many who work *within* the information industries). They tend to live in the space of places and are the more subject to historical condition and consequence. What is more they are now treated with the same systemized processes as machines.

Underlying all this is the dominance of the global, and information technology-driven, financial markets. Diverse levels of access to these markets account for new forms of social division, and the fate of any contemporary concern depends on these markets which become the 'nerve center of informational capitalism' (p. 374). The crucial point is, however, that the movements of these nerve centres are no longer ruled by the old market logic, despite the continued bleating of free marketeers. Such a logic is currently being erased by

> ... a combination of computer-enacted strategic maneuvers, crowd psychology from multicultural sources, and unexpected turbulences, caused by greater and greater degrees of complexity in the interaction between capital flows on a global scale (p. 374)

One reason for this is simply that the computerized global market simply moves too fast for the rest of the market to keep up with it. Social inequity is dramatically increased and the nation-state loses most of its legitimacy, perhaps to the new 'network state' (p. 378). Government loses any power beyond a certain 'influence'. Full power is transferred to the network itself and becomes somewhat 'immaterial' yet 'real'. Whole peoples are excluded from these markets in what Castells calls the 'black holes of informational capitalism' (p. 376). What results in the culture of real virtuality is a battle over the connections of perceptions.

Castells is arguing here for the enhanced power of culture, of symbolic manipulation, as this now forms the basis of capital. We need to think this through a little more as it is important to realize that this means that all cultural events are now in the circuits of the network society. Enlightenment itself is put to work in the market place, and the result is perhaps what Castells calls 'informed bewilderment' (p. 389), whichever way we move. Yet in another sense this means that the enlightenment continues for Castells, although through rather murky waters. The challenge for him will to be to realize its promise and to close the current 'extraordinary gap between our technological overdevelopment and our social under-development' (p. 390), although he does not believe in intellectuals giving a prescription to the world as to how this is to be done. We shall tentatively suggest some concepts with which to navigate these murky if open cultural waters in the next and final chapter. Here we ask the question of what kind of community, if any, can find its place within contemporary culture.

CHAPTER 8

Living with the Virtual

Asked recently how he saw the future, Matt Groenig, creator of *The Simpsons* and *Futurama*, said that the 'future is always presented as monolithic – people all dressed in the same spandex. I think it will have far more variety than the present. In the future everything is under construction. There are lots of loose wires sticking out of the walls' (Kelly and Groenig 1999: 116). In this chapter we will conclude by asking some questions about the variety of the future in the light of culture's new relations to technology. In accordance with our survey approach to issues in culture and technology, we will also give accounts of some thinkers who provide guidelines for living with the virtual. Crucial to these guidelines will be a brief account of community in the increasingly networked society.

Machines and the three ecologies

We begin with Guattari's essay, 'On Machines' (1995), to sum up the dynamic approach to culture and technology we have tended to favour. Although complex, this essay plays a series of variations on three things. Firstly, everything is interactive. Guattari is a theorist of networked, 'outside' thought. Secondly, this means that everything is implicated, ultimately, in the same shifting field of what he terms complexity. Thirdly, everything is a machine, in the sense that everything is involved in assemblages that form and unform within this complexity. Guattari assumes that we now live increasingly in a climate in which these 'machinic' issues can no longer be ignored, despite the fact that often 'the machine is treated as anathema and . . . there prevails the idea that technology is leading us to a situation of inhumanity and of rupture with any kind of ethical project' (p. 8).

Guattari does not define the modern machine as a threat

but instead as something that occurs as a crossroad, a point of trans-fer and exchange, an 'interface' or 'hypertext'. In other words, for Guattari the machine is interaction itself. The machine is therefore a very diverse object in his thought, if we can say that it is an object at all. For him, even our thoughts are interfaces, and our interfaces are ways of thinking. In general the machine is a concept much broader than technology, although they are important parts of the machinic. When technologies open out to seemingly non-technological objects and processes this leads us to what he calls 'machinic agencements'. Such machinic systems, as evolving systems, possess a new kind of collective agency. In the process this machinic evolution constantly creates new ways of existing, or what Guattari calls new 'existential territories'.

This may seem counter-intuitive and indeed it does contradict much of our normal thinking through of these issues. A more regular way of differentiating between technologies and life is that technologies are 'allopoietic' – they depend on processes from outside of themselves in order to survive, be 'born' and 'die' and so on. As we saw in Chapter 5, living things, on the other hand, are normally considered as 'autopoietic'. That is, they can operate themselves, be born and die themselves and are somewhat self-contained. Guattari, however, breaks down this opposition. He points out that there is always a relation between the two, and that most assemblages contain both. Allopoiesis relates to the side of a system in which everything is interactive – everything, even life, depends on all kinds of processes from outside in order to keep going – everything has a certain relation to alterity – to other things. Autopoiesis suggests that every system somehow maintains some sense of processual core – its own way of taking part in the process, which of course changes over time. The best example we can give here (following some Buddhists) is of the flame of a candle. It is never the same flame and it is always the same flame. Or, consider the Internet. It is never the same Internet from day to day. The people on it change, and the technologies and software involved change – from the first Netscape to Microsoft explorer to Java envi-ronments. Yet we still know what the Internet is. It has autopoeitic and allopoietic processes. Another example is of course, all of us, and the communities in which are involved. We – and our com-munities – are all autopoeitic and allopoietic machines.

The consequence is that 'we' are all, with our technologies, caught in complexity. In response, we live lives that fluctuate between complex organization and seeming chaos. However, what we call chaos is only, as Guattari points out, a level of hypercomplexity with which we have not yet managed to deal. Dealing with such levels of hypercomplexity, and giving us more effective ways of producing ways of existing within them is one of the driving forces behind technological development. Of course, as we more and more deal with complex processes, we no longer exist in the same way as before; as 100 years ago, or sometimes as we did yesterday. Our 'universes of reference' are constantly changing. The fact that we cannot avoid this change has been one of the major themes of this book. Guattari suggests that we should accept that today we have what he calls highly interactive 'partial subjectivities' – or partial senses of self – and that even these are dynamic rather than fixed. Guattari writes, for example, that 'Learning to drive . . . is a crucial moment for the psychotic, who may be totally incapable of having a conversation but is perfectly capable of driving a car' (1995: 12).

Guattari also asks about other forms of productive interactions with technology. For example, he thinks that

> . . . technological machines for information and communication operate at the heart of human subjectivity – not only within its memories and intelligence, but also within its sensibilities, affects and unconscious fantasies (1996: 194).

For Guattari this means that we have to take much more account of machines as the technosocial processes through which our senses of self and communities are formed and broken apart. What is more, he points out that thinking of machines as part of the process of constructing subjectivity and community means that we are talking about at least two very different types of sign systems that form the basis for such communities. First, there are sign systems that mean something – that signify. Second, and perhaps less obviously, there are those which just *operate*. The first signify community but the others often literally plug us into it – they operate rather than just communicate. Think of traffic lights, or the automatic bank teller and the pin number. Often they do not 'mean' anything but they produce community and subjectivity just the same. The broader implication here is that different media operate differently to produce the sense of self and community. They place us within the communities of the cinema or of the television set, of the chat room or email. We experience different senses of community – and experience different possibilities of community –

through being attached to a particular machine, on the Internet, in front of the enormous screen of the Imax cinema, or on the telephone.

Guattari gives an ethical dimension to this when he comments that:

> The machinic production of subjectivity can work for the better as for the worse. At best, it is creation – the invention of new universes of reference; and at its worst, it is the mind-numbing mass mediatization . . . (1996: 194).

As a response to the mind-numbing mass mediatization, Guattari significantly rewrites the notion of ecology. He suggests social and mental ecologies much broader than, if including, the rainforests and so forth we would normally think of in terms of ecology. He suggests in fact, not one ecology but three, and situates the ambiguous question of how we are coping with technological advance within the interaction of these three ecologies (1989). They echo cybernetic pioneer Gregory Bateson's earlier notion of three 'cybernetic or homeostatic systems: the individual human organism, the human society, and the larger ecosystem' (1972: 446). The first of Guattari's three ecologies is the environment. The second of the ecologies is the subject or the self. Thirdly there is the ecology of the socius.

This brings us to the central ecological question for this concluding chapter: what do we wish to conserve in our new configuring of the world? And here we do not mean what do we wish to preserve in formaldehyde. We mean a more dynamic sense of ecology – in the sense of which relations, possibility or degree of complexity of relation, we wish to conserve, or even enhance. Might we, in this case, talk of a series of diversities that we might want to conserve as well as biodiversity? We might talk of 'ideodiversity', a diversity of ideas. We might talk of 'technodiversity', a culture of constant technical invention and adaptation, not a monolithic technodeterminism where one solution 'fits' all. We might talk of 'communodiversity', or a diversity of communities and possible communities (De Certeau's 'community in the plural' or Agamben's 'coming community'). This implies a dynamic work of conservation – of communities, ideas and technical solutions as much as of old growth forests.

Verena Conley, developing Guattari's ideas, points out that although technological advances have enabled an unparalleled destruction of the environment, they have also enabled us to see the planet as a whole as never before (the famous images of the earth from space, for example). It is no longer 'us' versus 'the world'. It is us becoming with the world. This is a becoming – as Conley writes – 'in a nature redefined in terms of fluctuations, patterns, and randomness rather than of Newtonian immobility and timelessness' (1993: 80).

Third nature and the natural contract

McKenzie Wark points out that thinking these kinds of 'environmental' questions through will allow us a degree of sophistication as regards the employment and analysis of new technologies themselves. He argues that they will, in Guattari's terms, extend 'ecosophy' to that which Wark calls 'third nature'.

For Wark there was initially 'first nature' just as found or perhaps used in agriculture. Then there was 'second nature' – nature converted to a social space as in cities. This is nature conquered. It is nature operated upon and made abstract for the first time by the technologies such as railways, shipping, 'built environments' (1994: 99). We know that there are a series of ecologies involved in second nature – ask any architect. Third nature is a move to the more abstract flow of the instantaneous 'media vector' (ibid.). We have a nature in which the way we model it or overlay it with media vectors has a direct effect upon it. Our media impact upon the world as they simulate it. We live quite literally in an information landscape. For him third nature has recently become capable of organizing itself as a biodiverse eco-information system.

Michel Serres (1995) pushes this perhaps the other way, with a more critical view of technology. He suggests a 'natural contract' that will parallel and exceed the 'social contract' that binds us into a society that is relatively cooperative. Serres thinks that the social contract has come at a price. He points out, for example, that we have lost contact with the elements through our attempted technological control of the environment. He also points out that the complexities of the changes that our use of technologies brings about within the environment will paradoxically bring us back into contact with the elements quicker than we expect (in global warming and atmospheric pollution and so on). Crucially, for Serres this loss of contact with, and damage of, weather systems is not just industrial, material pollution. It is also 'cultural pollution'

(p. 31). Such damage results in part from our loss of important elements of community that arose from being in touch with the elements.

Serres ties this into cybernetics, which for him has not just been invented in the last 50 years. It has instead returned as a model for the natural contract, in an echo of the job of the person at the helm of a ship, trying to guide it through a series of difficult constraints (such as the weather). So Serres adds nature as an important part of our collective life, with 'rights' of its own. To repair our communities, we shall now have to rely more and more on a 'physiopolitics' (p. 44) – a series of contracts between the social and the environment, rather than attempts to dominate the latter.

Another form of 'new contractual' thinking focuses on the challenges within the social new relations to machines. This is found in Gray's ten-point 'Cyborg Bill of Rights' (2001: 27–9). None of these rights can currently be taken for granted. These include the right to freedom of: travel, whether 'virtual or in the flesh', 'electronic speech', 'electronic privacy', information and peace. Gray also suggests a 'freedom of consciousness', the ability to manipulate one's own consciousness rather than have it manipulated. There is also a 'right to life' by which he means that a cyborg citizen's body should not be unreasonably invaded by technology but that such citizens should be allowed to modify their own body as they will if it does not harm others. Likewise, there is a 'right to death' by choice if no one else is harmed. Perhaps most interestingly in terms of community, Gray defends the right of the cyborg citizen to 'determine their own sexual and gender orientations' (by which he means the full multitude of possibilities) or take on family life and/or parenthood 'and other forms of alliance' in whatever permutations they wish.

Perhaps the crucial question here and elsewhere, if we are to reach an age of multiple interactions, and new contracts or rights, rather than mass mediation, is one of what Guattari calls 'existential territory' (1996: 196). This refers to the physical and mental space that we are able to create for our own existence. In short, challenging received ideas is perhaps more important than ever. In this, Guattari once gain echoes Bateson's consideration of consciousness as primarily a component involved in the coupling of diverse ecological systems in all their natural, social or technical glory. This suggests once again that our sense of 'self in the world' allows us to participate in highly complex procedures, not to sit as a closed 'thing'. It allows us to insert ourselves into such complex physical domains as forests but also into activities as abstract as mathematics or music, for example. Subjectively, while we are doing a sum our self is part of a very complex world of numbers. While we sing a tune or play an instrument we are participating in a very complex and constantly redeveloping series of harmonies, acoustic patterns. In all such complex occurrences we are not living out a 'frozen subjectivity' but participating in a highly contingent process – a 'universe of reference' brought together only for that moment (p. 200).

It is through such participations that senses of self and community mutate and expand (thus dance and popular music as one set of refrains for the formation and mutation of existential territories). Obviously the possibilities of such mutations and expansions are enhanced by many recent technologies, as are the possibilities of forming more and more unique worlds – such as when one controls one's own 'media'. Wark points to the people of Yuendumu in central Australia broadcasting their own television as a good example of this subjective mutation of a technology in order to conserve an existential territory (1993: 101). The new cheapness and portability of visual production media in general are another case in point, as is the ability for more and more individuals and groups to broadcast their own sounds and images throughout portions of the network society.

Shifting communities and 'cyberdemocracy'

Echoing all the above thinkers, Howard Rheingold writes:

> Not only do I inhabit my virtual communities . . . my virtual communities also inhabit my life. I've been colonized; my sense of family at the most fundamental level has been virtualized (1994: 10).

This implies an increasingly dispersed, globalized and at the same time localized community and politics. Community is now often, as the term says, 'glocal'. Bulletin board systems, Internet relay chat, multi-user domains, email, the Web, are instantly everywhere in general, and anywhere in particular that you want to be. Community is everywhere, but in the sense in which it is normally understood, it is also nowhere, and this is problematic.

For some, this could in fact spell disaster. The relatively pessimistic theorist Neil Postman (1992) describes a form of 'technopoly' where technocracy moves to a heightened state. In technocracy, technology and tradition coexist in an uneasy tension, but they do coexist. However, in technopoly,

> ... one of those thought-worlds disappears. Technopoly eliminates alternatives to itself. . . . It does not make them illegal. It does not make them immoral. It does not even make them unpopular. It makes them invisible and therefore irrelevant. And it does so by redefining what we mean by religion, by art, by family, by politics, by history, by truth, by privacy, by intelligence, so that our definitions fit its new requirements. Technopoly, in other words, is totalitarian technocracy (p. 48).

Postman is no doubt right about the fundamental redefinition of the basic processes of community. We would suggest, however, that power is not a one-way street and 'technopoly' may be too simple a concept with which to approach these complex issues. For example, we have seen how the rather confused use of technological strength by the military has only highlighted a more general cultural confusion about the effects of technology. This confusion has only contributed to the undermining of the nation-state. This in turn has suggested at least the possibility of a new kind of community that can arise out of electronic culture and, as the examples of the Yuendumu people or even sampling in music show, the past is often reworked in these new communal expressions rather than thrown away.

Others might shift register and suggest, against Postman, that what we need is a community that deliberately exceeds the current definition of its inhabitants, a society that exceeds its certified (password possessing) members, a politics that exceeds traditional politicians and political machinery. Giorgio Agamben asks:

> What could be the politics ... of a being whose community is not mediated by any condition of belonging (being red, being Italian, being communist) nor by the simple absence of conditions, . . . but by belonging itself? (1993: 85).

There is of course no definitive answer to this question, but Agamben sees a 'herald' of the answer in the figure of the protester in Tiananmen Square in Beijing. This suggests a powerful sacrifice by those who forgo state organization for alternative communal networks (1998: 181). Yet it is perhaps neither always so tragic nor exceptional. For many, the question of how one belongs to a community without identity, though difficult, is an everyday question.

Douglas Rushkoff gives a similar diagnosis of the situation to Postman, but Rushkoff blames traditional institutions themselves. As he imagines the twenty-first century:

> The cultural institutions on which we have grown dependent... appear to have crumbled under their own weight. ... Without having migrated one centimetre, we have nonetheless travelled further than any generation in history (1997: 1).

One response to the crumbling of traditional institutions is to head for cyberdemocracy – a heavily mediated democracy which could extend the participation of citizens in government like never before. Others only see the increasing 'commodification of the public sphere' (Rheingold 1994: 279). Is commodification incompatible with electronic democracy? Is electronic democracy itself incompatible with democracy as we have known it until now?

Mark Poster (1997) questions whether the concept of the public sphere is in fact still valid in the face of new forms of social power. He thinks that the Internet in particular challenges nearly all our 'existing theoretical approaches' to democracy. For a start, the Internet for Poster is not just another enabling technology, but itself a new social space. Secondly, he follows John Hartley in suggesting that the media 'are the public sphere' (p. 208). Poster thinks that the old notion of the sacrifice of the public sphere to the 'media' has always been a false one, and that the Internet demonstrates this. Yet all this problematizes the very idea of the public/private divide that so much political theory is based upon. Poster asks whether individuals who never meet but communicate through 'pixels on screens' can be considered to be involved in public or private communication. In another context, Steven Jones points out that such communication is, at one level, far from public, but rather 'intensely local' (1995: 12). For Poster this highlights 'the fiction of the democratic community of full human presence' that has for some time hidden the fact that 'political discourse has long been mediated by electronic machines' (1997: 211). This suggests that new technology interventions into democratic and communal life could solve long-standing problems, not just create new ones. This is because they

> ... enable new forms of decentralized dialogue and create new combinations of human–machine assemblages, new individual and collective 'voices', 'specters', 'interactivities' which are the building blocks of political formations and groupings (p. 211).

Here we are again in the realm of Guattari's ecologies. For Poster, these 'interactivities', precisely in replacing autonomous agents with contingent 'ongoing dialogues' (p. 212), give more democracy not less. One cannot participate in communal processes without interaction, but one is not immediately constrained by a supposed fixed form, such as the 'gender and ethnic traces inscribed in face-to-face communication'. In this way all forms of cultural production are 'radically decentralized' along with the media that were often used in the past to impose old-fashioned and outmoded democratic forms. Moreover, one gets one's democracy not once in a while when one votes, but every time one joins in the communal discourse. And 'citizens' are not restricted to just one community and one communal identity, but are somewhat more mobile, more plural.

There are problems in these ideas. Steven Jones writes that the chaos that results from such radical decentralization and multiplication of community inevitably cries out for new forms of control. Yet he still thinks there are advantages to computer-mediated communities (CMCs). For a start, they are a 'form of efficient social contact' that permit 'us to customize our social contacts from fragmented communities' (1995: 16), thus again solving some of the problems older media have perhaps helped to create. CMCs, however, again imply a different kind of community in that they are about putting together fragments, and rarely operate to 'produce solidarity' in any broad sense (p. 22). In fact, the very nature of fragmented community means that 'computers just as easily create boundaries and hierarchies' (p. 30) as new freedoms. It is perhaps with the politics of the fragments that we can conclude, in a return to Jean-François Lyotard's account of the *petit récit* or little narrative.

Computers, knowledge and the *petit récit*

Jean-François Lyotard's 1979 account of what was to become the contemporary computer-based world in *The Postmodern Condition* seems perhaps more relevant today than ever, even if the postmodern itself may have run its course. We shall finish our survey of culture and technology with Lyotard's diagnoses of the major cultural breaks involved, and with the hope he sees within technological change.

Lyotard is particularly interested in the status of knowledge within culture. He starts from the premise that a computerized society will use knowledge differently. In fact, even the rules for what counts as knowledge will be different in such a society, along with the way in which it is possible to speak about knowledge. Accompanying this will be an emphasis upon sciences more and more premised on questions of how to speak about knowledge. From these new sciences (such as cybernetics) flow new technologies which are based upon a new *performative* understanding of language (as in computer programming languages that make things happen). Lyotard gave a long list of these developments when he first wrote *The Postmodern Condition*, pointing out that these were developments going back 40 years, roughly to the Second World War. This list remains largely pertinent and convincing today and includes '. . . theories of linguistics, problems of communication and cybernetics, modern theories of algebra and informatics, computers and their languages, problems of translation and the search for areas of compatibility among computer languages, problems of information storage and data banks, telematics and the perfection of intelligent terminals . . .' (pp. 3–4). As Lyotard points out, this list is not exhaustive but 'the facts speak for themselves'. Lyotard discusses the way in which such an enhanced technical determination of knowledge has in fact undermined more traditional forms of knowledge. In particular, he famously discusses the crisis in the grand narratives surrounding knowledge that maintained an idea of progress within modernity. We discussed this in Chapter 2.

This crisis can seem somewhat nihilist but it can be looked at as a kind of maturing of culture. In fact, Lyotard has no desire to mourn the loss of these narratives. This is because this loss indicates a release from some of the social fantasies that these grand narratives maintained.

There is, however, a concurrent crisis in the legitimation and justification of science and technology that had employed these grand narratives. If these narratives are not there, it is harder to justify our scientific research and development beyond profit and utility. Moreover, narratives generally – as cultural elements that hold the sense of societies together through space and time – are now in a state of collision, fragmentation, destruction and constant recreation.

All this leads to a series of societies – and social acts – based not upon grand narratives but 'little narratives' (*petits récits*) (p. 60). This idea refers to narratives that function specifically in specific times and specific places. They may even function in apparent contradiction and paradox at times but they do allow us a little cultural space. One way of summing all this up is that what we lose on the grand scale we gain on the smaller scale. On the other hand, forms of social control can also perform better at the smaller, local level, largely due to the increased specificity of technologies of social control. It is this increased performativity of social controls at the specific, everyday level of culture, not the loss of the grand narratives, that worries Lyotard.

This brings us to technology. Lyotard once again points out that new technologies affect both the production and transmission of knowledge. Knowledge itself cannot be expected to remain unchanged in this situation. This is one in which, to count as information, all knowledge must be able to be translated into languages that can be read and written by computers. Computers and accompanying machines control everything and with this comes a 'certain logic' (p. 4). This logic justifies some statements about what we know above others (purely because these statements are more likely to function and circulate in a computer-controlled society).

This means that knowledge is made exterior to the 'knower'. There is no need to remember things if everything is archived on your computer or on the Internet – and no need, incidentally, for professors (p. 53). When knowledge is made exterior in this way it also becomes more of a commodity, and as a commodity that can be bought and sold it 'ceases to be an end in itself'. Knowledge is then a power sold to the highest bidder in this situation – yet you literally cannot operate without it.

International corporations buy the research and inventions of many nations. Knowledge becomes, as recent events in the software, video and music industries have demonstrated, 'mobile and subject to piracy' (p. 6). Subsequently, the production of knowledge begins to respond to its own use within these new markets. There is a kind of feedback mechanism between the performance of knowledge and its production and distribution. Society as a whole, as something in which knowledge circulates according to various feedback mechanisms that measure the deployment of knowledge, becomes one vast complex cybernetic system. The

> . . . true goal of the system, the reason it programs itself like a computer, is the optimization of the global relation between input and output – in other words, performativity (p. 11).

This is a performativity of the machine that does not sit well with oppositional thinking (the kind that inspires the revolutionary grand narrative). Unlike revolutionaries or philosophers opposing the injustices or irrationality of society, this new performativity is quite happy to mix and match apparent contradictions, as long as the system performs.

The positive side of this is that, even if we are all more and more '"nodal points" of specific communication circuits' (p. 12) through which messages pass, we are not without power. Lyotard argues two crucial things here. The first is that not even the least privileged, once brought into the circuit of what he calls the various language games of the new communications networks, 'is ever entirely powerless over the messages' that pass through the points at which we find ourselves. In fact, even the system itself needs us to make unexpected 'moves' in these games or it will wind down through a kind of natural attrition.

It is the same with the information economy. This also feeds on new patterns and in the process sets up a kind of freedom of movement within it in order to gain access to the new. This freedom of movement works in a complex way as far as our own freedom in relation to the information economy is concerned. Lyotard envisages this as a freedom that enables us to establish our own performativity within the system. At the same time of course we place our own little narratives (*petits récits*) within the system, although these are as likely to disrupt the system's performativity as to support it. If they support it however, Lyotard is dubious. Lyotard raises the example of 'knowing how to live' (p. 18) which can, if we are not careful, become a purely performative, technical matter. A simple example might be the carefully programmed and optimized life: going to the gym, eating carefully nutritionally prepared foods heated in the microwave, making the best use of time management and electronic office assistants at work (all carefully debited from our credit card).

The consequences throughout society are that anything that does not perform tends to be excluded in an increasingly computer-controlled environment. Any kind of research that does not at least take up the language of performance is 'doomed'. This also affects education into knowledge. Education is not about finding one's own place, or self-expression, or even about the furthering of general speculative knowledge. It is about performance, and being about performance it is about becoming an expert. It is this, not just the prevalence of computers, which explains the expanded opening of education to the technical and anything to do with computers. Society needs experts, and *technical* experts for the information age in particular, because society now defines itself as technologically and performatively bound. Of course, this leads to a society controlled by technocrats who assume that society is best operated under the conditions of the optimal performance brought about by technological control. These technocrats 'cannot trust what society designates as its needs' (p. 63) by itself but rather tie in society's needs to the efficient functioning of its machines. Here is the crucial point. Do we want society thought about as a total system that can be optimized, regardless of the specific and sometimes contradictory or paradoxical needs and desires of the members of that society? Or, do we want society thought about as somewhat more plural, contradictory, fragmented and paradoxical than that? Lyotard obviously thinks the latter.

How do we get to the latter? Again the battle with – and within – computers is crucial. Computers could become what he calls the 'dream' technologies for optimizing the performance of the 'system' despite any deviations within it (the film *Gattaca* represents this idea forcefully). Computers could also, however, provide the information necessary for individuals and groups to decide on the best tactics for 'imaginative invention' (p. 60). How is maximum information to be given to the public? Lyotard's solution in 1979 was simple. It was to 'give the public free access to the memory and data banks' (p. 67). Then the hard work could begin. Several critics think this perhaps too idealistic. There will not necessarily be clear dividing lines between the *petits récits* and corporate networks. Even if simplistic, however, Lyotard looks to a creative future rather than a mourning of the past. He calls to us to use technology not to become more utilitarian or profitable, but rather to become more sophisticated, imaginative and inventive in the way we live.

Bibliography

Agamben, Giorgio (1993) *The Coming Community* trans. Michael Hardt, Minneapolis: University of Minnesota Press

Agamben, Giorgio (1998) *Homo Sacer: Sovereign Power and Bare Life* trans. Daniel Heller-Roazen, Stanford, Calif.: Stanford University Press

Amelunxen, Hubertus v. (1995) 'Photography after Photography: the Terror of the Body in Digital Space' in *Photography after Photography* Munich: Verlag der Kunst

Amerika, Mark (2000) 'What in the World Wide Web is Happening to Writing?' at http://trace.ntu.ac.uk/incubation/level2/speakers/salon.htm, accessed 15 November 2001

Anderson, Benedict (1991) *Imagined Communities* 2nd edn, London: Verso

Ballard, J. G. (1975) 'Introduction to the French Edition of *Crash*' (1974) London: Panther

Barglow, Raymond (1994) *The Crisis of the Self in the Age of Information* London: Routledge

Barlow, John Perry (1994) 'The Economy of Ideas (Everything You Know about Intellectual Property is Wrong)' *Wired* March: 85–90 and 126–129

Barrett, William (1978) *The Illusion of Technique: a Search for Meaning in a Technological Civilisation* New York: Doubleday

Barthes, Roland (1977) *Image–Music–Text* ed. and trans. Stephen Heath, London: Fontana/Collins

Bateson, Gregory (1972) *Steps Towards an Ecology of Mind: Collected Essays in Anthropology, Psychiatry, Evolution and Epistemology* London: Intertext

Baudrillard, Jean (1983) *Simulations* trans. Paul Foss, Paul Patton and Philip Beitchman, New York: Semiotext(e)

Baudrillard, Jean (1988) 'L'Extase de la Communication' trans. Bernard Schutze and Caroline Schutze, *Mediamatic* **3** (2): 81–5

Baudrillard, Jean (1994) *Simulacra and Simulation* Ann Arbor: University of Michigan Press

Baudrillard, Jean (1995) *The Gulf War Did not Take Place* trans. Paul Patton, Sydney: Power

Bauman, Zygmunt (1997) *Postmodernity and its Discontents* London: Polity

Bell, Daniel (1976) *The Cultural Contradictions of Capitalism* New York: Basic Books

Benjamin, Walter (1970) *Illuminations* London: Fontana

Bergson, Henri (1911) *Matter and Memory* trans. Nancy Margaret Paul and W. Scott Palmer, London: Allen and Unwin

Berman, Marshall (1983) *All That is Solid Melts into Air: the Experience of Modernity* London: Verso

Bernadelli, Andrea and Blasi, Giulio (1995) 'Introduction. Semiotics and the Effects-of-Media-Change-Research Programmes' *Versus* 72: 3–28

Bettig, Ronald V. (1996) *Copyrighting Culture: the Political Economy of Intellectual Property* Boulder: Westview Press

Bolter, Jay David and Grusin, Richard (1999) *Remediation: Understanding New Media* Cambridge, Mass.: MIT Press

Brosnan, Mark (1998) *Technophobia* London: Routledge

Bruno, Giuliana (1990) 'Ramble City: Postmodernism and *Blade Runner*' in Kuhn, Annette (ed.) *Alien Zone* London: Verso

Bukatman, Scott (1990) 'Who Programs You? The Science Fiction of the Spectacle' in Kuhn, Annette (ed.) *Alien Zone* London: Verso

Bukatman, Scott (1993) *Terminal Identity: the Virtual Subject in Postmodern Science Fiction* Durham, NC: Duke University Press

Bukatman, Scott (1997) *Blade Runner* London: BFI

Cameron, Andy (1991) 'Introduction' in *Digital Dialogues* special edition of *Ten8* 2 (2)

Castells, Manuel (1999) 'Flows, Networks and Identities: a Critical Theory of the Informational Society' in Castells, Manuel, Flecha, Ramón, Freire, Paulo, Giroux, Henry A., Macedo, Donaldo and Willis, Paul *Critical Education in the New Information Age* New York: Roman and Littlefield

Castells, Manuel (2000) *The Rise of the Network Society* 2nd edn, Oxford: Blackwell

Chesher, Chris (1996) 'CD-ROM Multimedia's Identity Crisis' *Media International Australia* 81, August

Clark, Andy (1997) *Being There: Putting Brain, Body, and World Together Again* Cambridge, Mass.: MIT Press

Conley, Verena Andermatt (1993) 'Eco-subjects' in Conley, Verena Andermatt (ed.) *Rethinking Technologies* Minneapolis: University of Minnesota Press

Constable, Catherine (1999) 'Becoming the Monster's Mother: Morphologies of Identity in the *Alien* Series' in Kuhn, Annette (ed.) *Alien Zone II* London: Verso

Creed, Barbara (1990) '*Alien* and the Monstrous-Feminine' in Kuhn, Annette (ed.) *Alien Zone* London: Verso

Crick, Francis (1994) *The Astonishing Hypothesis: the Scientific Search for the Soul* New York: Maxwell Macmillan International

Cubitt, Sean (1998) *Digital Aesthetics* London: Sage

Cyberarts99 (1999) *Cyberarts99* Linz, Austria: Prix Ars Electronica

Davis, Erik (1993) 'Techgnosis, Magic, Memory, and the Angels of Information' in Dery, Mark *Flame Wars*, special edition of *The South Atlantic Quarterly* 92 (4), Fall: 585–616

Davis, Erik (1999) *TechGnosis* London: Serpent's Tail

Dawkins, Richard (1989) [1976] *The Selfish Gene* Oxford: Oxford University Press

Debord, Guy (1994) [1967] *The Society of the Spectacle* trans. Donald Nicholson-Smith, New York: Zone

De Certeau, Michel (1998) *Culture in the Plural* trans. Tom Conley, Minneapolis: University of Minnesota Press

De Landa, Manuel (1991) *War in the Age of Intelligent Machines* New York: Zone

De Landa, Manuel (1997) *A Thousand Years of Nonlinear History* New York: Swerve

Deleuze, Gilles (1993) *The Fold: Leibniz and the Baroque* trans. Tom Conley, Minneapolis: University of Minnesota Press

Deleuze, Gilles (1995) *Negotiations* trans. Martin Joughin, New York: Columbia University Press

Deleuze, Gilles and Guattari, Felix (1987) *A Thousand Plateaus: Capitalism and Schizophrenia* trans. Brian Massumi, Minneapolis: University of Minnesota Press

Dennett, Daniel (1991) *Consciousness Explained* Boston: Little, Brown and Company

Dery, Mark (1996) *Escape Velocity: Cyberculture at the End of the Century* New York: Grove Press

DJ Spooky (1999) Interview *Revolver* Sydney, June: 47

Drexler, Eric (1986) *Engines of Creation: the Coming Era of Nanotechnology* New York: Doubleday

Drexler, Eric (2001) 'Machine/Phase Nanotechnology' *Scientific American* **285** (3), September: 66–7

Dreyfus, Hubert (1996) 'The Current Relevance of Merleau-Ponty's Phenomenology of Embodiment' *The Electronic Journal of Analytic Philosophy*, **4**, Spring, accessed 3 July 2000

Druckrey, Tim (1996) 'Fatal Vision' in Amelunxen, Hubertus v., Rotzer, Florian and Iglhaut, Stefan (eds) *Photography after Photography* Amsterdam: G + B Arts

Edelman, Gerald (1992) *Brilliant Air, Bright Fire: On the Matter of the Mind* London: Penguin

Egan, Greg (1999) *Diaspora* New York: HarperCollins

Eisenstein, Elizabeth (1979) *The Printing Press as an Agent of Change: Communications and Cultural Transformations in Early-Modern Europe* New York: Cambridge University Press

Elfstrom, Gerard (1997) *New Challenges for Political Philosophy* London: Macmillan

Ellul, Jacques (1964) *The Technological Society* London: Jonathan Cape

Eno, Brian (1996) *A Year with Swollen Appendices* London: Faber

Eno, Brian and Kelly, Kevin (1995) 'Eno: Gossip is Philosophy' *Wired* May: 146–51 and 204–9

Everard, Jerry (2000) *Virtual States: the Internet and the Boundaries of the Nation-State* London: Routledge

Feather, John (1998) *The Information Society: a Study of Continuity and Change* London: Library Association

Featherstone, Mike and Burrows, Roger (eds) (1995) *Cyberspace/Cyberbodies/Cyberpunk* London: Sage

Feenberg, Andrew (1991) *Critical Theory of Technology* New York: Oxford University Press

Foucault, Michel (1973) [1966] *The Order of Things* New York: Vintage

Foucault, Michel (1978) *The History of Sexuality: an Introduction* trans. Robert Hurley, Middlesex: Penguin

Foucault, Michel (1980) *Power/Knowledge* trans. Colin Gordon, Leo Marshall, John Mepham and Kate Soper, New York: Pantheon Books

Foucault, Michel (1988) [1961] *Madness and Civilisation: a History of Insanity in the Age of Reason* trans. Richard Howard, New York: Vintage Books

Foucault, Michel (1991) *The Foucault Reader* ed. Paul Rabinow, London: Penguin

Foucault, Michel (1997) *Ethics: Subjectivity and Truth* ed. Paul Rabinow, New York: The New Press

Galloway, Alex (2001) 'Conversions: a Phase Shift in net.art' *Working the Screen 2001* Sydney: Open City: 3

Gergen, Kenneth (1991) *The Saturated Self* New York: Basic Books

Gibson, William (1984) *Neuromancer* New York: Ace Books

Goodwin, Andrew (1990) 'Sample and Hold: Pop Music in the Digital Age of Reproduction' in Frith, Simon and Goodwin, Andrew (eds) *On Record* London: Routledge

Goody, Jack (1977) *The Domestication of the Savage Mind* Oxford: Oxford University Press

Gray, Chris Hables (2001) *Cyborg Citizen* New York: Routledge

Greenfield, Susan (1997) *The Human Brain* London: Weidenfeld & Nicolson

Guattari, Felix (1989) *Les trois Écologies* Paris: Éditions Galilée

Guattari, Felix (1992) 'Regimes, Pathways, Subjects' trans. Brian Massumi, in Crary, Jonathan and Kwinter, Sanford (eds) *Incorporations* New York: Zone

Guattari, Felix (1995) 'On Machines' trans. Vivian Constantinopoulos, *Journal of Philosophy and the Visual Arts, No. 6: Complexity: Architecture/Art/Philosophy*: 8–12

Guattari, Felix (1996) 'Subjectivities: for Better and for Worse' in Genosko, Gary (ed.) *The Guattari Reader* London: Blackwell

Habermas, Jürgen (1983) 'Modernity: an Incomplete Project' in Foster, Hal (ed.) *The Anti-Aesthetic* New York: Bay Press

Habermas, Jürgen (1996) *The Habermas Reader* ed. William Outhwaite, Cambridge, UK: Polity Press

Haraway, Donna (1991a) 'The Actors Are Cyborg, Nature is Coyote, and the Geography Is Elsewhere: Postscript to "Cyborgs at Large"' in Penley, Constance and Ross, Andrew (eds) *Technoculture* Minneapolis: University of Minnesota Press

Haraway, Donna (1991b) 'A Cyborg Manifesto: Science, Technology, and Socialist-Feminism in the Late Twentieth Century' in Haraway, Donna *Simians, Cyborgs, and Women: the Reinvention of Nature* London: Free Association Books

Harvey, David (1989) *The Condition of Postmodernity* Oxford: Blackwell

Havelock, Eric (1963) *Preface to Plato* Oxford: Basil Blackwell

Hayles, N. Katherine (1996) 'Virtual Bodies and Flickering Signifiers' in Druckrey, Timothy *Electronic Culture: Technology and Visual Representation* New York: Aperture

Hayles, N. Katherine (1999) *How We Became Posthuman: Virtual Bodies in Cybernetics, Literature and Informatics* Chicago: University of Chicago Press

Heidegger, Martin (1977) 'The Question Concerning Technology' in *The Question Concerning Technology and Other Essays* trans. William Lovitt, New York: Harper Torchbooks

Heim, Michael (1993) *The Metaphysics of Virtual Reality* Oxford: Oxford University Press

Hill, Stephen (1989) *The Tragedy of Technology* Sydney: Pluto

Hillegas, Mark R. (1974) *The Future as Nightmare: H. G. Wells and the Anti-utopians* Carbondale, Ill.: Southern Illinois University Press

Hindmarsh, Richard and Lawrence, Geoffrey (eds) (2001) *Altered Genes II: the Future?* Melbourne: Scribe

Holland, Samantha (1995) 'Descartes Goes to Hollywood: Mind, Body and Gender in Contemporary Cyborg Cinema' in Featherstone, Mike and Burrows, Roger (eds) *Cyberspace/Cyberbodies/Cyberpunk* London: Sage

Horgan, John (1999) *The Undiscovered Mind* London: Weidenfeld & Nicolson

Hughes, Robert (1991) *The Shock of the New* London: Thames & Hudson

Huyssen, Andreas (1986) *After the Great Divide* Bloomington: Indiana University Press

Hutcheon, Linda (1989) *The Politics of Postmodernism* New York: Routledge

Innis, Harold (1950) *Empire and Communications* Toronto: University of Toronto Press

Jameson, Frederic (1983) 'Postmodernism, or the Cultural Logic of Late Capitalism' in Foster, Hal (ed.) *The Anti-Aesthetic* New York: Bay Press

Jencks, Charles (1987) *The Language of Postmodern Architecture* 5th edn, London: Academy Editions

Jencks, Charles (1989) *What is Post-Modernism?* 3rd edn, London: St Martin's Press

Johnson, Steven (1997) *Interface Culture* San Francisco: HarperEdge

Jones, Barry (1988) *Sleepers, Wake!* Melbourne: Oxford University Press

Jones, Steven G. (1995) 'Understanding Community in the Information Age' in Jones, Steven G. (ed.) *Cybersociety: Computer-Mediated Communication and Community* Thousand Oaks: Sage

Joy, Bill (2000) 'Why the Future Doesn't Need Us' *Wired* (Australian edition), April: 238–62

Juarrero, Alicia (1999) *Dynamic in Action: Intentional Behaviour as a Complex System* Cambridge, Mass.: MIT Press

Kelly, Kevin (1997) 'New Rules for the New Economy: Twelve Dependable Principles for Thriving in a Turbulent World' at *Wired* http://www.wired.com/wired/5.09/newrules.html accessed 8 June 2000

Kelly, Kevin and Groenig, Matt (1999) 'One-Eyed Aliens! Suicide Booths! Mom's Old-Fashioned Robot Oil!: Kevin Kelly Tours the Theme Park inside Matt Groenig's Brain' *Wired* February: 114–21 and 158

Khan, L. Ali (1996) *The Extinction of Nation-States: a World without Borders* The Hague: Kluwer Law International

Kroker, Arthur and Weinstein, Michael A. (1994) *Data Trash: the Theory of the Virtual Class* New York: St Martin's Press

Kuhn, Annette (ed.) (1990) *Alien Zone* London: Verso

Kuhn, Annette (ed.) (1999) *Alien Zone II* London: Verso

Kuhn, Thomas S. (1996) [1962] *The Structure of Scientific Revolutions* 3rd edn, Chicago: University of Chicago Press

Kurzweil, Ray (1999) *The Age of Spiritual Machines* New York: Viking Penguin

Lacoue-Labarthe, Philippe (1990) *Heidegger, Art and Politics: the Fiction of the Political* trans. Chris Turner, Oxford: Basil Blackwell

Lessig, Lawrence (1999) *Code and Other Laws of Cyberspace* New York: Basic Books

Levinson, Paul (1999) *Digital McLuhan* London: Routledge

Levy, Pierre (1994) 'Toward Superlanguage' in *ISEA 94 Catalogue*, Helsinki: University of Art and Design

Levy, Pierre (1997) *Collective Intelligence: Mankind's Emerging World in Cyberspace* trans. Robert Bononno, New York: Plenum

Levy, Pierre (1998) *Becoming Virtual: Reality in the Digital Age* trans. Robert Bononno, New York: Plenum

Lewontin, Richard (1993) *The Doctrine of DNA: Biology as Ideology* London: Penguin

Lewontin, Richard (2000) *It Ain't Necessarily So: the Dream of the Human Genome and Other Illusions* London: Granta

Lunenfeld, Peter (2000) *Snap to Grid: a User's Guide to Digital Arts, Media, and Cultures* Cambridge, Mass.: MIT Press

Lupton, Ellen and Miller, J. Abbott (1992) 'Hygiene, Cuisine and the Product World' in Crary, Jonathan and Kwinter, Sanford (eds) *Incorporations* New York: Zone

Lyotard, Jean-François (1984) [1979] *The Postmodern Condition: a Report on Knowledge* trans. Geoff Bennington and Brian Massumi, Minneapolis: University of Minnesota Press

McCarthy, Phillip (1983) 'The Body Obsolete: Interview with Stelarc' *High Performance* **24**: 12–19

McIntyre, Paul (2000) 'eSony plays on the Web' *The Australian* Thursday 13 April: 24

Mackay, Robin (1997) 'Capitalism and Schizophrenia: Wildstyle in Full Effect' in Pearson, Keith Ansell (ed.) *Deleuze and Philosophy: the Difference Engineer* London: Routledge, pp. 247–69

Mackenzie, Donald M. and Wajcman, Judy W. (eds) (1988) *The Social Shaping of Technology* London: Oxford University Press

Mackenzie, Donald M. and Wajcman, Judy W. (eds) (1999) *The Social Shaping of Technology* 2nd edn, London: Oxford University Press

McLuhan, Marshall (1967) *The Medium is the Message* Middlesex: Penguin

McLuhan, Marshall (1974) [1964]*Understanding Media* London: Abacus

McQuire, Scott (1998) *Visions of Modernity* London: Sage

Madsen, Virginia (1995) 'Critical Mass' *World Art* **1**: 78–82

Manovich, Lev (2001) *The Language of New Media* Cambridge, Mass.: MIT Press

Marcuse, Herbert (1964) *One Dimensional Man* London: Routledge

Marinetti, F. T. (1961) 'Initial Manifesto of Futurism' [1909] in Taylor, J. C. *Futurism* New York: Museum of Modern Art

Marx, Leo (1995) 'The Idea of "Technology" and Postmodern Pessimism' in Ezrahi, Yaron, Mendelsohn, Everett and Segal, Howard (eds) *Technology, Pessimism and Postmodernism* Minneapolis: University of Minnesota Press

Mauss, Marcel (1992) 'Techniques of the Body' in Crary, Jonathan and Kwinter, Sanford (eds) *Incorporations* New York: Zone

Meyrowitz, Joshua (1985) *No Sense of Place: the Impact of Electronic Media on Social Behaviour* Oxford: Oxford University Press

Minsky, Marvin and Papert, Seymour (1988) *Perceptrons: an Introduction to Computational Geometry* expanded edn, Cambridge, Mass.: MIT Press

Moravec, Hans (1988) *Mind Children: the Future of Robot and Human Intelligence* Cambridge, Mass.: Harvard University Press

Mumford, Lewis (1934) *Technics and Civilization* London: Routledge

Mumford, Lewis (1967) *The Myth of the Machine: the Pentagon of Power* New York: Harcourt, Brace, Jovanovich

Murray, Timothy (2000) 'Digital Incompossibility: Cruising the Aesthetic Haze of the New Media' in *Ctheory*, http://www.ctheory.net/, accessed 19 November 2001

Nancy, Jean-Luc (1993) 'War, Law, Sovereignty – Techné' in Conley, Verena Andermatt (ed.) *Rethinking Technologies* Minneapolis: University of Minnesota Press

Neuman, Johanna (1996) *Lights, Camera, War: Is Media Technology Driving International Politics?* New York: St Martin's Press

Norris, Christopher (1992) *Uncritical Theory: Postmodernism, Intellectuals and the Gulf War* London: Lawrence and Wishart

Olalquiaga, Celeste (1992) *Megalopolis: Contemporary Cultural Sensibilities* Minneapolis: University of Minnesota Press

Ong, Walter J. (1982) *Orality and Literacy: the Technologizing of the Word* London: Routledge

Overall, Mary (1991) *Stelarc – An Event* (video) Darwin: Northern Territory University/Australian Film Commission

Pacey, Arnold (1983) *The Culture of Technology* London: Basil Blackwell

Patton, Paul (1984) 'Conceptual Politics and the War Machine in *Mille Plateau*' *Substance* **44/45**: 61–80

Pinker, Steven (1997) *How the Mind Works* New York: WW Norton

Plant, Sadie (1997) *Zeroes + Ones: Digital Women and the New Technoculture* New York: Doubleday

Poole, Ross (1991) *Morality and Modernity* London: Routledge

Poole, Ross (1999) *Nation and Identity* London: Routledge

Poster, Mark (1997) 'Cyberdemocracy: Internet and Public Sphere' in Porter, David (ed.) *Internet Culture* New York: Routledge

Postman, Neil (1985) *Amusing Ourselves to Death* New York: Viking

Postman, Neil (1992) *Technopoly: the Surrender of our Culture to Technology* New York: Knopf

Regis, Ed (1995) *Nano: the Emerging Science of Nanotechnology: Remaking the World – Molecule by Molecule* Boston: Little, Brown and Company

Rheingold, Howard (1994) *The Virtual Community: Finding Connection in a Computerized World* London: Secker and Warburg

Roberts, Joanne (1999) 'Theory, Technology and Cultural Power: an Interview with Manuel Castells' in *Angelaki: journal of the theoretical humanities* **4** (2), September: 33–9

Rochlin, Gene I. (1997) *Trapped in the Net: the Unanticipated Consequences of Computerization* Princeton, NJ: Princeton University Press

Rose, Hilary and Rose, Steven (2001) *Alas, Poor Darwin: Arguments against Evolutionary Psychology* London: Vintage

Rose, Steven (1992) *The Making of Memory* London, Sydney: Bantam Press

Rose, Steven (2001) 'Escaping Evolutionary Psychology' in Rose, Hilary and Rose, Steven *Alas, Poor Darwin: Arguments against Evolutionary Psychology* London: Vintage

Rosler, Martha (1991) 'Image Simulations, Computer Manipulations: Some Considerations' in *Digital Dialogues* special edition of *Ten8* **2** (2)

Ross, Andrew (1994) *The Chicago Gangster Theory of Life: Nature's Debt to Society* London: Verso

Rushkoff, Douglas (1997) 'Untitled' in *The Australian* 19–20 April *Syte*: 1

Rutsky, R. L. (1999) *High Techne* Minneapolis: University of Minnesota Press

Schwarz, Robert K. (1997) 'Music for 18 Musicians, Revisited', notes for Steve Reich, *Music for 18 Musicians*, Nonesuch CD

Scientific American (2001) 'Megabucks for Nanotech' *Scientific American* **285**, 3 September: 6

Searle, John (1990) 'Minds, Brains and Programs' in Boden, Margaret (ed.) *The Philosophy of Artificial Intelligence* Cambridge, Mass.: MIT Press

Serres, Michel (1995) *The Natural Contract* trans. Elizabeth MacArthur and William Paulson, Ann Arbor: University of Michigan Press

Simpson, Lorenzo C. (1995) *Technology and the Conversations of Modernity* New York: Routledge

Smalley, Richard E. (2001) 'Of Chemistry, Love and Nanobots' *Scientific American* **285**, 3 September: 68–9

Sobchack, Vivian (1999) 'Cities on the Edge of Time: the Urban Science Fiction Film' in Annette Kuhn (ed.) *Alien Zone II* London: Verso

Spinoza, Benedict de Davis (1952) *Ethics* trans. W.H. White, Chicago: Encyclopaedia Britannica

Springer, Claudia (1996) *Electronic Eros: Bodies and Desire in the Postindustrial Age* Austin: University of Texas Press

Staiger, Janet (1999) 'Future Noir: Contemporary Representations of Visionary Cities' in Kuhn, Annette (ed.) *Alien Zone II* London: Verso

Stelarc (1996) 'On the Future of the Net: Phantom Bodies, Fractal Flesh and Collective Strategies' *ISEA96 Book of Abstracts*: 12

Stephenson, Neal (1995) *The Diamond Age: Or a Young Lady's Illustrated Primer* New York: Bantam

Stix, Gary (2001) 'Little Big Science' *Scientific American* **285**, 3 September: 26–31

Suzuki, David and Knudston, Peter (1989) *Genethics: the Ethics of Engineering Life* Sydney: Allen & Unwin

Tapscott, Don (1996) *The Digital Economy: Promise and Peril in the Age of Networked Intelligence* New York: McGraw-Hill

Ten8 (1991a) 'Esther Parada: Historical Revisions in Time and Space' in *Digital Dialogues* special edition of *Ten8* **2** (2)

Ten8 (1991b) 'Eva Sutton: Nostalgia Subverted Space' in *Digital Dialogues* special edition of *Ten8* **2** (2)

Tisdall, Carolyn and Bozzolla, Angelo (1993) *Futurism* London: Thames & Hudson

Tofts, Darren and McKeich, Murray (1997) *Memory Trade: a Prehistory of Cyberculture* Sydney: Interface

Tomas, David (1995) 'Feedback and Cybernetics: Reimaging the Body in the Age of Cybernetics' in Featherstone, Mike and Burrows, Roger (eds) *Cyberspace/Cyberbodies/Cyberpunk* London: Sage

Turing, Alan (1990) 'Computing Machinery and Intelligence' in Boden, Margaret (ed.) *The Philosophy of Artificial Intelligence* Cambridge, Mass.: MIT Press

Turkle, Sherry (1984) *The Second Self: Computers and the Human Spirit* New York: Simon and Schuster

Turkle, Sherry (1995) *Life on the Screen: Identity in the Age of the Internet* New York: Simon and Schuster

Ulmer, Gregory (1989) *Teletheory; Grammatology in the Age of Video* New York: Routledge

Ulmer, Gregory (1994) *Heuretics; the Logic of Invention* Baltimore: Johns Hopkins University Press

Van Creveld, Martin (1989) *Technology and War: From 2000 B.C. to the Present* New York: Free Press

Varela, Franciso J., Thompson, Evan and Rosch, Eleanor (1991) *The Embodied Mind: Cognitive Science and Human Experience* Cambridge, Mass.: MIT Press

Venturi, Robert (1972) *Learning from Las Vegas* Cambridge, Mass.: MIT Press

Virilio, Paul (1983) *Pure War* New York: Semiotext(e)
Virilio, Paul (1986) *Speed and Politics* trans. Mark Polizzotti, New York: Semiotext(e)
Virilio, Paul (1989) *War and Cinema: the Logistics of Perception* trans. Patrick Camillier, London: Verso
Virilio, Paul (1990) 'The Image to Come' trans. Stephen Sartarelli, *Art and Text* **36**: 90–4
Virilio, Paul (1991a) *The Aesthetics of Disappearance* trans. Philip Beitchman, New York: Semiotext(e)
Virilio, Paul (1991b) *Lost Dimension* trans. Daniel Moshenberg, New York: Semiotext(e)
Virilio, Paul (1993) *L'art du moteur* Paris: Galilée
Virilio, Paul (1997) *Open Sky* trans. Julie Rose, London: Verso
Walker, John A. (1983) *Art in the Age of Mass Media* London: Pluto
Wark, McKenzie (1993) 'Suck on This, Planet of Noise!' *Media Information Australia* **69**, August: 70–6
Wark, McKenzie (1994) 'Third Nature' *Cultural Studies* **8** (1): 115–32
Warrick, Patricia (1980) *The Cybernetic Imagination in Science Fiction* Cambridge, Mass.: MIT Press
Wertheim, Margaret (1999) *The Pearly Gates of Cyberspace* Sydney: Doubleday
Wheale, Nigel (1995) 'Modernism and Its Consequnces: Continuity or Break?' in Wheale, Nigel (ed.) *The Postmodern Arts: an Introductory Reader* London: Routledge
Wiener, Norbert (1961) [1948] *Cybernetics: or Control and Communication in the Animal and the Machine* 2nd edn, Cambridge, Mass.: MIT Press
Williams, Raymond (1975) *Television: Technology and Cultural Form* New York: Schocken Books
Williams, Raymond (1983) *Keywords* London: Flamingo
Wilson, Robert Rawdon (1995) 'Cyber (body) Parts: Prosthetic Consciousness' in Featherstone, Mike and Burrows, Roger (eds) *Cyberspace/Cyberbodies/Cyberpunk* London: Sage
Winner, Langdon (1986) *The Whale and the Reactor* Chicago: University of Chicago Press
Winston, Brian (1998) *Media Technology and Society* London: Routledge
Wollen, Peter (1989) 'Cinema/Americanism/The Robot' *New Formations* **8**: 7–34
Woodmansee, Martha and Jaszi, Peter (eds) (1994) *The Construction of Authorship: Textual Appropriation in Law and Literature* Durham: Duke University Press
Zurbrugg, Nicholas (1995) 'An Interview with Paul Virilio: the Publicity Machine and Critical Theory' *Eyeline* **27**, Autumn/Winter: 8–14
Zurbrugg, Nicholas (2000) *Critical Vices: the Myths of Postmodern Theory* Amsterdam: G + B Arts

Index

219

CPSIA information can be obtained
at www.ICGtesting.com
Printed in the USA
LVHW050513210123
737604LV00003B/252